ONCE UPON A TIME THERE WAS
A THREE-YEAR-OLD GRANDPA

Once Upon a Time There Was a Three-Year-Old Grandpa

A Kaleidoscope of Farmer-Boy Stories with Reflections on Character, Wisdom, and Community

by
DAVID JANZEN

Foreword by Nancy and Joe Gatlin

RESOURCE *Publications* • Eugene, Oregon

ONCE UPON A TIME THERE WAS A THREE-YEAR-OLD GRANDPA
A Kaleidoscope of Farmer-Boy Stories with Reflections on Character, Wisdom, and Community

Copyright © 2024 David Janzen. All rights reserved. Except for brief quotations in critical publications or reviews, no part of this book may be reproduced in any manner without prior written permission from the publisher. Write: Permissions, Wipf and Stock Publishers, 199 W. 8th Ave., Suite 3, Eugene, OR 97401.

Resource Publications
An Imprint of Wipf and Stock Publishers
199 W. 8th Ave., Suite 3
Eugene, OR 97401

www.wipfandstock.com

PAPERBACK ISBN: 979-8-3852-1525-6
HARDCOVER ISBN: 979-8-3852-1526-3
EBOOK ISBN: 979-8-3852-1527-0

07/09/24

Contents

Foreword by Nancy and Joe Gatlin | ix

Acknowledgments | xiii

Introduction | xv

MIRROR # 1: A MENNONITE FARM BOY TAKES ROOT

Chapter 1 Sitting on the Steps—The Art of Contemplation | 3

Chapter 2 How the Cutest-Ever Little Lamb Turned into a Bicycle—Attunement between Souls | 13

Chapter 3 My Worst and Best Grade School Year Ever—Mentors Who Shaped Me | 25

Chapter 4 Take a Kid Along—Learning to Mentor in Turn | 36

Chapter 5 The Last Threshing Circle—The Curse and the Redemption of Work | 43

MIRROR # 2: WHAT'S A HONYAK?

Chapter 6 Honyaks—From Youthful Mayhem to Prophetic Mischief | 51

Chapter 7 HeckuvaRanch and other Pranks with Words—How Play and Work Team up for Good Writing | 60

Chapter 8 Not My Enemy—Reweaving the Human Fabric in Time of War | 66

Chapter 9 Hedgewood—Our Stubborn Roots in Kansas Soil and History | 76

Chapter 10 About Chicks, Imaginary Chicken Hawks—
 And an Inconsistent Vegetarian | 81

Chapter 11 My Brief Career as a Champion Major League Rock
 Batter | 86

MIRROR # 3: SEVEN CAREERS FOR SEVEN DECADES

Chapter 12 Memories of Cows, a Milking Barn, and a Hobble-Dance—
 Practical Wisdom Is a Thing | 97

Chapter 13 Fighting Bookworms on the Farm—History as Science,
 Art and Craft | 110

Chapter 14 Building the ALCAN Highway—What Goes into Good
 Work? | 120

Chapter 15 New Shoes for DP's—The Holy Work of Restoration
 after War | 130

Chapter 16 Section Hands in the Garden—From Model Railroading
 to Affordable Housing | 142

Chapter 17 When the Ruts Get Too Deep—From Family Trips
 to the Nurturing Communities Network | 149

Chapter 18 Career Number Seven—Si Dios Quiere* | 159

MIRROR # 4: FAMILY TIES THAT BIND AND LOOSE

Chapter 19 Thanksgiving Blizzard of 1952—Through the Snow
 to Sudan and Back | 165

Chapter 20 Lost, But Not Really Lost | 173

Chapter 21 Lessons our Piano Taught Us—About Pride, Humility,
 and Solidarity | 176

Chapter 22 Climbing, Jumping, and an Unforgettable Pain in the Butt | 184

Chapter 23 Father Teaches Me to Survey Terraces—
 And Join the Fifth Agricultural Revolution | 187

Chapter 24 Driving Cattle to the Kansas City Stock Yards—
 and Proposing with Manure on My Boots | 194

Chapter 25 Marrying a Stranger | 200

Chapter 26   Natasha in War and Peace—Intuiting
              the Condition of Souls | 211

Chapter 27   James—A Calling to Rescue the Underdog | 217

Chapter 28   A Family without Borders—Eric Revises
              Our Family Tree | 226

Chapter 29   From Farm Boy to Communal Life | 232

MIRROR # 5: BEARING FRUIT IN OLD AGE

Chapter 30   I Remember Beans—From Peasant Village to Urban Soil | 243

Chapter 31   Sorghum Day—How Refugees Remember
              and Give Back | 248

Chapter 32   Our Half-mile Cottonwood Tree—
              Bearing Fruit in Old Age | 257

Appendix: A Chronology of Selected Writing Projects | 267

Foreword

Blessed are the pure in heart, for they will see God. Matthew 5:8

We (Joe and Nancy) are of that generation that is saddened by the fact that not many people read books anymore. So, right out the gate, let's ask and answer this question: should you keep reading?

Yes, keep reading, if you are:

- One of David's and Joanne's grandchildren or any of their other relatives on down the line. Memoirs are apparently in the Janzen DNA. David and several of his forebears have taken seriously the debt we should all owe to those who follow us to share the path we have traveled.

- A practitioner or seeker of Christian community. We have now for several years continued the work, started by David, of the Nurturing Communities Network. "Once Upon a Time…" is another addition, and the most entertaining one, to David's contribution of indispensable books and reports to further this movement.

- A lover of tales that are taller, stranger, and funnier than fiction.

- And, should none of the above categories apply to you, continue on if you are a human being who would seek purity of heart or have a desire to see God.

Speaking of purity-of-heart, here is the second question. Why would that apply to the three-year-old grandpa and "Once Upon a Time"?

It's not that David is blameless or bland or boring (learn herein the definition of a *honyak*). He's certainly not faultless or infallible (he once showed up at the Waco airport to help us celebrate the twentieth anniversary of our community — a week early!).

And pure-in-heart should not be equated with simple-mindedness. As you will see, David's curiosity and joy in learning has been stoked in vastly diverse settings such as a cattle truck on its way to market, a dorm room at Bethel College in the heart of rural Kansas, and around a flagpole at Harvard Divinity School where *honyak* mischief and solidarity unfolded. He has drawn his lessons of life from faithful people of all ages, in many walks of life, and from opposite sides of the globe, among them a pastor preaching Christian non-violence in the aftermath of a civil war in the Democratic Republic of the Congo and a *campesina* in the rural jungle of El Salvador managing her daily household, again in the aftermath of a civil war. David also takes dives into Tolstoy, quantum mechanics, the fine points of slaughtering chickens, and the merits of agriculture's fifth revolution over the pretensions of permaculture.

Make no mistake, the vast and sprawling experiences of David's life do not signify flightiness. Through the decades there has been a consistency of commitment—to his wife Joanne, his children Natasha and James, and his extended families in New Creation Fellowship, Reba Place Fellowship, and the many individuals and communities that he has mentored—that shines a light of faithfulness. His purity in heart is seen in his single-minded commitment to God's realm, a daily devotion to the shared life of those bonded together as disciples of Jesus.

As Jesus promised, David's purity in heart has given him the gift of seeing God. He sees God in the simple and the complex, in the rural and the urban, in grief and celebration, in the silly and the serious, in housing and in agriculture, in trees and in machinery, in childhood and adulthood, in conflict and in harmony. Everywhere David looks he sees God. This vision is not naive. David understands brokenness, suffering, and sin. But in these he always sees the passion of the cross and the hope of the resurrection.

Seeing God also means hearing God. David has nurtured a lifelong habit of listening and contemplation that began when his mother would respond to his throwing blocks against the wall, pulling his sister's hair, or some other manifestation of his childhood temper, by grabbing him by the neck and walking him to the basement stairs. "Sit and think about it," she would tell him. Over the years, as David tells the story, through times of silence he learned to listen and hear the Holy Spirit, to draw the connections between diverse events, and to recognize the common experiences, deep motivations, and needs of human beings.

David's giftedness is not just his 20-20 vision and his acute hearing but also his ability to communicate. His stories and memories are framed as a wonderful and entertaining memoir for his grandchildren that will help them understand part of their origin. For all of us, as we take a step back, we can see a tapestry that David has woven, a metanarrative that becomes an invitation for each of us to join that band of believers walking at Jesus's side. With pure hearts we will see God at work in both the dramatic events and the mundane hours of our lives, in tumult and in peace, in community and in solitude, in beginnings and in endings.

We think you will enjoy "Once upon a Time There was a Three-Year-Old Grandpa." We will even venture to say, we think as a result of reading this book, you will have a number of laughs and guffaws, you will be inspired, and you will grow in wisdom. The chapters are short enough in length and large enough in number that you could use this book as a morning devotion time for a month. Or you could get engrossed in it and just read it through in a couple of sessions. Or you could read it just a bit at a time so you can pause for a week or so to reflect on its fundamental truths.

Enjoy your read and may your heart grow evermore pure.

Nancy and Joe Gatlin,
Hope Fellowship, Waco, Texas
On behalf of the Nurturing Communities Network

Acknowledgments

It is my joy to thank the persons who have shaped my life journey and, more particularly, contributed to this memoir in various helpful ways. My parents (Louis and Hilda Neufeldt Janzen) and mentors (Al Meyer, Mukuna Joseph, Jake Pauls, Virgil Vogt, Julius Bleser, Allan Howe, Hilda Carper, and Sally Youngquist, among others) have already been mentioned more fully in the body of this memoir.

I want to also thank those who heard me read portions of this memoir in various "Lack of Talent" shows and encouraged me to keep writing. Thank you to son James, daughter Natasha, and my siblings who have read portions about them and have given me the green light to pass it on to you. Special thanks goes to teacher Harold Regier who took the gritty photos of our grade school years. I must also mention my dear wife, Joanne who has, thank God, walked with me through all weather and has helped me find the right place for my misplaced socks, punctuation, and spelling since 1964.

Finally, I want to thank persons who have read portions of this memoir and given their encouragement and comments like Tim, Mike, Sally, Joe, Nancy, Greg, and another Tim. . . . My memory is not good enough to recall everyone on this list, but you are nevertheless in my gratitude. I owe a heap of thanks to Susie Kaufman who volunteered her services as a copy editor, catching all the glitches that would have otherwise irritated you and our publisher, Wipf and Stock, where I count a number of good friends in the family of faith.

Introduction

I REMEMBER SOMEWHERE IN my childhood a moment of recognition that the adults around me had forgotten what it was like to be a child. I vowed that I would never forget. And in a way, this book is the fulfillment of that vow.

If you read on, you will discover a rather eccentric memoir, with a childhood farmer-boy story introducing most chapters, thereby launching a theme that arcs forward to splash down in later decades of my life. The title, "Once upon a Time There Was a Three-year-old Grandpa," comes from a collection of tales I first told my grandsons at bedtime. This farmer-boy narrative approach has made the chapters lots of fun to write, and therefore, I hope, more enjoyable for you to read. It has also given me the freedom to let stories follow their own scent trail wherever that might lead. I'm trusting that curiosity will pull the reader along as much as it has driven the writer. In any case, a strict chronological narrative doesn't allow me to develop the wild diversity of themes you will find here including imaginative play, construction crew humor, animal intelligence, journal writing, rural and urban farming, communal wisdom, along with a few serious pranks and the prophetic mischief that follows.

This memoir is also a confession, a genre that Augustine of Hippo first ventured, where he offered to God reflections on his waywardness, gratitude for grace, and his whole-hearted worship. Augustine also found in this confessional format a freedom to ask essential wisdom-seeking questions about the journey of life, and to reflect on them theologically with the reader. This mode of confession allowed Augustine to reflect profoundly on the inner workings of the spirit in a way that seems completely contemporary. Following Augustine's lead, I believe that the more honestly I can face the hard questions of my life, the more you might discover echoes of your own struggles in mine. We are different and we are the same—that's the paradox we share as human beings. And this mystery, I believe, can be a source of fruitful reflection on character development and community in the pages that follow. Hang around and see how the experiment turns out.

Here and there in this memoir, I share excerpts from my prayer journal in the form of intimate conversations between Jesus (JC) and myself (DJ). Some may find this habit of reflection disconcerting. Do I profess to know what Jesus is saying to me? Is this just an artifice of creative writing? Or is Jesus really with us the way he promised? (Matt. 28:20) What can I say to explain the mystery of the most intimate, free, and trustworthy source of guidance in my life? It will have to speak for itself and you are free to draw your own conclusions.

Why the five-part structure of this memoir/confession? At my fifth birthday I was given a kaleidoscope—something called a "scientific toy" in those days. I was totally captivated by its variety of geometric shapes, vivid colors, and dramatic glints of light as I peered into the eye-hole and rotated the cardboard tube before me. In fact, curiosity about how it worked soon compelled me to take it apart, whereupon I discover nothing but three long rectangular mirrors and a few shards of colored glass. Alas, you guessed it—I was never again able to put my dear kaleidoscope back together. In one day, I both welcomed and killed my birthday present, which introduces the question of later reflection—is curiosity a virtue or a vice?

But the wonder of that moment has come back to inspire me, to picture the structure of this book as five mirrors in a kaleidoscope that, when rotated, might reveal new ways of seeing and reflecting upon the mysteries of one life when held up to the light. As you read ahead you will encounter breaks in the narrative marked by five asterisks (*   *   *   *   *) which you can consider as a twist of the kaleidoscope, resulting in a different view of the same story. This structure does not result in a tightly integrated system where everything fits in logical sequence. Some stories will explicitly connect with their neighbors, while others seem to stand alone, leaving you, dear reader, to discover how they might connect. These chapters, like parables, might appear as unfinished dialogues awaiting further conversation. Hopefully, this structure may allow for random kaleidoscopic elements to emerge as patterns to the discerning eye. Now, permit me to introduce these five mirrors.

MIRROR # 1: A MENNONITE FARM BOY IS GIVEN ROOTS.

Like the overture of an opera, this section is meant to introduce a few major themes that follow. This first mirror begins with stories from my childhood on the farm twelve miles east of Newton, Kansas, called "HeckuvaRanch." It recalls an era in American history that began with Laura Ingalls Wilder's *Little House on the Prairie* stories, and runs through Willa Cather's classic Midwestern tales in an era when half the people in America lived in small towns or on family farms, a time when my life seemed perfectly normal because almost everyone we knew came from a similar background. But my childhood also marks the end of an era with the story, "The Last Threshing Circle." Now, seventy-five years later, my farmer-boy stories appear amazing, almost unbelievably quaint to my urban millennial friends and mentees who know no one else that grew up on a farm like me.

MIRROR # 2: WHAT IS A HONYAK?

A honyak is a rogue, a prankster, a misguided youth, and perhaps a gem in the rough. In any case, God seems to use honyaks in exceptional ways because they don't know when to be afraid. Here is a collection of stories that explore how honyaks happen and what it takes to turn a honyak into someone whose unconventional energy might be redirected into prophetic mischief.

MIRROR # 3: SEVEN CAREERS FOR SEVEN DECADES.

It may be restless curiosity or it may be Providence that led me to multiple careers as a youthful farmer (which never really took off), as an historian, a general contractor leading a community-based construction crew, a refugee resettlement ministry coordinator, a developer of affordable housing, and as an apostle called to gather something called The Nurturing Communities Network. It may be that God gives me the grace to dabble with a seventh career, and another decade of life, as a thinker and mentor in Christian community. Time will tell!

In all these career changes, my vocation as a follower of Jesus in community, did not change. Each of these career transitions was discerned by my community at the time, and the fruitfulness of these changes, I believe, bear witness to the Spirit's leading. Each of these careers resulted in a new set of disciplines, a unique kind of know-how, a practical wisdom that Aristotle first wrote about and that we reflect on together in this mirror #3.

MIRROR # 4: FAMILY TIES THAT BIND AND LOOSE.

This is a collection of stories and reflections on the ways that families inherit and pass on traits of character demonstrating both continuity and surprises. For me, the arc of family passes beyond kith and kin to land in intentional Christian community as a witness to the new humanity a reconciling God has in mind for the world. In God's kingdom, adoption is the main strategy of family building—so these stories illustrate a strange family tree without borders. Love comes first, sometimes followed by understanding—sometimes not. But the adventure of trying to embody and to understand the diverse family God has given us is totally worth it.

MIRROR # 5: BEARING FRUIT IN OLD AGE.

This mirror also begins with childhood stories and leads to a journey where we discover the difference between conventional wisdom (about how to succeed in the world the way it is), and how the wisdom of God's kingdom transforms us (and the world) if we seek it first. This section concludes the book with the story of a colossal cottonwood tree that dominated my childhood landscape, and later became a metaphor for fruitfulness in old age.

There is in these stories the obvious theme of play—the childhood delight in creating imaginary worlds and systematically exploring them with their improvised casts of characters and rules of engagement. Play for children is never aimless, but usually involves intense hands-on exploration of the reality that they imagine awaits them when they become adults. I've come to the conviction that this kind of curiosity-driven play is the most creative way of dealing with life as an adult as well. "Unless you become as little children, you cannot enter the kingdom of God."

Finally, you might ask, for whom was this book written? Let's keep it simple. It was written for you, me, and God.

It was written first of all for my own clarification of thought, my own attempt to be honest with God and myself. But, as I've shared portions of this memoir/confession with friends and family, co-workers and colleagues, on long car rides and at informal talent shows, folks have strongly encouraged me to keep writing and sharing the fruit of these farm-boy inspired reflections. This looser format of curiosity-driven adventures in early and later life, naturally leads to wisdom-seeking digressions—one of the assignments God and society give to people with grey hair. By now I've written several serious books about Christian community. For folks who have read those books, this one I hope, can follow those main-course entrees as something of a dessert. So, if this whimsical memoir allows you to catch a few glints of wisdom kept aloft by the winds of childish hilarity, that would complete my joy. See you in Chapter One.

Mirror # 1
A Mennonite Farm Boy Takes Root

Chapter 1

Sitting on the Steps

The Art of Contemplation

"Once upon a time there was a three-year-old grandpa," is how I began the bedtime story.

"That's impossible," my grandsons replied. "Grandpas can't be three years old."

"But this story is about a three-year-old who was me, your grandpa."

"That's crazy."

For a couple of weeks one summer Joanne and I hosted two grandsons, Damien and Derrek, who, in order to postpone the finality of bedtime, would beg me for a story from my childhood. So, I began to tell the tales that eventually led to the farmer-boy collection that introduces the chapters of this memoir.

That summer the nights were so hot we gave up on indoor sleeping and set up camping mats next to each other on the second-floor back porch, hoping for a little breeze. The boys settled down quickly because they wanted to hear another once-upon-a-time story. And each time, almost like a ritual, they'd object to my silly infant grandpa beginning.

"But you didn't have white hair and a beard when you were three. Just tell us the story, Grandpa. Okay?"

All right. So, once upon a time there was a three-year-old grandpa who decided to run away from home. In those days whenever I lost my temper and threw blocks against the wall, or pulled my sister's hair, or screamed at the world in frustration, my mother would grab my neck and walk me to the basement steps where I was supposed to "sit and think about it," whatever that meant. Sitting on the steps, I never knew what I was supposed to think about until one day I had an idea.

Mom holding me up to the light.

In my own mind mother compared unfavorably with Aunt Helen who always thought I was cute, worthy of cookies, and who never scolded me and made me sit on the steps "to think about it." Aunt Helen's house beckoned from across the Henry Creek Valley beside the Rock Island railroad tracks only half a mile west of our farm.

So, I set my determined little feet to go live with Aunt Helen and Uncle Johnny, and with cousins Herman, Edna, and Doris where I had always been a welcome darling. Happily, I left behind my first earthly home, kicking rocks and dust as I strolled along the country road, trying to whistle like my older brother, John. I was moving up in the world.

Then, alas, over my shoulder I spotted my mother walking after me in strides far longer than I had ever seen before. But no problem, I knew how to run, something that, to my knowledge, mothers could not do. So, I kicked into high gear, trusting these fast legs that would safely carry me to the city of refuge up the road.

Horrors, Mother could run. Who knew? And what's more, she was gaining on me. I reached the bottom of the hill and grabbed the bridge railing with all my might while mother's hands turned into talons, twisting and wrenching harder and harder until I lost my grip, and became her prisoner.

Back up the hill she trudged, my feet dragging a double line in the dust, my wrist manacled to her steely hand. I got to hear all the warnings in her frightened mother's heart. "What were you doing running in the road? You could have been hit by a car and killed."

"I am going to live with Aunt Helen who isn't mean to me," I answered in my defense.

"You're *our* child," Mother replied, "and besides, Aunt Helen would never agree to it." What a sinking realization that children don't get to choose their parents! My life plans so quickly dashed in the dust!

Somewhere on the uphill road my feet began to walk of their own accord. My mother's fierce grip relented. When we entered the yard and opened the gate she bent down and faced me: "Are you listening?" she asked.

"Yes," I mumbled.

"Don't ever try to run away from home again. You're our son. We love you. You understand?"

I don't know what turned my heart, but I gave her a quick hug and ran into the house.

Several times in the following weeks, mother arranged for me to play at Aunt Helen's house, and every time I lost my temper, I was scolded and made to sit on the steps "to think about it."

* * * * *

When I was courting Joanne at Bethel College, she often told me her troubles and fears of which there were plenty. I liked Joanne, attracted by her beauty, but I wondered if her anxieties might overwhelm me. However, since I otherwise enjoyed being with her, l decided to make an experiment, to just listen. I noticed that when she got to the bottom of what troubled her, she became peaceful, grateful, and even affectionate. I liked that too. I thought, I know how to give Joanne joy and she gives me joy. I think I can get used to this and find meaning in caring for her by the way I listen.

Joanne caught my eye.

* * * * *

While attending Harvard Divinity School, I landed a field-work assignment (1963–64) at the Massachusetts Mental Health Center where I listened to patients tell their stories, and then I wrote up personal profiles to share in our once-a-week sessions with a psychotherapist. I discovered that these troubled people with mental illness, whom society counted as bottom-of-the-heap, had an infinite depth of character such that getting to know them in an active listening mode opened as much geography and culture for exploration as an entire continent. In fact, I started to look forward to these listening sessions as high points in my week. Because these patients had hit rock bottom in their lives, if I listened sympathetically, they became increasingly honest and real to me. By contrast, my dormmates who were so ambitious about climbing the academic ladder only talked about their achievements, so I seldom got to know the real and often broken persons behind the masks.

I recognize now that the strategy of my field work assignment was an application of Carl Roger's non-directive active listening therapy, not as a mere technique that parroted back what we heard from patients, but to express genuine empathy and excitement over their discoveries. This emotional connection seemed to validate the personhood of those we listened to and gave them courage to face the hard stuff of their lives.

In a few instances I could listen to my dorm mates in a similar way, and they thanked me for taking their personal struggles seriously. I wondered, is this what pastoral care is like?

* * * * *

I don't remember where I heard this bit of advice, but when shaking hands with a newly-wed groom, I might let him in on a secret, "The sexiest part of a man's anatomy is his ears—that is if he really listens."

* * * * *

When Joanne and I were just married and in graduate school at the University of Kansas (1964–66), we often attended a traditional Quaker meeting. I was intrigued by this hour of silence where we sat in a square room facing each other, waiting for the Holy Spirit to reveal something which we might then share with the group. This was my first serious immersion in the art and practice of contemplation. By listening to silence I became aware of the wild and disorderly river that tumbled by in my stream of consciousness. But I found that if I let the crazy stuff just pass, often the Spirit would work with the themes of my life and bring up some insights that had not appeared before. I began to see how the Holy Spirit was, indeed, active in shaping and guiding my thoughts into the ways of peace, perhaps recalling someone to whom I owed an apology. It was as if the Spirit was looking out for my integrity and that of our community. And when someone spoke up in the meeting, I was surprised at how often their words touched the need of my own soul.

About that time, I became fascinated by the *Journal of George Fox*, a spiritual classic by a founder of the Quaker movement. He was a wild man who acted courageously on the promptings of the Spirit, often landing in jail for his denunciations and prophetic actions against the injustices of his day. I also read the journal of Quaker, John Woolman, a gentle and persistent 18th century colonial American anti-slavery advocate. These journal writers persuaded me to keep a spiritual log, which I have continued in one form or another until this day. Thus, as an adult I found a fruitful and voluntary way to do what my mother had commanded of me, to calm and center my unruly spirit, to "listen and think about it."

* * * * *

In the 1970's our community, New Creation Fellowship, was actively involved in the peace-movement, protesting the Vietnam War and the nuclear arms race. Brent Koehn and I were sent to support a non-violent direct action at Rocky Flats, Colorado, where the plutonium triggers were manufactured for the thousands of Hydrogen bombs in missile silos and submarines that the U. S. deployed around the world, aimed at population centers in the Soviet Union. And the Soviets had a similar, though much smaller, arsenal aimed at us. We were at Rocky Flats when Ladon Sheets and others cut through the fence and entered the grounds where they were soon arrested in a Plough Shares action like the Berrigan Brothers' witness on the east coast.

After we returned from Rocky Flats, the Spirit moved me to begin a monthly vigil at a missile silo in our area, and others joined the witness. Sometimes there was only one other person with me. On one Good Friday, about two hundred people gathered to lament and protest this crucifixion of the human race threatened by the two dominant military powers, as helicopters hovered overhead to keep an eye on us all.

One beastly hot summer day in 1978, as I took quiet time and journaled in our cool cellar, I was given the words of a prophecy to deliver at a convocation of peacemakers in an upcoming Mennonite World Conference gathering in Wichita Kansas. The title of this prophetic word was "My People, I Am Your Security." New Creation Fellowship members read it over, suggested a few changes, and commissioned me to share it at Wichita. There, without much effort on my part, the Spirit seemed to open doors for this prophetic word to pass up the hierarchy of conference planners, till it was read by John Stoner, head of the Mennonite Central Committee Peace Section to the whole conference assembly. A few weeks later the piece was published in *The Post-American*, a forerunner of what is now *Sojourner's* magazine. This kind of prophetic witness was clearly in the tradition of George Fox and John Woolman. Our community discerned with me whether it was my calling, to plunge deeper into the peace movement and to listen for other prophetic words. One time a similar prophetic word was instrumental in launching the Newton Area Peace Center. But the needs of Joanne and our family persuaded us that I was not available at this stage of my life for the role of a public prophet.

*   *   *   *   *

Soon after our move to Reba Place Fellowship in 1984, we met Jim Stringham, a retired psychiatrist and former missionary to China. Jim encouraged just about everyone he met to read his pamphlet, *God Wants to Speak to You: Are You Listening?* In it he advised us to practice a form of contemplative prayer that he had followed daily for years. His practice was to ask God "What do you want me to hear?" and then write down what follows?

Usually, when Christians pray, it is a one-way communication of praise, petitions, and thanksgivings—good things to do. But "Listening to the Lord" ends up becoming a two-way conversation. My journal has preserved these daily dialogues with Jesus in which I feel a total freedom to share my heart and where I find Jesus's delight in my mustard seed of faith. I also receive guidance on occasional prophetic initiatives. When I lack the will to do what needs to be done, that small voice promises me, "I am with you. Let's do this together." So, with a courage that is not my own, we step forward as a team.

Jim Stringham's pamphlet also gives a few cautions like don't go around pointing fingers at people and denouncing them with, "Thus saith the Lord. . ." Test what you hear with a mentor or small group before you go public with your spiritual intuitions—advice which we happened to follow in Wichita in 1978. This journal record of my conversations with Jesus has allowed me to go back in times of retreat to review how these intimate words of love and guidance have panned out in my life. They have, indeed, marked all the turning points in my spiritual journey.

As I wait for the still small voice to outlast the turbulence of my own thoughts, I discover that even when I hear nothing, listening for God in silence has its benefits. It increases my capacity to listen to others, now with a heightened interest and curiosity because the silence has opened a space within me for their concerns.

* * * * *

When our son, James, was raising his boys, I once caught grandson Damien sitting on the steps. I asked James, "Where did you learn that parenting trick?"

"From you, Dad—Don't you remember?"

Three generations of enforced contemplation.

* * * * *

A second fruit of "listening to the Lord" is that I have a more authentic self to share with others when they ask that often awkward question, "How are you doing?" Instead of telling them *what* I'm doing, I can talk about my latest conversations with Jesus. Likewise, I can ask, "What has God been showing you?" Even if this question is a surprise, it turns out that people usually "get it" with something thoughtful and revealing to share from the core of their being.

* * * * *

Journal: 3-23-20

D.J.   Jesus, here I am, a mess. What do you want to show me?

J.C.   David, I love you. If you've not noticed, I love you through James and Natasha, through Tim and Sharon, through Eric, through Joanne, through all the people who look upon you with good will. Soak that up and let it set your heart free.

D.J.   But I've been such a poor steward of your grace. I've not brought you my hurts for healing. Instead, I've mostly escaped into self-pity and tried to comfort myself.

J.C.   You are human. I know and see all that too. But you've been forgiving of others, especially Joanne. I'll be forgiving of you too. And even if you didn't forgive others, I'd still show you love. The Father's desire is that all humans find redemption. Our source of grace and forgiveness in the Father is infinite. I understand your wish to be worthy of grace, but don't try to keep score. Just accept God's love for you in your shortcomings.

D.J.   I've not begun to confess everything. I don't think I can remember everything that needs confessing. I'm still a mess.

J.C.   Here, watch me. I'm giving you a fresh newly laundered heart that smells like the out-of-doors on a breezy spring day with birds singing in the background, and all that good green stuff growing toward the light. I want to be with you, you understand? In this time of the of the Corona Virus pandemic—no social distance between us! I'm contagious goodness. Stay close to me and let it infect you. Rest your soul in my love. There is enough grace for you and everything you face. Behold, I make all things new. How does that feel?

D.J.   It feels like a great way to start the rest of the day.

* * * * *

In the last decade, since 2010, as my work has taken me to visit and consult with other Christian intentional communities, people have often thanked me for my wisdom. At first this made me uncomfortable, a feeling I might shrug off with a joke: "When I was young, I got blamed for a lot of things I didn't do. Now that I'm old, I get praised far more than I deserve. In the long run, you see, it all equals out." If people laughed, then I was off the hook and we moved on to other topics.

But the topic of wisdom haunted me. I had a philosophy major in college, and philosophy is supposed to mean "love of wisdom." However, the study of philosophy did not make me wise, it just taught me a lot about philosophers and their philosophies. I'm sure these communities I visited didn't want me to lecture them on the history of Western Philosophy. They wanted me to help them get wise about their calling to live peaceably and to grow to maturity in Christian community.

So, at the age of seventy I "majored" once more in philosophy, this time from a more committed angle, eager to learn—how do individuals and communities grow in wisdom?

The image that came to me was of wisdom as a three-layered cake of a very special kind—the kind where you can both have it and eat it too. *The first layer is knowledge*, what children pursue avidly well before they go to school. Everything seems bright and shiny to them, and they are eager to absorb it, testing what they learn by role play and interaction with peers. School and study are further ways of gaining knowledge to pass exams and, hopefully, to be useful someday in ordinary life. Our brains are almost infinitely capable of storing and organizing information. But knowledge, however high the tower, does not add up to wisdom.

The second layer of the wisdom cake is experience or skill. This is what Aristotle, and others since, have called practical wisdom. Society has organized a lot of practical wisdom for us in terms of professional know-how—butcher, baker, candlestick maker. Each profession has its training regime which used to progress through stages of apprentice, journeyman, and master. Now school and internships largely take that place. A professional has at least ten years of training and proficiency in his or her field, which provides a wealth of experiences to draw on, allowing for quick intuitive and accurate decisions about how to repair a house, diagnose a patient, or teach a classroom of children.

Life experience alone, however, isn't enough to result in wisdom either. Conventional wisdom—what everyone in the dominant culture assumes is true—can often mislead us in individualistic and imperialistic directions. People and communities keep making the same mistakes again and again. What is missing? Experience, however much of it you have, does not add up to wisdom either. Alcoholics Anonymous, and similar groups, have demonstrated a path of salvation and wisdom for many people trapped in their addictions. The way out is at the same time personal, communal, and spiritual.

The missing ingredient, the third layer of the wisdom cake, is reflection, an attentive and honest conversation with one's own soul, with others of similar brokenness, and with God whose love gives us courage and motivation to face the hard issues we otherwise would flee.

This three-layer cake analogy is a brief orientation to the subject of wisdom, which I hope to explore further with you across the terrain of my own life experience in subsequent chapters of this confession / memoir. The point I want to make here is that reflection is essentially the same as deep listening—what happens in times of personal contemplation, in conversation with a community of wisdom seekers, and in dialogue with God.

This deep listening, this habit of reflection is what I now see my mother hoped I'd catch onto by sitting on the steps to "Think about it"—reflecting on my own behavior, how it affected those around me, and how, with God's help and the help of others, I might find a more peaceable path of life.

Jesus said, "Unless you become as little children, you cannot enter the kingdom of God." This book is an experiment in truth, an exploration beginning with childhood and arcing into subsequent decades, to see what clues we might find for growing in the wisdom of Jesus, perhaps the only goal worthy of a life's devotion.

Chapter 2

How the Cutest-Ever Little Lamb Turned into a Bicycle

Attunement between Souls

ONE MORNING WHEN I was four years old our Uncle Will drove onto the farmyard and called us children together—that would have been sister Sara and my older brother, John, and me. Mark was still a baby then. Out of the backseat Uncle Will lifted a cardboard box with something special wrapped in a towel—a little wobbly-legged half-wet lamb.

Looking back at that moment with the eyes of an adult, I can understand Uncle Will's strategy of showing a newborn lamb to us children before our parents ever got involved. Father soon showed up, and Sara, John, and I all began to beg at once. "Please, please, let us keep the lamb as our pet." . . . "Yes, yes, we will care for him, we will feed him, we will love him, we'll give him chicken feed, whatever he wants, we will do it. He's so cute! Oh please, please, please!"

Uncle Will, father's older half-brother, ran a sheep ranch a mile and a half to the west. It was lambing season and a ewe (that's a mother sheep) had, apparently, given birth to twins. As sometimes happened to inexperienced ewes, she accepted the first one and did not recognize the next one as her own. Lamb number two went bawling pitifully through the flock and found no one who volunteered to be his mother. Uncle Will had no idea who might be its mother as several other ewes had given birth that same night.

Of course, each of us clamored louder than the next one for the privilege of loving and caring for this lamb forever and ever, world without end, Amen! I must have begged the hardest because the lamb became mine to keep and care for. Mother found a narrow-mouthed bottle with a rubber nipple that fit neatly on the end. We filled it with warm cows' milk and inserted the dripping nipple into the lamb's mouth. Very quickly he was sucking down the milk and vibrating his whole back end with ecstasy. We petted the lamb from all sides, this lonely orphaned soul who finally felt welcomed into the world.

I declared that the lamb's name was "Scoochie" for reasons no one remembers, and the name stuck. My older sister and brother then went off to school while I, a pre-school kid, stayed home and spent hours every day carrying Scoochie around the yard in my arms and playing with him whenever either of us got lonely.

One day, soon after Scoochie came to live with us, I suffered a major life trauma. Father announced that Scoochie was old enough to have his tail docked. Do you know what it means to dock a sheep's tail? "Sheep tails have no use," father explained. "Manure sticks to them and then they get maggots. It's better to cut them off." I didn't listen, I just screamed, begged, and even pled with tears to my mother, but the Supreme Court turned down my appeal. Father gathered Scoochie in his arms, laid his butt on a chopping block, and, with a hatchet, whacked off all but three inches of his tail. At the sight of blood, I cried inconsolably. I think Scoochie got over the trauma sooner than I did. Apart from a scab on his tail stump, he showed no sign of loss and soon was playfully skipping around, worried not at all about his amputated self-image. Scoochie let me comfort him as he, in turn, comforted me. I refused to talk to Father for several days.

On the farm we had a well-established routine for feeding the pets. Every morning and evening after John, Sara, and Father hand-milked our five cows, they carried the stainless-steel buckets of frothy milk across the yard to the house followed by a parade of dogs, cats, Scoochie, and me. In the back porch, behind the screen door pulled shut by a spring to keep out flies and pets, the milk was poured into the cream separator. It was an appliance that every farm had in those days with a spinning core that separated the milk from the cream.

My job was to fill a tin can with skimmed milk and pour it into a wide bowl where the dogs and cats all scrambled, slobbered, and argued over their share. Then I'd hold Scoochie's bottle under the stream of skimmed milk until it was full and pull the nipple over the bottle spout. Scoochie was waiting for me, dancing in anticipation till I came out the screen door with his dinner.

Scoochie and I must have made a cute scene because one Sunday, when I was dressed up in my very special mother-pleasing-going-to church-maroon corduroy outfit with a matching maroon cap, suddenly, mom got an idea. She commanded me to quickly fill Scoochie's bottle with milk from the refrigerator. "What? Aren't we going to church?" I protested. But mother lined up Scoochie and me in the best sunlight and took our photo as my pet pulled at this improbable extra snack.

David, Scoochie, and an improbable Sunday morning bottle of milk.

We were cute enough to make the family album for guests to "ooh and aah" over. And then we hit the "top ten" when Mother had the photo enlarged and mounted for everyone who passed through the house to admire. In the last years of Mother's life, she gave away all her pictures and works of art to us children, at which time Scoochie, framed-for-posterity, came to Joanne and me as part of our inheritance.

I learned a lot about sheep and about Life (with a capital "L") from Scoochie who regarded me as his mother. He ran to me whenever I came outside the house, and he followed me wherever I roamed.

I remember one cold spring day lying down in a pile of straw on the sunny side of our horse barn with Scoochie snuggling close beside me as we experienced attunement with each other. And there we rested in wordless bliss for most of a morning while various dogs and cats came by and joined in the love pile.

From Scoochie I first learned about communion, about the unity of spirit that is possible between souls of very different types, souls who recognize in each other the blessing of God's presence and stay huddled close to enjoy more of the same. Later, as an adult, I discovered that philosophers and gurus of many cultures have spoken about this spiritual reality, too, and consider it the highest form of contemplation—a participation in the eternal awareness that "All is One."

Scoochie also taught me about keeping faith and being faithful. If I got distracted in my play and forgot his mealtimes, he would remind me with insistent bleating at the house back door. And if that didn't fetch me, then my siblings would. So early on I learned to be dependable for someone who depended on me. It was love that first taught me discipline and responsibility.

Sometimes Scoochie would get sick, get diarrhea, or a fever, and I'd report this to my parents who would adjust his diet and come up with miniature portions of the pills meant for cows. Scoochie learned to eat the mash that we fed chickens, and in a few weeks, he was grazing on the grass in our front yard. He never wandered far away because his instinct was to stay close to the flock—which in his case was the people, and the dogs and cats of our farmyard.

Scoochie grew quickly and soon was too heavy for me to carry around. He got more rambunctious and loved to butt me and engage in a sparring match where I'd push his horn buds and he'd push me back. As he grew older, he lost interest in the milk bottle and discovered how much he enjoyed eating the kernels of corn that dropped through the slats of a corn crib in our yard.

Soon Scoochie was no longer a lamb, but a full-grown sheep, and not just any kind of sheep—he was turning into a testosterone-fortified muscle-bulging buck who felt a need to assert his dominance in the herd. Cats now knew better than to slither between his legs. He sent the chickens squawking in all directions as he drove through their flock. We had to alert friends to look out for Scoochie, who loved to butt people from behind and send them sprawling. However, with some of our less-favorite guests, we would "forget" to warn them and then laugh cruelly when Scoochie got a good run at them from behind and knocked them flat. Sometimes I'd pretend to be a matador and hold out a cape for Scoochie to charge at me and then bow out of the way at the last instant to the roar of cheering crowds—Ole!

We children pondered how to wring something useful out of Scoochie's existence. He was probably depressed over having no other bucks to compete with, no flock to bully around. A psychiatrist would have noted how he self-medicated his sorrows with the high-calorie fare that fell through the slats of the corn crib where he had burrowed and hollowed out a comfortable couch of dust. Cows give milk, horses pull wagons, chickens lay eggs, dogs chase rabbits and cats eat rats, but what do surly old bachelor bucks do with no flock to hassle? He knew how to charge at a pretty high speed. Ha, we figured, he could be trained to pull a chariot like pictures we'd seen of war horses in ancient coliseums. So, from the farm junk pile we yanked a pair of wheels, fastened two "tugs" to the axle for our steed to pull, and laid a board across them for a seat. Then we fastened leather straps around his shoulders which made a Scoochie harness. Now we were ready to race. Only Scoochie had no interest in racing. Not one bit.

Scoochie hitched to a racing chariot—spurns our dreams of glory in the colluseum.

We wrestled and tugged him away from his corn crib lounge where he had turned into a miserable couch potato. So, when the three of us pulled him into position and strapped him into the harness, he just stood there. We shouted, taunted, slapped him with a stick, and flashed the matador cape in front of his nose, but he wouldn't budge. We had all the time in the world to call mother to come out of the house with her camera and take a picture—a still life photo it was. We still have that picture on our wall and after all these years, he still has not budged. Brother John is in the background solemnly looking on while Scoochie stands there, obviously thinking of nothing but "when can I get back to my couch?" For all the glory in the Coliseum, and with David Ben Hur at the reins, Scoochie wouldn't pull the chariot, not one inch. We learned that if a buck doesn't want to, you can't make him.

Finally, we relented and unharnessed him. With a sour attitude he sauntered back to his couch under the corn crib, laid down with a sigh, and began to nibble on the corn kernels just in front of his nose. What a lazy good-for-nothing corn-pilfering ungrateful cellulite-encumbered bad-attitude-toting double-chinned and pathetic super slob Scoochie had turned out to be.

One day, not long after Scoochie's unceremonious retirement from chariot racing, and without any further comment or announcement, Father tugged Scoochie into the stock trailer that was hitched to the back bumper of our car and drove away. None of us said a word about what we feared might be happening. In the evening Father returned to the farm with no Scoochie in the trailer, but in his place, there was a shiny new bicycle—a girl's bike it turns out. "This," Father explained, "is because Sara is the oldest, and a girl's bike is easier for short boys to learn on than a men's bike with a crossbar."

"What happened to Scoochie," we cautiously asked? "He sold for $48.00 at the Wichita Stock Yards," Father reported, "which happened to be the price of a new bicycle at the Newton Bike Shop. Maybe the bike will prove more useful." We paused for a moment of silence to respectfully give Scoochie our last regards, and then turned our attention to the shiny chrome pet in front of us, each one taking our turn trying to figure out, how *do* you ride this thing?

And that is the sorry tale of how the cutest-ever little lamb turned into a bicycle.

* * * *

In the summer of 1970, I became a vegetarian, and here is how it happened. Joanne and I were leading a Mennonite Voluntary Service unit in Denver Colorado, of about eight young people engaged in organizing resistance to the U.S. war in Vietnam. We all read Gandhi's autobiography, *The Story of My Experiments with Truth*, in which he challenges his readers to make the experiment, to refrain from eating meat out of respect for all sentient life. (My definition of "sentient life" is any critter who looks you back in the eyes, with whom there is some kind of soul-to-soul recognition.)

We agreed to eat vegetarian for a week, and I've never turned back. I immediately appreciated the moral coherence of vegetarian eating with non-violence and respect for animal life that obviously is conscious and capable of deep relationships. At the time we reflected on the universal taboo of eating animals who have become our pets. Apparently, Scoochie's sad demise continued to trouble me. Eating lower on the food chain also appealed to us as good stewardship of the earth's resources, especially when some people are hungry. Furthermore, my body felt more alive and my mind more alert as we learned to prepare a balanced vegetable protein diet. Joanne's hypo-glycemic metabolism is not like mine, so she has continued to eat some meat, and I've consented to eat some fish so we can share the same meals.

* * * * *

My Father's memoir has a chapter on the series of dogs that helped raise our family as we raised them. Likewise, I could tell about Jiggers who was my companion growing up, and for whom I wrote a glorious somewhat enhanced obituary while I was in divinity school, and that father preserved in his memoir

I could tell about Mac, the dog who raised our children by his loving attention, and whose need for walks taught both Natasha and James how to be faithful in their chores. Mac moved with us from small town Newton, Kansas, to urban Evanston Illinois, sitting faithfully on the truck seat next to me, his driver. In town he was terrified by sirens and fourth of July celebrations and tried to hide under the couch. But he forgave us for bringing him to the city because he loved us. Each day he would get a scoop of dried dog food and some canned horse meat. In his twelve-year lifetime, we calculate that he ate two horses and a small truckload of Purina Chow. He was worth it. We buried him in our back yard where he was honored with a ceramic marker that Natasha fashioned in her high school pottery class.

Joanne and I have not seen fit to get another household pet, but we have instead made friends with the wild animals who already live on our block. We love to sit on our 2nd floor back porch and get to know the same robins, cardinals, and house finches who return each spring. Joanne puts out pie crusts and other leftovers too rich for us, which a possum cleans up in the night. We love the bunnies that are born each spring, who fearlessly dance across our small back lawn where they find enough food for growing up.

We appreciate what Evanston resident and author, Gavin Horn, has written about the concept of "reconciliation ecology." (See *The Way of the Coyote: Shared Journeys in the Urban Wilds.*) Everyone knows about conservation ecology where wildlife habitats are protected, where wilderness is preserved and observed, but basically left alone. This is a great improvement from the kind of war we waged on nature when I was a child. In that era, we learned to hunt rabbits and other beasts because, otherwise, we believed, they would eat our livelihood. It was us or them. In those days there were no deer, bobcats, foxes, turkeys, or migrating geese around. We killed off the last jackrabbits when I was young. Now, we observe that all these species have returned to the countryside around our Kansas homestead, "Heck of a Ranch," where appreciative farmers are learning to live at peace with our wilderness cousins.

A similar thing has happened in the city where humans try to see how close we can live to the local wildlife. Falcons are nesting on our local library's third floor window ledge. Foxes, deer, beaver, and geese inhabit our cemeteries, golf courses, and nature preserves. Here in Evanston, we try to see how close we can live with the local wildlife and thus, learn how close they are willing to live with us. We have our limits, of course, but they are generally non-lethal. We have a screened back door to let in the air and keep out the bugs. We try to keep the rabbits out of our garden greens with chicken-wire fencing. Ant traps at the bottom of our climbing beans discourage these "aphid farmers" whose "cows" suck our vines dry and cut into our bean harvest. We've not yet figured out how to keep squirrels from picking tomatoes and then leaving them to taunt us, half-eaten, on our 2nd floor back porch. At least they stay out of our compost bin, a forever-fortress built out of planks made from recycled plastic. Sometimes in the winter, we use our back porch as a second refrigerator, but usually with a tight lid on the box to keep our local raccoon at bay.

But contrary to the ethos of war against pests and rodents that I grew up with, we live in a zone of negotiated peace and mutual (we hope) appreciation. Humans and wildlife have a long history of living in each other's company. Their wildness and our modest attempts to tame them have created an ethos of life-giving mutuality which deeply nourishes our souls.

* * * * *

Journal: 5-16-19

This afternoon I looked into the eyes of three sets of geese who looked into my eyes with both judgment and grace. Joanne and I journeyed to Emily Oaks, a small well-managed nature preserve in the neighboring suburb of Skokie. Emily Oaks is a few acres of woodlands surrounding a pond we can easily circle in ten minutes, only it always takes us much longer because we can't help but stop, look and get carried away by some new discovery.

HOW THE CUTEST-EVER LITTLE LAMB TURNED INTO A BICYCLE

Gander, goose, and gosslings, warned us to back off and respect their lebens raum.

This time I approached a family of geese with a camera because they looked so impossibly cute. However, when the parents saw me squatting to take a picture, they immediately moved toward me, deliberately clacking their beaks, shaking their necks, flapping their wings. I could tell they were studying my face, trying to read my intentions. Their clear message was for us to back away and leave their goslings to graze in peace.

Adult geese are surprisingly big when they come close, and they know their power. We each stood our ground about five feet apart as they hissed their demands. So, why did we back away and then walk off? I knew they could take a nasty bite of my shins or beat some bruises into my knees with their wings, not to mention flying at our eyes. I had a long look into their eyes as they looked into mine. Though we do not speak a common language, communication was going on—furiously. It's clear they had some knowledge of the human race and how to negotiate a safe space around their family. They were respectful, but insistent. "Back away. Leave us be. You squat like that and I'll beat you up. I don't want to, but I will if you insist." They may have added, "And don't even think about posting our kids on Instagram."

I was only curious, but for them family *lebens raum* was at stake. The memory crossed my mind of how it felt to be parents of little children. My ego didn't need to win this showdown. So, we turned and respectfully walked away.

Later, Joanne and I found our way to a favorite pair of benches three paces from the water's edge. But two geese stood preening themselves right where we hoped to sit and enjoy our snack. The goose pair was combing their breast feathers and digging in to scratch whatever itched them. As we came closer, one of them threatened us with a glare and a step in our direction, but the other one turned and walked to the water where she slowly paddled away, looking back to see if her partner was following. She seemed to say, "Leave 'em be. They're not worth it." We waited. He searched our eyes, then seemed to shrug and walk away, ceding the bench to us. They didn't need a bench to do their thing, we did. It was a soft negotiation.

We had come with a pomegranate that I proceeded to cut up into wedges, red juice dripping on the stone bench. Looking across the water we spotted a goose standing guard. With my telephoto lens I snuck up to within a few feet of his nest. Then with goose bobbing wildly in the camera monitor, I clicked the shutter and froze him on his perch among the cattails. That's when we discovered a partner behind him, probably sitting on eggs.

Once he spotted us, he entered the water and paddled straight in our direction. Was he going to aggressively demand our departure? We were a long way from his nest. It seemed unlikely. He marched onto land and scanned our eyes as we looked into his, gauging each other's intentions. But he seemed more interested in what we were eating. When we tossed a few pomegranate seeds in his direction, he snapped them up with expert memory of where each one landed, missing not a single seed. We tested how close he would come, and he tested us whether we were safe. Finally, he consented to quickly snatch up a seed between my sandals and then back away. We had found a mutual comfort zone. It was obvious he had done fund-raising (or food-raising) before with other humans in this place and had perfected his solicitation technique by repeated practice.

There is a purist notion of wildlife conservation that says humans should only observe, not feed or interact with wild animals. That kind of conservation ecology certainly has its place. I think we should be knowledgeable about what is healthy for animals in nature and not feed gobs of white bread to deer, for example. But eating together is a way of falling in love, of satisfying our curiosity, of both taming and wilding one another as God's beloved creatures.

When our pomegranate was all gone, we apologized that there was no more, got up and stepped back, and so did the gander. We nodded to each other and moved on. But something wordless lingers from the "conversations" between geese and humans this afternoon mediated through eye contact and body language, through gracious and not-so-gracious requests, learning how to accept each other in our common world. Joanne and I went home feeling deeply renewed in spirit and amazed that we are permitted to share life with "alien" beings who are, we realize, our distant kin with similar recognizable needs, and yet, possessing an attentive consciousness so wonderfully other than our own.

Modern science has no category for souls, but whatever a soul is, if we have one, so do sheep, geese, pets, and all other living creatures who have the courage to look us in the eyes and try to read our intentions.

*****

Prayer Journal:

4-12-20

JC: David, do you love me?

DJ Yes, I love you right now. But obviously, a few minutes ago, I loved you less than I loved following my curiosity wherever it took me through a maze of web articles, which was a waste of time.

JC Don't try to curb your curiosity with shame, willpower, or some other technique of self-improvement. Only love is powerful enough to tame your natural desires. I use the word "tame" because curiosity is a God-given gift. But this gift is also wild and 'wants' to rule your life rather than be your servant. That is how idolatry works. You get attached to the gift and forget the giver. But it won't work to hate the gift because you need it, your community needs it, the world needs it. I delight in seeing your gifts functioning rightly in service to the kingdom, in service to those around you in community. That gives God glory. What do you think of that?

DJ: It reminds me of the way a horse is tamed. First one befriends the horse by feeding it, currying its coat, leading it around, giving it joy. And then after the horse knows it is loved and has nothing to fear, you can ask it to do your bidding. And out of a feeling of security in your leadership, it will comply.

I see something in horses and in dogs that has been bred into them over many generations, where they have evolved to enjoy a relationship with humans and want to collaborate in common activity. I remember sensing this as a child when I was learning to ride horses. The pony under me probably weighed twenty times my weight. Obviously, the horse could have easily hurt me if it wanted to. But it didn't want to. It had some instinct that was protective of me as an eight-year-old child. It could get frustrated and bored with my indecisive and clumsy riding technique. Admittedly, it could get wild in an instant if it was startled, because horses have a deep instinct to protect themselves, to run from danger in an instant. But somewhere in that big body of a well-trained horse lives a desire to cooperate and belong to a herd which can include humans.

I remember how, once the pony I was riding understood that I wanted to round up a herd of cows and bring them home, it would anticipate my signals and start to do the job on its own. That really thrilled me. We were doing this together. We were in synch, our wills meshing. I enjoyed it and so did the horse. Is that what you're trying to do with me, Jesus?

JC: Well, almost. You think you know what I want and do it on your own, and soon you have forgotten about me, and have taken over the project rather than check in with me. You think you are doing my will, but we are no longer attuned to each other. Then you start to feel oppressed by the work or get lost in distractions to escape the feelings of oppression. Eventually, you discover that we are disconnected, just like you were for twenty minutes before our quiet time, when your curiosity took over. Other times you get carried away by your work. Remember, I am not like your father who felt obligated to discipline you to stay on task and did not know how to stay relationally connected with you and your spirit. I love you and hope your love for me can keep us close and attuned to each other all day long—in play, work, and quiet contemplation.

DJ: Wow. I see it's never too late to learn how to grow closer to you. It's like Augustine said, "Our hearts are restless until they find their rest in you." It's like that late-winter love pile of lamb, boy, dog, and cats on a mound of straw on the sunny side of the barn.

CHAPTER 3

My Worst and Best Grade School Year Ever
Mentors Who Shaped Me

LOOKING BACK AT THE shortened year that she taught at our one-room rural Kansas grade school, I view Mrs. Hackler with a lot more sympathy now than I did when I was her rebellious eighth-grade student. I recognize that she was on the verge of retirement after a career of just-barely-making-it as a grade school teacher. I imagine that our school board of three farmers had a hard time attracting a good teacher with what little they could afford to pay in an era when rural grade schools were going out of business. Mrs. Hackler also was at the end of her rope, needing a job when she probably wanted to retire but couldn't afford it. The two desperate parties fell into a co-dependent relationship. For better or worse, she was our teacher at Trainview where the Rock Island Railroad ran right by our school yard.

The Busenitz family "school bus" saves some students the two-mile rainy-day ordeal of walking through mud.

It didn't take long for the fourteen of us in grades one through eight to recognize Mrs. Hackler's limitations. Besides her snicker-worthy name, another reason she lost our respect was because she did not play with us or supervise recess times. Without a responsible adult, our squabbles tended to escalate until someone cried or got a bloody nose. Academically, she was weak, relying on the answers in her teacher's manual rather than deeply understanding the subjects she taught. By Christmas break we were still on the first chapters of our textbooks. She tried to discipline our misdeeds by making us sit in our desks and miss five minutes of recess. Hah! We were used to much harsher punishments than that! We started to brag about how many demerits we got. With my pocket knife I cut a growing row of notches in the library bookcase to keep a public score of my infractions. At report card time, however, we were surprised to see we all got A's and B's. We suspected Mrs. Hackler was just treading water till the end of the year and did not want our parents to know we were learning almost nothing.

The last studentbody photo in 1955, as the one-room school was then consolidated into the Elbing district. Yours Truly behind the bow tie.

A couple of times in the play yard we "accidentally" overthrew the softball and cracked her car windows. On another occasion eager hands and buckets moved all the sand from the sandbox into Mrs. Hackler's Packard trunk so that the back bumper just barely cleared the ground. When she tried to drive home, we were hiding behind the hedge watching her car snort and sputter, barely getting underway. She must have complained to the School Board, so one morning Albert Busenitz, chairman of the board, sat in a school desk on the back row to make sure we respected our teacher, which, of course, we did while he was there. At noon he gave us a tongue-lashing and we promised to do better, a resolve that lasted until his dust had settled on the road.

One rainy day when the school yard was muddy, all our pent-up recess energy had to recreate indoors. We played tag, running around and jumping over desks, yelling at the top of our lungs, and knocking over little kids who couldn't keep up. Meanwhile, Mrs. Hackler, somewhere far in the background, was rapping her ruler on the desk and pleading with us, "Be nice." At that point Donnie conceived of a new Olympic event called "desk running," which he practiced by bounding from one desk to the next around the room while we timed him. At the finish line, the last desk broke loose from its mount and Donnie toppled with it to the floor, grabbing his bruised elbow, and wailing to high heaven. At that we all grew quiet, the teacher rang the bell, and we returned to our seats momentarily sobered.

I remember feeling protective that year toward first-grader John Mark and took him under my wing, so to speak. In free-for-all situations like that it's often the littlest ones who get hurt. In return John Mark would do whatever I asked of him. One day, in the back of the classroom I advised him to call the teacher "A big black witch," which he proceeded to do in a loud and gleeful voice. This caused Mrs. Hackler to boil over in rage. She pulled a yard-long hose out of her desk drawer and ran at John Mark, grabbed him by the shoulders, and dragged him out the door. We were petrified to hear the smacks of the hose and the terrified wailing of our first-grade darling.

The breaking point in this increasingly chaotic drama came that evening when John Mark's father took his battered son to Albert Busenitz, lowered his pants and showed off the bloody bruises on his legs and back. At that Albert declared, "She's fired."

In those days, parents and teachers had the right to inflict corporal punishment, but to make an example of a first grader who had been put up to it by an eighth grader, was deemed beyond the pale. John Mark's parents had had enough. Up to that point their first-grade son had learned nothing, they said, except to print the letters of his name—backwards. Anyway, that's the last we saw of Mrs. Hackler.

A few days later we heard that our Zion Mennonite Church pastor, Rev. Cornelius J. Dyck, had agreed to lay aside most of his church duties and to teach the remaining six weeks of our school year. What a huge relief for us all! C.J. was an inspiring teacher; he knew his stuff, enjoyed joining us for recess, and could tell fascinating adventure stories of his time helping resettle WWII refugees in South America. He had our total respect and attention without ever needing to command it. It didn't hurt his cause that C. J. could throw a mean fastball and run the bases like the wind.

I remember whizzing through my homework and then getting a thick book, Charles Dickens *Tale of Two* Cities, plopped on my desk. C.J. said, "This might be more at your level." Wow, did I sit up straight and dig in to prove him right! In those six weeks we learned more than in the whole rest of the year. We had a proper end-of-school-year celebration in which I gave the valedictorian address (since I happened to be tops in my class of two.)

Interim teacher, Cornelius J. Dyck, presiding over the valedictorian's speech.

By the next fall, not surprisingly, Trainview Elementary School was shut down, and all the students went to a consolidated district in the village of Elbing, where a new gym was under construction. Ours was the last graduating class—end of an era.

* * * * *

Now, more than sixty years later, I look back at the dramatic turn-around in the spirit at work among us that school year, and I wonder how did we go from an appallingly calloused and alienated gang of rowdies to highly motivated model students in one short weekend? The 1954 novel by British author, William Golding, *Lord of the Flies,* describes a gang of children stranded on a Pacific Island who, deprived of parental figures, descends into brutal rivalries and, eventually, the ritualistic sacrifice of a scape-goat child. The Bible tells about "principalities and powers" that rule over people groups in a way that transcends the individuals in them. We were still the same kids before and after that fateful weekend, but a certain power over us was broken. Of course, the character of our two teachers had something to do with this transformation, but more was at play.

According to anthropologist Rene Girard, the rivalries of unacknowledged envy and competition within every society keep rising until they settle on a common enemy, a scapegoat that becomes the target of their collective wrath. And when that scapegoat is sacrificed, there is peace—at least for a while, until the whole dynamic of sin and the search for an atoning victim starts up once again. In many ancient societies this dynamic was ritualized in annual cycles of human sacrifices. With the Hebrews this impulse was transformed into a literal "scapegoat," a sacrificial goat on whom was laid the sins of the nation. This shift away from human sacrifice has its origins in the story of Abraham, Isaac, and the atoning ram that God provided.

According to Girard, Jesus was the one who most clearly unmasked this enemy-making scapegoat mechanism by teaching love of enemies, and by letting goodness incarnate be sacrificed to show what human wrath (not divine wrath) will lead to. In so doing he exposed our persistent human tendency to project our sins onto a common enemy whose death we imagine might save us. This explains a lot in our unredeemed national politic where leaders try to consolidate power around themselves and against some faction or enemy by projecting our unacknowledged sins onto "the other" whom we rally to defeat—as if this will save us from chaos.

At Trainview School, lacking a credible role model, we descended into petty power struggles with each other and eventually organized our aggression against Mrs. Hackler, our unifying scapegoat. Then when she was suddenly gone, we were all appalled at what we had done and what we had become. We never talked about it with each other in those terms, but a spirit of shame and repentance was manifest in the way we quickly buckled down to study and cooperate under C. J.'s leadership.

Years later, C. J. Dyck became a highly respected professor of church history at the Anabaptist Mennonite Biblical Seminary in Elkhart, Indiana. About once a decade I would run into him at some church conference, and he would ask what had become of me as a good mentor should do. He remembered our intensive six weeks together with genuine fondness, and at every stage of life I've wanted to make him proud. In the words of Dickens, I remember that last year at Trainview as "the worst of times and the best of times" all wrapped up in one.

* * * * *

During childhood, the significant adults around me wanted to save my soul or get me to behave, or both. I resisted these pressures to conform by stubbornly thinking my own thoughts, and by getting into provocative arguments with my Sunday-school teachers. A spirit of alienation and reactive mistrust of authority grew in me.

In Bethel College, (1958-62) I had a few inspiring professors whose excitement about life-long learning was contagious. Though I had academic advisors with professional expertise, that is not where my values and vision for life were shaped. The real integration of education happened for me in late-night peer groups, where we tried to put together what the academic world was segregating into specialties and professional silos. This is where we worked out what a life of integrity might look like, and in these settings, I sharpened the philosophical arguments to support an anarchist politic.

There was one college mentor, however, who made a significant dent in my alienation—not by direct assault, but by an intense interest in what I was thinking, and who shared his own critique of establishment assumptions with similar enthusiasm. Al Meyer, our academic dean my junior and senior years, became a genuine mentor, as he was for a group of other student leaders, including Joanne. His office door was always open to us, inviting us to interrupt him any time we wished. He was young enough in spirit to remember what we were going through. He had a Ph.D. in atomic physics but was on fire to see the radical discipleship of Anabaptist and Early Church experience be reborn in small intergenerational groups of students and faculty. We were impressed by Al's top-notch intellect similar to his brother-in-law, the budding Anabaptist theologian, John Howard Yoder.

Rather than challenge my radical inclinations, Al Meyer encouraged them with the revolutionary insight that Jesus, the Early Church and our Anabaptist spiritual ancestors were radicals too. "Radical" meant not just opposed to the status quo but getting at the root of any issue at hand. After all, Jesus came to demonstrate a kingdom that turns the conventional wisdom of the world upside-down with the power of fearless truth telling, servanthood, and suffering love. Both Joanne and I were pointed by Al in the direction of intentional Christian community where we found a life-long expression of the call to radical discipleship in the life of Jesus with his followers.

In the Congo, soon after we arrived at our teaching post in Bibanga (1967-69) I had a visit from a bright young pastor, Mukuna Joseph, fresh out of seminary, who had learned that I was a conscientious objector to military service. He confessed that he had always seen Jesus as an advocate of prophetic non-violent social change and peacemaking—somewhat in the pattern of Martin Luther King, Jr. Until then his pacifist convictions had been put down by his seminary professors and by white Southern-Presbyterian missionaries more generally. Did I have any resources on Christian pacifism in French, he asked? I lent him a couple of books right down his alley by Andre Trocme, the French pastor whose congregation sheltered and spirited to safety hundreds of Jews fleeing Nazi genocide during World War II.

Pastor Mukuna, I soon learned, had similarly risked his life during a recent Congolese civil war, assisting tribal enemies to escape their persecutors. The next Sunday, Pastor Mukuna began to boldly preach Christian non-violence and enemy-love from the pulpit.

But the blessing of our relationship more often flowed in the other direction in that Mukuna became our trusted pastor and coach in cross-cultural matters. He was a creative leader in welcoming indigenous cultural expressions like drumming, dance, and spontaneous singing into the worship setting.

Pastor Joseph Mukuna (white collar) greeting worshipers at the Bibanga church.

He advised us on how to behave as Jesus-followers in an awkward post-colonial era where Africans were coming into leadership. Nevertheless, as whites, we were automatically counted among the power elite and ushered to the podium (for example) simply because of our skin color. We asked his counsel: Should we hire servants to chop our wood, cook our meals, plant our garden, care for all our menial needs like other privileged white people around? Yes, we should hire a cook so we could both focus on teaching. No, it was good to chop our own wood to let neighbors know we did not put ourselves above others. He urged us to take time to listen to the stories of suffering around us. This was our first experience of submitting our spiritual and economic lives to someone who was racially and culturally very different from us, and yet with whom we found a profound meeting point in our love for the prophetic enemy-loving Jesus. We were excited to experience such a depth of community across the barriers of conventional racism and felt a call to somehow bring our discoveries back home with us to America.

At New Creation Fellowship (1971–84) community leader, Jake Pauls, did not impress me as a sharp intellect, rather he won my trust by patient and sincere friendship, by the joy he expressed in being around me and others in community. It was a delight to work together whether on the construction crew or in community leadership meetings since we always connected with a round of prayer and personal sharing before we tackled the agenda before us. Jake's presence in a group, or on a crew had the effect of settling everyone down so that we could do our best without stress. His hugs were always hearty and steadying.

Some leaders are strong on giving advice. Jake was quick to pitch in on whatever practical help might be needed. I remember one time when our family took a much-needed vacation trip. We came home to a house where all the rooms had been painted, completing a project that had drug on way too long under our own flagging energy. The folks who did the work were as excited as we were over this surprise.

As a mentor, Jake provided steady good cheer, spontaneous help, sincere friendship, and a freedom to pray whenever we felt stymied in our community life, trusting that God would bring good out of whatever we were facing.

It was during this period of my life that I discovered I was beginning to mentor others in a natural way like Al Meyer, Mukuna Joseph, and Jake Pauls had done for me. Now, I naturally took an interest in the spiritual life of those who worked next to me, who were in my small group. When the need came up, I could channel my mentors and give to others what had been given to me. What divinity school had failed to produce now emerged in the context of thick Christian community. Intensive discipleship in community is the way Jesus did it, and that's what made an unofficial pastor of me. It was not a transmission of knowledge so much as an imparting of character from one life to another, a flame passed on, a spiritual insight that appears when needed.

Similarly, I could tell stories of other mentors in my life at Reba Place Fellowship (1984 to the present)—Virgil Vogt, Allan Howe, Hilda Carper, Sally Youngquist—to name a few. But to save my words and your patience, I will conclude this section on the gifted mentors who have poured into my life by borrowing a few reflections from my journal as my mentor of thirty-four years, Julius Belser, was leaving us behind.

* * * * *

Journal 12-13-18:

I wake up this morning with both a heavy and a grateful heart because my compassionate friend, faithful mentor, best advocate, inspired co-worker, unstoppable visionary of new projects to bless the last and the least, this prophet of God for almost nine decades on earth, Julius Belser, is dying. This is no shock. His stooped body more and more often in recent times would fall asleep in mid-conversation, but then his eyes would open, and he'd ask us to sing with him, "Soon and very soon, we are going to see the King."

I've been looking over a collection of photos from Julius and Peggy's sixtieth wedding anniversary. Among them is one with Julius surrounded by a motley crew of mourners and oak trees in the humble Plow Creek Cemetery. There he stands in his lanky frame, slightly bowed, reading from the Bible, presiding at the burial of George Busse. George was a nobody in the world's eyes, someone with limited intelligence, few earthly possessions, mostly abandoned by family, and yet beloved by God, and accompanied in his final hour. Here is his body awaiting burial in a finely crafted homemade casket of knotty white pine, a casket with perfect angles and proportions, crafted by Julius and his helpers. Now George's friends are gathered to give him a loving and decent burial. I have joined Julius in building a few other caskets in the Reba Shop and hope to help his family build a coffin to honor him as he has honored others.

Julius Belser presides at George Busse's funeral in the Plow Creek Fellowship cemetery.

In the early eighties, Julius Belser, one of three elders at the helm of Reba Place Fellowship, was in anguish of spirit. His imagination was seared by images of thousands of Central Americans fleeing north from death squads and a brutal civil war of the rich against the poor. In a Passion Week drama at Reba Place Church, Julius played the role of Pontius Pilate, who turned Jesus over to be tortured and killed by those who hated him. Pilate then ceremoniously washed his hands of any guilt. In that moment Julius knew prophetic action was called for.

Julius led the way in imagining a network of folks reminiscent of the Underground Railroad, secreting slaves to freedom in Canada. Since the railroad that Julius dreamed up and organized was mostly legal, he called it the Overground Railroad and invited others to join in its operation.

In 1984, our family moved to Reba, and I became Julius Belser's assistant, helping him manage this growing network of churches, intentional communities and volunteers linking hands across the U.S. and Canada. Julius lined up Spanish-speaking volunteers to interview those refugees in shelters and detention camps on the southern U.S. border, where they selected those most in need of protection. We'd bond them out of prison, arrange for rides to temporary hosts, communities who could teach them how to survive in "El Norte" Eventually they would land with sponsors in Canada. For a decade we ran this railroad together. He was the imaginative chairman of the board, and I was the director. He was the humble stepladder that I climbed to take over his job even as he held me up so I could do my best.

Then when the civil wars in Central America came to an end, we turned our attention to affordable housing needs in Evanston. He was chairman of the board, and I was the Executive Director, of Reba Place Development Corporation. There I learned that when I knocked on the doors of City Hall, and they heard I worked for Julius Belser, I'd describe the project and they'd ask, "How much money do you need?"

Later, Julius and a few African American pastors teamed up to organize the Evanston Community Development Association for a similar mission of providing affordable housing in the African American neighborhoods. When they learned I was with Julius, I got immediate credibility and welcome. I remember Bishop W.D.C. Williams grabbing my torso with a linebacker's hug and bellowing in my ear, "I love you with the love of Jesus, and there's nothing you can do about it." Then Bishop took me under his wing and coached me on how to use my gifts in service of an organization with mature African American leadership, moving forward in the wake of my mentor Julius Belser.

I could tell many other stories from our thirty-four years of Monday morning mentor meetings where I mostly talked, and Julius listened. Together we hatched schemes that organized many others in doing good for the last and the least. Wherever I went, I learned that Julius had already earned the trust that I needed to do my job. Again and again, Julius would dream up some new community-sized project responding to needs of the poor and oppressed. I'd say, "That's a great idea, but who will administer it?" Never dismayed, he would come up with another dream which we'd problem-solve into a viable project. At that point Julius would knock on doors, and because he was Julius, they would open. Minority leaders would usually get on board first because they were already Julius's friends.

There is no end to Julius stories I could tell. But now it is time to build Julius's coffin in the traditional Belser pattern. We want to honor his body as his spirit passes on "to see the King" from whom he will surely hear, "Well done good and faithful servant."

Chapter 4

Take a Kid Along

Learning to Mentor in Turn

My Uncle Johnny and my dad were stockman-farmers with ranches half a mile apart, making it easy for them to share a cattle truck, swap implements, or borrow boys as needed. I remember Uncle Johnny once reprimanding his younger brother—my dad—for going to town and failing to take a boy along. What was that about? Was there a family tradition that Uncle Johnny was obliged to pass on to his younger brother?

On Saturdays, or in the summertime when we were not in school, my brothers and I were supposed to work non-stop on some useful farm project. Father would set us up with chores in the field, garden, or barns—and then go to town, perhaps to get some implement repaired or to bring home a load of gravel. Father's economic reasoning was that if he took a boy along, the farm would be less productive. But Uncle Johnny had a different economy in mind—a father should not waste an opportunity to talk with his boy one-on-one, not just to pass on wisdom and skills, but also to learn what was going on in that lad's head.

True to form, Uncle Johnny rolled onto our farm in the cattle truck one day and asked, "Does any boy want to go with me to the Wichita stock yards?" Of course, I volunteered. Sitting high in the truck cab to survey the farms going by, I relished the status and honor of Uncle Johnny's company. Along the way he told me stories and relayed information about the towns and the farms we passed by. He'd ask me to estimate how big was that field? Or how many cattle in that herd?—Skills a farmer would need. We talked theology too. Uncle Johnny understood that raising spiritually awake boys, rather than alienated brats, was a more important farm product than any crops that might be sold on the market.

Along the way I remember Uncle Johnny making fun of lazy farmers who go to town in the middle of the day to "eat beer and drink pie" when they should be out in the field. I laughed and repeated the punch line so I could get a rise from my friends later. On the way home we did not "eat beer and drink pie," but we did pause at an ice cream shop to get cones which we licked and nibbled on, seeing who could make his last the longest in the hot summer wind.

After Uncle Johnny's reprimand to my father, I remember father making more of an effort to take one of us boys along when he went into town. Since mother didn't bake pies, which was my father's favorite desert, invariably, on the way home from town we would stop at a café where the waitresses all just happened to know my father's first name and preference. "Louie, what'll it be today? Apple pie?" Sitting down on the stool in front of the pie case, I made my choice, which was usually cherry pie, with ice cream on top if Father was in a good mood.

At the age of fourteen I got a driver's license—Kansas law permitted farm kids this privilege because they were needed to drive wheat loads to the grain elevator in harvest time. But well before my fourteenth birthday Father would take me along for driving practice. Without him realizing it, father gave me a big honor by falling asleep as I drove our semi-trailer cattle truck home from Kansas City through the rolling Flint Hills, trusting me to shift up and down as needed without instructions. I felt big, raising my index finger off the steering wheel at the passing truckers who did the same for me, mistaking me for a grownup.

While Uncle Johnny indulged his nephews, he was a harder task master on his own son, Herman, who grew up to be a rather alienated and rebellious teenager. Herman, a few years ahead of my brothers and me, was our larger-than-life role model, already over six feet tall and 200 pounds as an eighth grader. As a freshman in high school, he got his own car and loved to give rides to us, "Louie's boys." He exceeded every speed limit and showed us how to "fly" cars and farm tractors around corners, expertly down-shifting, hitting brakes and then the accelerator to take off in a cloud of dust as we hung on for dear life. Our big cousin loved to take us along on his errands or joy rides, which usually ended with the consumption of a six-pack of pop and as much ice cream as we could find in the refrigerator. Herman loved to share with us his own dare-devil X-X-Large Falstaffian style of life.

A few years later, when I had kids and led a construction crew, I enjoyed taking James and Natasha off their mother's hands and driving together to the lumber yard in our rusty red New Creation Builder's truck to bring home a load of supplies. We enjoyed non-stop conversation and then a stop at the Dairy Queen where the take-a-kid-along tradition melted and messily trickled down to another generation.

* * * * *

Given my earlier vow to become the mentor I wished I'd had when I was young, how did that commitment pan out? One mentoring strategy is to open doors, to involve younger disciples in my work and ministry as Julius did for me. I used to invite teenagers from Reba and other communities to accompany us on delegations to our sister community in El Salvador, Valle Nuevo. For some of them it was a rite of passage, a formation in community and the politics of Jesus, a concrete way they could engage in the work of reconciliation. We stressed in our orientation that these delegations were not "mission trips" where imperialist-minded do-gooders pretend to have the answers for poor third-world heathens. Rather, we came to learn from a people who had suffered immensely and, nevertheless, held onto their faith. We prepared by learning Spanish songs familiar to the community, watching the Romero video, practicing how you wash your hands and face from a poured pot of water, and preparing to enjoy tortillas and beans at just about every meal. These teens participated in the delegations by playing with Valle Nuevo kids and listening to the agonizing stories of suffering and loss by a people who had been targeted for extermination, and yet rescued by God like the Children of Israel at the Red Sea. (You'll catch the fuller story of this sister community relationship in chapters 8 and 15.)

The impact of these annual Valle Nuevo visits from 1992 to the present has been profound for the young people. Here are some of the things I've heard them say on the way home: "I want to be baptized because now I know what faith looks like;" or, "I want to study Spanish and major in community health;" or, "I'm done complaining about the latest stuff I don't have;" or, "I never thought of myself as privileged before, but now my eyes are opened to the real world;" or, "I brought my guitar along because I wanted to teach them a few lessons, but instead, my friends taught me so much more, and I'm leaving my guitar with them."

Sometimes this "take a kid along" tradition would take a giant leap into deeper collaboration. On one early trip to Valle Nuevo, Sara Belser, who had grown up at Reba, surprised me by taking a seat beside me on the bus and asking, "David, would you be my mentor?" She continued. "I realize that by growing up in community at Reba, I've absorbed a whole way of life without thinking about it. I wish we could organize a seminar where community elders (like her grandparents, Julius and Peggy Belser) could tell their stories about what they have learned." So, instead of her?

going to college, Sara and I dedicated the next year to researching internship programs in other communities and recruiting an intern class to join her in an intensive year of discipleship to Jesus in the light of Reba's experience. This program included Monday night seminars taught and attended by the whole community, including an "Intentional Christian Community" class from North Park University. Our intern class often pulled away for campouts and retreats. We made no bones about it—we were in training to become saints. In our lighter moments, we even played at giving each other halos.

How we honored our Reba interns with halos in their pursuit of sainthood.

This program continued with strong community support for a decade or more, usually led by Yours Truly and a younger assistant.

I've had several younger assistants in my writing projects. *The Intentional Christian Community Handbook* (Paraclete Press, 2013) evolved through several planning retreats such that the voices and quotes of about fifty emerging community leaders are included in the book—a rich and rewarding period of my life. This large extended family of younger mentees has healed the loneliness wounds of my childhood and helped keep my spirit young to this day in ways I never could have imagined.

I believe these transforming conversations and relationships are what the prophet Joel (2:28–32) anticipated in times of renewal when "Your sons and your daughters shall prophesy, your old men will dream dreams, and your young men see visions." This is the sustaining "food" that Jesus talked about after his breakthrough conversation with the Samaritan woman at Jacob's well, food that his disciples (at that time) still knew nothing about.

* * * * *

I see now, looking back on my childhood trips with grown-ups, they represent an era of patriarchy, of fathers passing on a legacy to their sons. I suppose mothers took trips with their daughters back then too, but I don't remember. However, in my elder stage of life I've been blessed to not just to make long trips with Alan, John, James, Adrian, Chico, and Russ, but also with Sarah, Celina, Monica, two Natalies, and Anali—to name just a few. It's been my joy to see these young adults blossom and bear fruit in their own next steps of life. And we're connected in an undeniable bond that comes to life whenever we see each other again.

I cannot explain my technique because the essentials of mentoring are not techniques. We are talking more about character formation, and character grows from the inside out according to the gifts God has planted there, and the circumstances of life where these gifts are matured in service. I find it insightful to ponder the counsel of Lau Tzu: "Watch your thoughts, they become your words; watch your words, they become your actions; watch your actions, they become your habits; watch your habits, they become your character; watch your character, it becomes your destiny."

I've used the label "mentor" thus far in this chapter to describe what I've received and what I try to pass on. The role of mentor goes back to Greek mythology when Odysseus goes off to fight the Trojan War and leaves his trusted friend and advisor, Mentor, to raise his son Telemachus. And thus, the word, "Mentor" passed on into common usage. In my mind other terms are also useful. "Pastoring," "offering spiritual direction," "discipleship," "accompaniment," and "friendships of virtue" (Aristotle's word for it) are somewhat overlapping categories with a variety of emphases that cover much of the same territory. All these fields have their libraries of resources worth exploring, but the real work of character transformation is relational and communal rather than intellectual. Nevertheless, intellect does play a servant role in reflecting on and consolidating discoveries out of our experience. This reflection usually results in life wisdom. But wisdom is not a body of knowledge, it is a gift that shows up as Jesus promised, that he would be with us wherever "two or three are gathered in my name." There we will discover his life and character channeled in and through us by means of the Holy Spirit. The following section tells one such story of a friend and seeker after the wisdom of Jesus.

* * * * *

Journal: June 2017: Lilies and Sparrows Community.

Here in the Melas-Blanton living room a big grandfather clock behind my rocking chair solemnly chimes 6:00 AM. Outside, in this corner of Harrisonburg VA, the dawn is serenaded by a lyrical robin and occasional whimpers from baby Yani, who is teething a new set of molars. Beside me a candle spreads its warm glow, chasing the shadows into the corners of the room in this house without electricity, in this community without a car. We are in a swath of "liberated urban land" that includes a community center, a fishpond fertilized by chicken-yard run-off that ends up down-stream on the gardens. The sign above the front porch names this house "The Downstream Project," recalling Wendell Berry's ecological revision of the Golden Rule: "Do unto those downstream as you would have those upstream do to you."

Ever since Nicholas and Rachel Sarah met in an ecology club in their senior year at George Madison University, they have tried to pursue a lifestyle that would be sustainable for seven billion people on this earth with its limited resources. They continue in this way, now seven years and two children later, not just for the sake of the earth and future generations, but also because they believe this is what the coming kingdom of God will look like.

Soon Nicholas and Rachel Sarah (she goes by two names because there's another Rachel in the community) are up and making breakfast for the others of their group, scrambling a dozen eggs on a wood-burning kitchen stove with fuel easily available in the Appalachian hills around town. We met all day yesterday in a workshop exploring the covenant-making process that is background to all of scripture. The "Lilies and Sparrows" told their stories of liberation and commented on the latest draft of their rule of life. They are bracing for the coming year when the Melas-Blanton family takes a sabbatical year in France with a community called "The Ark of Lanza Del Vasto."

Lanza Del Vasto was a disciple of Gandhi, who launched a community and a movement in France marked by the clear non-violent witness of Jesus along with a beautiful way of living simply on the land sustained as much as possible by hand-labor. In a few years, the "Lilies and Sparrows" hope to give expression to such a life in the countryside somewhere near Harrisonburg.

The Lilies and Sparrows find strong support and encouragement in their local Mennonite congregation prophetically named, "The Early Church," where we met for worship and fellowship on Sunday morning. The congregation is small, about forty adults plus children, most of whom intentionally live in the immediate neighborhood. The gathering for worship has a "home-made" rather than professional feel to it. They take a long time for announcements and prayers because so many people are involved in community needs and local justice issues. Several homeless persons and recent immigrants are in attendance. They feel at home because the church meets in a space that, for most of the week, is open to them as a drop-in center. Next door is a tent with picnic tables full of potted plants and a "donations can" if you wish to contribute for what you carry home.

On my way to the airport, Nicolas spoke of his calling to holiness as one important reason why he feels committed to life in covenant community. He longs to become a saint in the simplest way—words you'd hardly expect to hear from someone so obviously gifted as an intellectual and a community leader. He longs for the structures of accountability and mutual encouragement so that community folk can speak into his life, and without which he knows he will not make much progress in godly character development. He is seeking a relational wisdom that comes from a community where members listen deeply to each other. This life together of the Lilies and Sparrows is fragile and yet, so clearly animated by the spirit of Jesus. They are no longer starry-eyed idealists; they have been on this journey a long time now and are building carefully, with a wide network of support, for a kingdom that will last. Thanks be to God for trusted friends and a movement of the Spirit like that!

CHAPTER 5

The Last Threshing Circle
The Curse and the Redemption of Work

WHEN I WAS SIX years old, I witnessed the last grain harvest the old-fashioned way in our rural Kansas community. By threshing time, all the fields of wheat, oats and rye had been cut with a binder and the twine-bound sheaves were hand stacked into shocks that dotted the straw-colored landscape. A dozen farmers joined in a threshing circle that worked together on each one's farm in turn, until all the harvest was in. On threshing day, the farmers and their boys all showed up with horse-drawn hayracks and began to pitch the bundles into the racks as the horses walked forward under voice commands.

The center of the drama was my Uncle Johnny's huge threshing machine with its hundreds of clattering, shaking, and roaring parts, driven by his big Case tractor with a long flapping traction belt. The noise was so deafening that everyone around had to shout to be heard. The fully loaded hayracks pulled up on each side of the machine where brawny farmhands pitched bundles into the "mouth" of the devouring beast. Chaff and straw blew out of the long rear spout onto a growing golden mountain on the plain, while wheat poured out of a side auger into a waiting wagon. Since I was too little to be trusted around horses or pitchforks, my job was to level the mound of wheat with a shovel as it poured into the grain wagon. Fascinated by numbers, I kept checking a little odometer at the base of the grain spout that counted the bushels, and tried to estimate how many bushels to the acre the wheat crop was making. I've been estimating whatever I could, ever since.

At noontime the threshing machine stopped, and everyone made their way to our house where tubs of cistern water, soap and a wash line of towels were waiting for the threshers who might strip to the waist to wash up muscular bodies streaked with chaff, dust, and sweat.

Suddenly, someone started a good-natured water fight that would stop, and then start up again until the call went out that lunch was ready. Then all the men, suddenly subdued, marched into the fully extended dining table groaning under the food that the women and girls had been butchering, cooking, and baking all morning to prepare. A solemn prayer thanked God for the wheat that grew and for the loving hands that prepared this bounty set before us.

Then with elbows spread, hungry threshers dug into mashed potatoes, fried chicken, gravy, roasting ears, sliced tomatoes, and succotash fresh from the barnyard and garden. The meal usually ended with apple pie—and complaints to the hostess that "I couldn't possibly eat any more. . . . Well, maybe one more piece."

While the meal was a high point, and the end of the day with its bath in the stock tank (before you were allowed in the house) was memorable, the climax of the harvest season was still to come—an ice cream social hosted by Uncle Johnny and Aunt Helen, home of the threshing machine. The ostensible reason for the event was for the farmers to pull check books from their bibbed overalls and settle each one's share of the threshing costs. I don't know what else the mothers and fathers did for the rest of the evening, but the event was a riot for us kids.

We had to outdo each other in games of tag, silo climbing, calf-chasing, and more ice cream eating. Cousin Herman suggested we all try to pull farm implements as if we were horses, and there were enough of us kids to roll the hayracks around the yard and into the barn. Finally, the little ones circled back to their mothers' laps, and fathers decreed that it was time to go home—the grand finale of a glorious summer season.

I think if I'd have experienced more such community on the farm, I might still be there. But soon farmers bought their own combines that did the work of binders, threshing machines, horses and hayracks. They could harvest on their own schedule, independent of neighbors they no longer needed. Soon there were fewer and larger farms with bigger equipment; small towns died out, schools were consolidated, and almost all the farm kids moved to the cities. An agrarian way of life with mostly self-sufficient family farms was coming to an end.

Contrary to my glowing childhood memories of communal work on the farm, the predominant experience of my teen years was the lonely toil of driving back and forth across endless acres under a hot summer sun. I could not imagine working alone and oppressing myself like this for the rest of my life.

"You can't stop Progress," was a slogan we often heard in that era. Since "progress" was inevitable, you might as well become its cheer leader and go along for the ride. But now, in the 21st century, a younger generation has grown up in the cities that can see through the systems of mammon that grind down the poor, abuse the earth, and alienate us from each other as consumers in the individual pursuit of wealth. Many of them are volunteering on organic farms, and hoping to relearn the way of life that I left behind.

Nevertheless, every summer, wherever we've gone, Joanne and I have tilled a garden to remember our roots and to feed our souls. And in the city, because community does not happen organically with neighbors, or by tradition and custom anymore, we joined Christian intentional community (in Newton and Evanston) and have become part of a different kind of work and harvest. Just as Jesus promised Peter that he'd be fishing for people, our harvest has been to grow the virtues of Jesus in our common life and to make disciples in all the ways he has taught us.

* * * * *

WORK: THE BLESSING, THE CURSE, AND THE NEW CREATION.

When strangers meet the question soon comes up, "What do you do?" This is a polite way of asking "What is your niche, your status in the capitalist economy," and from that answer one can infer a person's value (salary, wealth, status) according to the system. America's careerist culture encourages us to develop false selves that are nourished by job success and our consumption of material goods. Inevitably, this creates a system of "haves" and "have nots," of competition as if there is not enough dignity for all. When I'm getting to know someone, I've found a more interesting question to be, "Tell me about your work." I learn much more than just what happens nine-to-five.

In the second story of creation (Genesis 2–3) God gives Adam and Eve two tasks—tending the Garden that provides him food, and naming all the living species that dwell on earth. This latter is a serious research project still ongoing because naming something, in the Hebrew understanding, both reveals and carries the meaning of what that something actually is. Work is meant to be a joyful collaboration between God, humankind, and the awesomely bountiful creation.

But with disobedience and the fall, this harmony is broken. "Cursed is the ground because of you; in toil you shall eat of it . . . thorns and thistles it shall bring forth . . . By the sweat of your face, you shall eat bread until you return to the ground. . . You are dust and to dust you shall return."

In our post-industrial capital-serving economy, work still is under a curse, producing wealth for some, poor wages and unemployment for many, pollution and exhaustion of the land, misuse of creative gifts to produce what humans do not need, competition for survival, and joyless striving.

Nevertheless, the blessing of work also remains. Work conveys some dignity to the worker, a way to develop gifts and disciplines, an opportunity to produce the things that sustain life for family, and community. Thus, work carries both a curse and a blessing. But no work is even worse.

"When people lack work, they also lack hope. The resulting despair eats into a community like an evil spirit, and the violent results can be seen everywhere: in self-hatred, increased crime, the drug trade (often the only jobs available), a bloating of the prison population, racism, resentment, fear, alcoholism, break-up of families, domestic violence, children born without stable and secure homes, lack of commitments, and abuse of God-given talents of mind, heart and imagination." (Matthew Fox, *The Reinvention of Work*, p. 10)

REDEEMING WORK:

For people of faith, no matter what our job, the curse does not finally determine who we are. We are invited by Jesus to participate in the Kingdom of God that is already present for those with eyes to see it. This is the same "freely you have received, freely give" reality that Wendell Berry calls, The Great Economy: all that nature provides freely, all that spouses give out of love, all that families invest in the next generation, all that comes to life in the generative power of the Holy Spirit.

In this context William Cavanaugh reminds us of our call to demonstrate the New Creation by the way our work is structured and motivated in the creativity and collaborative harmony of the original garden. "Christians . . . are called to create concrete alternative practices that open a different kind of economic space—the space marked by the body of Christ. (*Being Consumed: Economics and Christian Desire, viii.*) This new creation is actually larger than the GNP, than the world's mammon economy. Everything else depends on it. It shows up wherever work is done for love rather than money. Intentional community is an especially effective way to make this economy real and visible.

WE ARE CHRIST'S WORK IN THE WORLD.

Normally, when we consume something, what we consume becomes a part of us. At breakfast Joanne and I consume a vegetable omelet, oatmeal, prunes and orange slices—and it all becomes a part of us. However, according to Augustine, when we consume the bread and wine of communion, we become it—we are consumed by Christ and become his body in the world. Doesn't that twist your mind into some new ways of thinking?

Our human tendency is always to come to Jesus hoping he can fix what is broken in us so that we can go on being our old selves with less pain and grief. And Jesus does graciously heal us—restoring life and meaning. But he also calls us to become his disciples, that is, to be changed into his likeness, to become his work in the world, reshaped by the imperfect communities of love he's given us to grow in.

God is a doer, a maker, a lover, and we are called to be his apprentices. As Jesus describes himself, "The Son can do nothing of his own accord, but only what he sees the Father doing. . . The Father loves the Son and shows him all that that he himself is doing." (John 5:19-20) The Master-Father shows his apprentice-Son all the art and mystery of his craft. The son watches and listens; he learns obedience and becomes like the father through what he suffers. (Hebrews 5:8) In the upper room, Jesus tells his apprentices that they will in turn do greater works because he goes to the Father (John 14:12) and his spirit will be with them, and us, to the end of the age. This is both how work is redeemed and how we become the redeeming work of God in the world.

(If you want to reflect further with me on what makes for good work, jump ahead to chapter 14.)

Mirror # 2

What's a Honyak?

CHAPTER 6

Honyaks

From Youthful Mayhem to Prophetic Mischief

OFTEN, IN MY EXUBERANT childhood at HeckuvaRanch, whenever I made a mess of things, I heard that epithet flung at me, "You honyak!"

It turns out this word is not a Janzen family invention but came from Germany and Poland where it meant something like White Trash—a person who is unaware of social norms, a bit rowdy and rough around the edges. Another definition I found online says a honyak is "A cross between a hillbilly and a redneck, only a bit dumber." But you'll get a better idea of the honyak disease if I tell a few stories.

My Janzen ancestors came to Kansas in the 1870's, a decade after the first settlers began to plow up the prairie. This land was stolen from the Native Americans, who followed herds of bison across the open range with their teepees in a semi-nomadic way of life. The first generation of farmers tended to be honyaks, people who were fleeing debts and angry relatives back east, who wanted to make a break from civilization and get rich quick. I'll tell you the story of one toxic specimen because his story spills over into our Janzen family history.

This particular honyak was named Frederick Remington. Is this name familiar? Later in life he became a famous painter and sculptor who brought to life scenes of the cowboy and Indian era of the Wild West. Well, Frederick Remington, at the time of this story, was a twenty-two-year-old New York boy with an inheritance burning in his pocket, and with dreams of making a quick killing as a sheep rancher on the frontier in Kansas. He bought a farm near the present-day town of Potwin but soon found actual farm work boring, and instead, entertained himself by sketching farm life—bucking broncos, and imaginary encounters between the U.S. Cavalry and Indian warriors that happened decades before he ever came out west.

Frederick Remington's latent honyak character showed up on the community stage when he fell in love with a local "school-marm" who had better sense than to fall for him. One evening the jilted and jealous lover showed up with a few rowdy friends at a social event at the schoolhouse where the said teacher was present. Remington and friends made a loud ruckus to disrupt the party. Then they piled hay against the schoolhouse wall and set it on fire. The folks at the party stomped out the fire, but from that day on, Frederick Remington's name in the community was "mud." So, he decided this was a good time to cash out and move on.

Well, this story connects to the Janzen family because it was my great grandpa, Johann Janzen, who wanted to retire in 1884 and sold his farm to the young upstart, Fredrick Remington, who quickly made a mess of it.

The irony of this tale is that, despite his ignominious departure after only one year of failed farming, Frederick Remington eventually became famous enough that the locals, in 1961 named their newly constructed regional high school after Frederick Remington. So, there you have honyak story number one, about a high-spirited, lazy, mean-tempered brat who later on made good according to the American Dream.

* * * * *

In my childhood we engaged in numerous honyak adventures, but one will suffice as a sample lesson in how not to behave. One lazy Sunday afternoon when our parents, Louis and Hilda Janzen, were away visiting neighbors, and our sister Sara was absent for some other reason, we were four restless boys left behind. There was my two-hundred-pound high-school-aged cousin, Herman, whom my parents trusted as our baby-sitter. Did they know that Herman was an irrepressible instigator of pranks, someone my siblings and I would follow anywhere in blind imitation? Together we hatched the idea of climbing our thirty-foot tall windmill tower, where a couple of us sat on the platform under the fan blades. We rigged up a bucket on a rope with which we'd haul up rocks to heave into the stock tanks below, to make the biggest splash we could.

But that wasn't exciting enough. With a pebble, some string, and our farmer bandanas we rigged up little parachutes and imagined that a plane was going to crash so the pilot had to jump out with a parachute to save his life. Sometimes the parachute opened up just in time and the pilot survived. Sometimes it didn't open, and he died a tragic death. But even if he died, he got another ride up the windmill, another parachute launch, and another chance at glory.

But soon jumping out of doomed imaginary airplanes was too predictable for us bored kids. Didn't we still have a real model airplane that brother John had built out of balsa wood, that would fly if you wound up the rubber-band-powered propeller? Sure. So, the plane went up in the bucket and was launched. It flew unpredictably, and crashed occasionally, but with a little tape and glue it would fly again.

But that still wasn't exciting enough. The plane was badly battered, but we reckoned it had one more flight left in it. This time we'd make it as dramatic as possible and light it on fire before we launched it on its ultimate journey. But we weren't dumb honyaks, we knew the wind was blowing from the south, and the barns and haystacks were north. No, siree. We were going to carefully launch the plane into the wind and away from all hazards.

So, matches and a gasoline-soaked airplane went up in the bucket for one glorious final denouement. With the tail on fire and the propeller spinning, we launched that doomed plane into the wind—where-upon a gust immediately spun it around and drove it north, past the silos, over the cattle loading pen, and beyond the cow barn where it disappeared from view into a stack of dry prairie hay.

Horrors! We scrambled down the windmill tower and ran toward the rising column of smoke. "Quick," brother John yelled at me, "get milk buckets full of water." Brother Mark tried to line up hoses from the garden faucet, but they were way too short. I filled a bucket and ran to the fire where cousin Herman and brother John were trying to stamp out the blaze or pitch the burning hay away from the stack. We dashed a few buckets of water on the fire, stomped some more, and eventually were satisfied that we had extinguished the conflagration. But now we had soot all over our clothes, hands, and faces. Quickly we rearranged the hay to cover up the sooty evidence, and then washed up the buckets and ourselves in the back-porch sink to look as presentable as possible.

And just then our folks returned, greeting us with good cheer. "Hey, did you boys have a good time?" they asked. "Yeah, we had a good time," we mumbled, not daring to look at them, or in each other's eyes. We older boys were worried that little Mark would be a tattle tale, but he was good, or as bad, you might say, as the rest of us. Our unspoken pact of solidarity held firm. When Mother asked if we'd like some ice cream, we all quickly agreed. Each of us sat around the kitchen table digging into our bowls, saying not a word. Soon we excused ourselves and went off to do our evening farm chores, without any adult reminder. Our parents must have wondered why we were so uncharacteristically quiet and well behaved.

Mother and Father never heard this honyak story until about twenty years later at a family reunion. In his old age, Father admitted that as a child, he and his brothers had performed equally dangerous high jinks, crawling up silos and exploring grain elevators with their spirited female cousins.

* * * * *

Eventually, I grew up and went to college where I fell in with another gang of honyaks who formed a prank committee. As serious philosophers, we worked late into the night hammering out both the theory and the practice of "the perfect prank." Theoretically, the perfect prank would wake up a bored campus with an event daring enough to be talked about for weeks involving no serious danger or loss to other parties, remain forever anonymous, and (there's a contradiction here) be worth bragging about to one's grandchildren. Our committee hatched a plan to raid the empty women's dormitory during supper hour, kidnap as many pillows as we could, and then leave a ransom note saying they would be returned upon receipt of ten dozen chocolate chip cookies. The idea was that we'd show up with pillows and all our friends so that the culprits might remain anonymous and enjoy a chocolate chip cookie party with the gals.

However, as often happens with honyak plans, something went awry. Emil Kreider took way too long with his pillow heist and missed the get-away car. So, he ended up running across campus loaded with a dozen pillows, whereupon he was caught by the Dean of Students and was soon sentenced to two days of obligatory community service. The rest of us, moved by regret, made a quick drop-off of the stolen pillows without getting caught. The chocolate chip cookie party never happened. And good old Emil did his slave labor without ratting on the rest of us.

Now I reflect back on this failed honyak episode and wonder, how come ten years later, all these energetic honyaks from the prank committee had Ph.D.'s and were teaching at the college level except for me. Perhaps that was their last prank, and they learned their lesson. Apparently, I did not.

* * * * *

Once again, this time at Harvard Divinity School, I fell in with another gang of honyaks who decided that the campus needed some comic relief in the high-pressure run-up to final exams. We determined that the tower and flagpole atop Andover Hall, central administration building with our dorm rooms on the second and third floors, needed a big black flag with the word "REPENT" emblazoned on it, to shame all those who had put off studying to the last minute. Our reconnaissance team determined that we would need a ladder as there was no rope through the pulley at the top of the pole.

At midnight our gang assembled with flag, a long ladder borrowed from maintenance supplies, and plenty of bungie cords. We quickly realized that no one wanted to climb the ladder fifty feet above the ground since the flagpole was weak and unstable. How to improvise? We made a human tower of guys surrounding the pole—heavy-weights on the bottom, welter-weights, then lightweights, and finally, one fly-weight guy who climbed over us all to the top and tied the flag tight every which way with bungie cords. Then we unborrowed the ladder and went to bed.

The next morning, we looked up like everyone else, as a fine breeze extended the flag, and remarked, "What an amazing flag! What an amazing feat! How timely this call to repentance!"

Later in the day we noticed that the Divinity School administrators had called in a firetruck with long extension ladder so a fireman could climb up and cut down the flag.

That evening all the guys in the dormitory, about twenty of us, were summoned to an urgent and serious meeting by the assistant dean of students. There we were informed in solemn and authoritative tones that somebody had degraded the reputation of the Divinity School with this shameful prank, grievously endangering the school's reputation with donors and prospective students. Furthermore, we had put at risk the lives of the maintenance crew who refused to retrieve the flag. So, the school had to pay the fire-department to bring it down. Therefore, we were all commanded to sit there until the culprits of this heinous deed came forward and made their confession.

So, we sat for a long time, and a longer time, with tension mounting afraid to look anyone else in the eye for fear of breaking down in laughter. Valuable time to cram for tomorrow's exams was slipping away. What should we do?

Absolutely no one in our prank committee anticipated what happened next. Thomas Stover, who had nothing to do with our gang, suddenly got down on his knees, began to pound the floor and wail at the top of his voice, "Mea culpa, mea culpa, mea grand culpa. I can't take the shame and embarrassment any longer. I'm the one who did it. I'm sorry I forever besmirched the glorious name of Harvard Divinity School. Have mercy on me. Have mercy."

At that we were all astounded, flabbergasted, falling out of our chairs, and leaning on each other in helpless laughter. We could not believe our eyes or ears—Thomas Stover, the wimpiest physical specimen on campus, Thomas Stover with delicate fingers and most refined tastes, mentally and physically incapable of climbing a pole three feet! We gagged and staggered about, apoplectic with astonishment and hilarity. Who knew this spindly esthete could be such an over-the-top actor!

Thomas went on and on: "It was all my fault. I'm sorry I made you all wait so long and miss your exam study time. I implore you, Mr. Assistant Dean, to let these others go, they had nothing to do with it. I'm so ashamed. I'll just have to live the rest of my days with this black mark forever on my record and on my soul. Have mercy on me. I plead with you, have mercy on my black, black soul."

At that the assistant dean of students closed his ledger of student names, gave up and rose to leave. As he walked away, Thomas called after him and asked in a pleading voice, "Sir, one last request: Could I please have my flag back?"

At that we mobbed Thomas and declared him forever our hero. Who knew he had it in him? What a honyak?!

Did we lament the anguish we caused divinity school authorities who feared that we had turned off donors and prospective students forevermore? No, we lamented their lack of humor that could not imagine how healthy it was for us to break the tensions of exam week with a little hilarity, with a prank far better than drunkenness and panty-raids, something donors and prospective students could probably sympathize with from their own experience. We were convinced the episode might, at least, be worthy of a few lines in the Divinity School newsletter.

* * * * *

Perhaps you've noticed a progression in these honyak stories from opprobrium to affirmation, from shame to glory, from bungled performance to surprising perfection. You might notice that even now, fifty years later, I'm still not ready to repent.

Nevertheless, I feel compelled to compare these prank stories to the one that has provoked the most frequent retelling and moral examination in Western History—Augustine's infamous pear thief episode as told in his *Confessions*, Book II. At the age of sixteen, he, along with some friends, shook down and stole a load of pears from a neighbor's tree and threw them at a herd of pigs. Their thievery, Augustine recounts with total remorse, was not motivated by any personal need nor any appreciation of the pears, but by a simple delight in the solidarity of doing wrong. This story of depravity becomes the occasion for Augustine to reflect at length both on his own sin and on the fallen nature of humanity in general, on the power of peer groups to corrupt the individual, and on our disordered desires that love created things more than the creator. He concludes with a theological generalization, that his wanton act of wrong doing, like all other sin, was a human perversion of our God-given goodness. The gifts that God had given him were squandered in doing wrong, in striving to be like God, reveling in his power to do evil while spurning God's perfect love for us. What do I make of Augustine's arguments?

I think Augustine's high-spirited, though inconsiderate, teenage prank has more in common with Frederick Remington's mean-spirited shenanigans than it did with our botched pillow raid or flagpole hoist. There is something natural, and potentially holy, in the raw energy of youth that wants to break out of the narrow confines of social conformity, that needs to court danger in heroic feats of valor, that finds meaning in the solidarity of a common high-spirited adventure. This need is especially strong in boys and young men. (Is there a female equivalent to honyakism?) The conventional outlet for this energy has often been harnessed by military recruiters in the direction of warfare where the goal is described as righteous victory without a thought given to the suffering of the losers who have already been dehumanized by their propaganda.

You will notice that the progression of these honyak stories moves from violence to non-violence, from mayhem to some attempt at redeeming social value, from pure delight in wrong-doing to deliberate prophetic mischief. So, what do we make of Jesus' carefully thought-out cleansing of the temple? In his day the temple authorities were incensed by his disruptive street theatre and schemed to kill him. But most Jews in his day would have recognized his action as a symbolic prophetic judgment on a corrupted system that tried to monopolize and profit from the universal human need of forgiveness for sins.

I really appreciate Robert Ellsberg's outstanding collection, *AllSaints*, 365 stories of peace-maker saints like Gandhi, Martin Luther King, Jr., Dorothy Day, and Jesus—one for each day of the year. Likewise, I've recommended and given away copies of the New Monasticism movement's *Common Prayer: A Liturgy for Ordinary Radicals*. I believe we need more stories of improbable saints that show how this honyak energy for daring and danger does not need to be squashed, but instead channeled and trained toward the kingdom of God, toward valiant peacemaking in a world that has corrupted this energy to its own ends.

How about one more honyak story, hidden for fifty years, and now revealed to the light of day

* * * * *

In early December of 2019, Bethel College, my Mennonite alma mater, invited people to return for a 50th reunion of the Moratorium Day participants from the fall of 1969 when school was canceled for teach-ins protesting the Vietnam War. At that time, I was an adjunct history professor just returned from two years of teaching in the Congo as part of my alternative to military service. Since I already participated in all the peace movement events at the time, the faculty named me a sponsor for the Bethel Peace Club. We staged demonstrations, marches, and protests of various kinds. The most dramatic event was reading the names of all the 30,000 Americans killed in Vietnam while tolling a large bell over a period of 48 hours. ABC News came out to film this event and to display it on national TV. Later that winter we took a caravan to Washington D.C. to join in a million-person Vietnam War protest on the Washington Mall. That was a lot of honyak energy directed toward opposing a futile, misguided, and genocidal war.

Participating in a million-person Anti-Vietnam War rally in Washington, D.C., 1974.

At this fifty-year Moratorium Day reunion, I asked Ron Flaming, a peace-movement activist fifty years ago, if he wanted to talk about our prank committee that "bombed" Newton with anti-war leaflets. He said that he'd never told anyone that story before, but we agreed that now, five decades later, this was a fitting time for confession.

Four of us honyaks conspired to "Xerox" several thousand leaflets that would be "bombed" on the city of Newton from an airplane. The message, as I remember it, was something like this: "If you were in North Vietnam, this leaflet would be a bomb and you would be dead. Please consider if you want our country to bomb civilians as innocent as you are, in a cruel and unjust war that has already killed millions."

Ron Flaming, at the time, was a college freshman who also, providentially, happened to have a pilot's license, perhaps "for just such a time as this." He arranged to rent a plane from the McPherson airport—a sufficient distance from Newton, we believed, to stay anonymous. So, with an accomplice, they "bombed" Newton with thousands of leaflets, which folks soon picked up from sidewalks, lawns and streets. The local paper, *The Newton Kansan,* called for an investigation and the arrest of the people who had littered the city with communist propaganda. Isn't it fitting that Ron Flaming went on to seminary and a career as a highly trusted Mennonite pastor and denominational leader?

I have a theory about honyaks with their dangerous excess of energy and youthful tendency to overlook the consequences of their behavior. My theory is that unless guys start life with some high-spirited vitality and a zest for danger, they end up grumpy old men who missed out on life, who are set in their ways, and who have no crazy stories to tell their grandchildren—which is a shame.

Chapter 7

HeckuvaRanch and other Pranks with Words

How Play and Work Team up for Good Writing

FATHER CALLED OUR FARM "HeckuvaRanch," which is as close as a Mennonite in our rural Elbing, Kansas, community could get to swearing without catching a reprimand from the local Pharisees. Morally, "heck" represented a last-second verbal U-turn just before the gates of hell. My dad got a buzz from the wave of anxiety and uneasy laughter that this mildly risqué label provoked from our conservative friends and neighbors.

The word "heck" marked another kind of boundary because if Father lost his temper at four straight days of rain, he might take out his foul mood on a mud puddle, driving through it at top speed with the farm tractor, yelling "Hachickapuya!" splashing water as far as it would fly. This is how he vented his wrath and scattered his depression without actually sinning.

Father also believed in the malevolent intentions of inanimate objects. If a wrench slipped off a nut and bloodied his knuckles, he might throw the devil-possessed tool at the wall and stomp around, swearing in an unknown language—what we children called, "Cussing in Greek." Ecstatic charismatics "speak in tongues." Father "swore in tongues" so as not to take the Lord's name in vain—at least not in English.

But Father had another purpose in mind by calling our local agricultural enterprise "HeckuvaRanch." By that label he also meant to show that Janzen farm standards, though strong and capable of mass production, would not result in an picture-perfect Dutch-looking farm with every building and picket fence painted white, with equipment all parked in neat rows,

HECKUVARANCH AND OTHER PRANKS WITH WORDS

with top-quality live-stock in the pens and no visible manure on the lot, like the D. B. Neufeldts of rural Inman, Kansas, where he had courted, married and carried off a beautiful daughter who kept our house and gardens up to artistic Neufeldt standards, and whom Father affectionately called "Madam Queen," just to see her blush. Did you notice how that run-on sentence kept you in suspense all the way to the end, even wondering if there would be an end? That's how Father liked to talk.

* * * * *

So far you might have thought this chapter was about our farm, but really, it is about Father's boredom with conventional language and his need to make something surprising happen with words. So, for your enjoyment, here's another sample of Father's typically tangled run-on sentences lifted from his memoir *Eighty-Plus and Looking Back* (p. 38), where he reports on a family vacation trip, when, as a boy he discovered the difference between Kansas and Texas small towns.

> We learned that while in Kansas some people would spend a part of Saturday evening in town because the stores were open, in Texas, it seemed every mother's son and daughter, plus any other human beings who might be around, went to town and stayed as long as the stores were open, and the stores stayed open as long as there were people around.

Father was incapable of using the clichés that people expected of him but had to give his sentences a novel and loopy twist before he could lay them down.

Father also had a knack for launching good dinner table conversations with our many guests, often beginning with bolts out of the blue like, "Anything get you riled up lately?" Father was also an avid listener, following up on whatever our guests chose to reveal. A year later, he might meet the same person again at a church conference or farm sale, and immediately continue the same conversation without transitions because he remembered their last words and had been thinking about them. While Father had a light and playful touch with words, at the same time people felt that he took them and their concerns seriously.

* * * * *

As children, we were disappointed in Father's refusal to play with us. He believed, like a good Prussian, that play was beneath his adult dignity. He feared that if he came down to our level, he would lose authority in our eyes.

Father, Louis, giving camel rides to grandchildren, Natasha and James.

So, it teed us off that in later years Father easily forgot his dignity and allowed a mob of grandchildren to turn him into a camel on hands and knees, willing to give rides wherever they steered him by their voice commands. Why didn't he ever play with us like that? We'd have loved him so much more.

However, Father did teach us by example how to play with language by his unique brand of swearing in tongues, his ad hoc verbal concoctions, and his loopy run-on sentences. This was his way of giving listeners a suspenseful and improbable camel ride of another kind. I think his fun with language rubbed off on me, which has made me an avid conversationalist and a player with words who, like pets, also sometimes like to play with me in return.

Over the years I've become a writer of sorts, combining my mother's knack for good organization and my father's gift for loopy storytelling with interesting detours that somehow, eventually, by unexpected routes, manage to make their point. In my college sophomore year, I won the dubious distinction of failing my first try at a compulsory English competency exam, (Why should I care about spelling and punctuation if you already know what I mean?) and at the same time, managed to win the Bethel College Thresher Award for the best short story of the year. After marrying a good proofreader, her spelling and punctuation gifts have made my second drafts look quite respectable.

Writing my Masters thesis on a Royal Standard in 1966.

* * * * *

I've often heard, "You're a good writer," and "You should write more." Given all the wide reading I've done in a lifetime, I'm aware that my gift is a modest one. I've never aspired to being famous (except on my mother's coffee table).

Usually, when I've dedicated serious time to writing a book, I've been accountable to a local Fellowship committee that reads, critiques, and encourages me as they see fit. These folks not only know my gifts as a writer, but also my weaknesses, my home life, my practical work commitments, and what earning the Fellowship needs of me. I like that way of staying rooted and balanced in our real life of relationships and economic necessity.

I feel motivated to explore the many ways I could become a better writer. Back in the days of the typewriter, I'd typically leave ten pages on the floor for each page of final draft. Good art, as I've learned from watching painters, is usually the result of many layers of construction. Even if I'm on my twentieth draft, I still can see ways to make it better—a more apt image here; seeing from another angle there; an insight from another author; a way to be more vulnerable with my pronouncements; simplifying till only the essentials remain; recalling what Jesus has to say about the theme; testing how the words flow when read aloud; what does Joanne think about it; and most importantly, what has the Spirit shown me after sleeping on it for a night?

It seems that suffering is needed in order to write from the heart rather than just from the head. A wise person does not waste opportunities to suffer well. Avoiding the hard-to-face issues of life is our natural human temptation. It is, however, the path of mediocrity, spiritual stagnation, and eventual death of the soul. In our tribulations is where we meet Jesus most intensely, and where inspiration often breaks through.

The gift of good writing, I believe, lies in the intuition that the work is never done: it always could be better. The result of this process of playing and tinkering with layers of insights is that the writing becomes increasingly fresh and simple—almost inevitable in the way the story unfolds.

Aiming for fame or keeping up a reputation feels wearisome to me, especially in this season of life. Rather, I want to aim for the truth of what I have experienced and trust the Spirit to awaken in the reader something of the inspiration that moved me to write it.

* * * * *

I believe my gifts as a writer also have something to do with my ambivalent relationship with work and play. (See "Combatting Bookworms on the Farm.")

So why did I just detour for 15 minutes to knock out a Sudoku Puzzle? Is this an addiction or a necessary way to relax my mind in order to return to my work with refreshed energy and attention?

In 1967, Joanne and I became teachers in the Democratic Republic of the Congo, our first professional jobs, you might say. After a day of classroom instruction, a mid-day siesta to beat the heat, various meetings, coaching basketball, entertaining guests, and supervising evening study hall, at 10:00 pm with the kerosene lamp burning before me and bugs flying around my head, I still had six lesson preparations to go. That's when I discovered that if I interspersed times of concentration with times of puzzle play, I finished sooner and fresher than if I tried to bulldoze my way with uninterrupted effort. Prolonged concentration would freeze up my brain. I had no choice but to break for play or curiosity-driven reading. Fortunately, or unfortunately, that is how my mind works, and has worked ever since. If my work is more like play than work, I've found I can go farther and smarter than with sheer plod.

This dynamic has been a source of tension with Joanne at times when she catches me playing when she "has to work," and I should be working too. Still, somehow, I get done what I need to do as fast as most others and have more fun in the doing of it. That's not fair. Or is it? I don't know. It seems like that's how God made me. Or am I making excuses? Maybe, when I get to the other side of eighty, then I will confess like my hard-working Father, that he was always a lazy person at heart who could finally in retirement, allow himself to be himself and play around with writing his memoir. No, that's not quite true for me either. I don't think I'll ever fully retire because I don't want to quit this alternate striding of work and play, of concentration and contemplation, because I love what I do.

So, in conclusion of this brief essay on almost-but-not-quite swear words, and other pranks with language, I prescribe for you my father's favorite all-purpose expletive that allowed him to be angry and sin not: "Hatchickapuya!" *(Rx: Use as needed.)

*In case you were wondering, that "Greek swear word" is pronounced with an explosive saliva-scattering emphasis on the "p."

(P.S. At the end of this book you will find an Appendix, a chronological bibliography listing some of the writings I have completed over the years.)

Chapter 8

Not My Enemy

Reweaving the Human Fabric in Time of War

Toward the end of World War II, and for some months after its conclusion, there was a camp of German prisoners of war in Peabody, Kansas, just five miles north of our farm. The government brought these captives to the U.S. in hopes of wresting some labor from their otherwise idle bodies. Farmers were encouraged to pick up prisoners each morning as day laborers. Along with two or three prisoners came an armed guard. Of course, we children were most fascinated by this new development and the prisoners seemed drawn to us in response. Before they did any work, Mother brought out breakfast for the prisoners who had very skimpy rations in their camp.

Since our family spoke German in the home, there was no language barrier between the prisoners and us. They eagerly engaged us children and answered our questions. The armed guard, on the other hand, was unrelational, showed us no interest, and seemed at a loss of what to do with his time. How were these prisoners, brought to the middle of a strange and distant continent, ever going to escape and return to Germany on their own? So, the guard spent most of his day reclining somewhere within range of the working prisoners, taking a nap with his gun leaned against a shade tree. I remember my brother John daring me to sneak up on the snoring guard and touch his gun. Did I do it, or just remember the dare? Neither of us can recall for sure.

At lunchtime, everyone was invited to our dining table—prisoners, guard, and family. Mother would not allow the guard to sit at table with his gun, so he set it aside for the meal. The conversation was mostly in German.

According to my brother John, who would have been seven at the time, we used our imaginations to dramatize our understanding of the adult roles around us. So, for a few days we played "Prisoners and Guard." Of course, as pacifist Mennonites we boys were forbidden to have toy guns, but we could not be prevented from picking up sticks, reshaping them a bit, and pretending they were army rifles. We'd march imaginary prisoners with our guns on our shoulders. And then when the prisoners tried to escape, we'd shout, "Stop or I'll shoot." We don't remember what happened after that. For us it was unthinkable to actually shoot someone. After a week or two, the guards stopped coming to our place because, apparently, they were bored with the game of "Prisoners and Guards" too, because nothing ever happened that needed their attention.

Once there were no guards on hand, our relationships with the prisoners relaxed and warmed up. They were hard working, self-motivated, and familiar with farm work. Our lunchtime conversations often ran on into work time. We quickly learned their names and became friends as the same fellows usually kept coming to our place. Kurt Knittle, Paul Lehman and Horst Schellenberg are names I still remember. We boys would follow them around on their jobs and keep the conversation going, and sometimes join in the task. They were willing to talk about their families and about their present circumstances, but questions about the war were met with very brief answers and awkward silence.

Paul Lehman was a smoker who rolled his own cigarettes, which fascinated me with its novelty. Paul had a neat kit about the size of a wallet where he laid a cigarette paper moistened on one edge, and a ridge of loose tobacco in the middle. Then he'd close the kit and open it again, revealing a neatly rolled cigarette. Magic! I begged Paul to let me roll cigarettes for him, which he did. This was a somewhat risqué trick for us to pull off since our parents did not approve of smoking. So, Paul and I had our little secret—except that, at the age of four, I was a blabbermouth who could not stop bragging about my new expertise.

This arrangement of daily farm help from prisoners coming out from their guarded Peabody stockade went on for about half a year, as I remember. Then we heard the news that the prisoners would be going home, for which we were both sad and rejoicing. They gave us going-away presents. One of the gifts was a realistically carved two-engine model airplane painted silver with gold insignias on the sides, propped on a stand which was displayed in a prominent location in our home for the years of my childhood.

Our parents corresponded with these returned prisoners for at least a decade. We also sent our version of CARE packages to them and their families in the years of dislocation and famine that ensued in Germany after their return. Coffee was, we learned, a scarce and valuable commodity after the war, often used as currency, so my parents were careful to include several tins of it in each package. According to the story I was told, one prisoner was able to trade his coffee for a pair of starving work horses, and thus begin to farm on a more productive scale.

What I remember most prominently from that experience is how our parents were able to create family with these prisoners of war, and how they became like uncles to us children in a way that, I'm sure, pleased God who wants to see his people put an end to the hatreds that so often divide the human race. It's a mystery how the same people under one set of political circumstances can hate and seek to destroy each other, and in other circumstances, quickly become families of mutual support. I'm grateful that our parents introduced us to creative ways of fulfilling the calling to "Seek peace and pursue it." (Psalm 34:16)

Brother John recalls an inspiring sequel to this brief chapter of life shared with German prisoners on our farm. About 1970, twenty-five years after they were repatriated, John, now married to a German wife, arranged to meet one of these former prisoners and his wife at the home of John's parents-in-law in Goettingen, Germany. As a retired couple, this one-time prisoner with his wife got permission to leave East Germany for a "Janzen reunion" before The Wall came down. "They had along a few photos of our family back in Kansas in 1944–45," with fond stories of his experience in that era. "It was quite moving," John reports, "and a tribute to our parents' loving hospitality across the dividing lines of nations at war."

* * * * *

Our parents understood that as Mennonite followers of the Prince of Peace, we did not automatically accept that the enemies of our nation would be our enemies too. They gave us children an identity rooted in our Anabaptist heritage of being resident aliens, chased from one country to another, never fully at home—potential refugees who needed to remember, like the Children of Israel, that we too had been slaves in Egypt. I think this memory was a reason why my life story became enmeshed in the peasant people of Central America in an era when President Reagan and most of America labeled them "communists" and "the enemy." Peacemaking, we learned, is not just about abstract causes and news-worthy social movements, but must become personal, communal, and faithful over time.

Here is how, in 1984, we were drawn back into that reconciling work. At that time, New Creation Fellowship, in Newton, Kansas, was a stop on the Overground Railroad, a network of refugee interviewers in South Texas, volunteer drivers, and hosts on the way to asylum in Canada. (The

Overground Railroad name recalled the Underground Railroad that spirited escaped slaves to refuge in Canada.)

That's why we happened to host a fellow named Eliceo Sosa and others in a carload headed from Harlingen, Texas, to Reba Place Fellowship in Evanston, Illinois. We heard the short version of Eliceo's story at the supper table—that he had fled El Salvador because of death threats over his participation in protests opposing army violence against civilians.

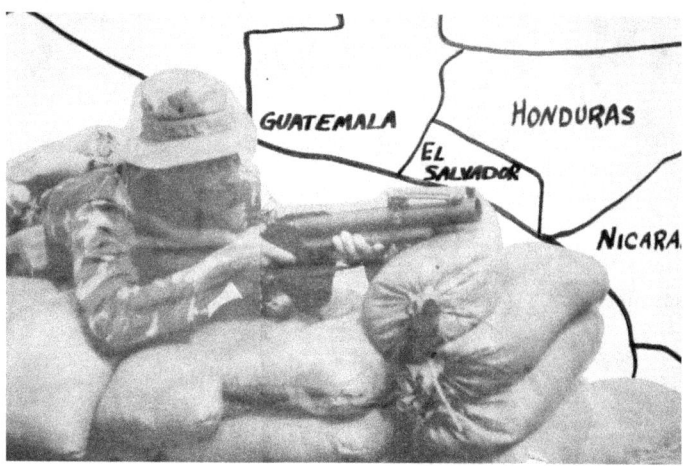

Right-wing death squads targeted those who organized for social change in Honduras, El Salvador and Guatemala.

After fleeing north, across the Rio Grande River, Eliceo found a niche as a cook in a shelter for homeless and fleeing refugees in South Texas. He was lucky because many refugees were caught at the river, detained, and sent back to their deaths.

At that time, Eliceo met Richard and Ruth Anne Friesen, leaders of the Overground Railroad team in South Texas, who interviewed and selected candidates for asylum in Canada. At that point, Eliceo was "undocumented," so at the Friesen's advice he applied for U.S. asylum, knowing that he would be denied, but it gave him temporary status in the U.S. until his court date—enough time to be interviewed by Canadian authorities for a more likely acceptance into Canada. That is how our "Railroad" became more "Overground" than "Underground" in those days.

Central American refugees were detained in concentration camps along the southern U.S. border where the Overground Railroad interviewed and selected those most in need of protection.

I tell this story of Eliceo because it illustrates on a personal level how the Overground Railroad worked for the Sosa family and for about two thousand others over eight years, whom we helped to find refuge. This story is a microcosm of the larger story of the half-a-million refugees who fled to the U.S. from a civil war and wide-spread military terror against civilians in El Salvador. (Watch the movie, *Romero*, if you want to understand the times.)

I never expected to see Eliceo again, but Providence seems to like surprises. Half a year later, on our "Sabbatical" from New Creation, I was working at Reba Place Fellowship as an assistant to Julius Belser, helping to run the "railroad" that he had founded. Our office was in the basement of the Clearing household where Eliceo also happened to live, where he was the breakfast cook. In that basement office a small team of volunteers came together and worked the phone lines (before there were fax machines, home computers, and e-mail) to arrange for volunteer drivers and hosts who would keep refugees and their families for six months to a year, until Canada had sponsors lined up to welcome them. After a few months, my mentor Julius asked me to replace him as the Director while he stepped back to support our team as chairman of the Overground Railroad Board.

The "line" from Texas to Evanston was a minor route on "the railroad." The main line ran through Jubilee Partners in Comer Georgia where their Anno de Jubileo bus periodically brought thirty Salvadoran, Guatemalan, and Honduran refugees out of South Texas for six weeks of orientation at Jubilee's refugee center.

A sign at Jubilee Partner's summarized their resettlement ministry to refugees from many lands in conflict.

That's where the Canadian Consul from Atlanta would come by and interview all heads of households in one day, giving them the eventual green light to Canada. From Jubilee they went on to host churches that the Overground Railroad lined up till Canada was ready.

Normally, that's how the railroad ran, but there were many crises that called for extraordinary responses. While waiting for his asylum hearing, Eliceo got work as an electrician's helper and started sending money back to his family. Then a desperate phone call signaled that his family was in grave danger. His two sons, Nelson and Carlos, aged fourteen and fifteen, had been press-ganged by military recruiters at a soccer game and hauled off into a prison-style boot camp where they were brutalized every day. Emma, the boys' mother called and reported this devastating news to Eliceo and Julius, pleading for our prayers.

But Emma was not going to let the military take her boys without a feisty response. She stormed into the boot camp, showed the officer in charge of her boys a copy of Eliceo's U.S. asylum application, and bluffed him with her demand that the boys must be immediately released because this official paper (in English, which he could not read) claimed they were to appear in a Chicago court hearing with their father. While the officer left to confer with his superiors, Emma walked out of the camp with her boys in tow. Without going home, where she knew the military police would soon follow them, she caught the first bus north where she deposited the boys in a Quaker house of hospitality in Mexico City. Again, she called the Clearing household to discern what to do next. Her boys were in Mexico, and her three younger daughters still at home in San Salvador. Julius advised her to contact the Mennonite Central Committee team in El Salvador where Reba could wire funds to bring the whole family north.

A couple of weeks later, after crossing the Rio Grande River at night, the family was caught in the Harlingen, Texas, airport, attempting to buy tickets to Chicago. At that time, the "migra" (Immigration and Naturalization Service) had no place to keep a family with little children, so they were allowed to fly north with court orders to appear before an immigration judge in Chicago. What a celebration we all had seeing the Sosa family reunited!

Reba Place Church arranged for the Sosa family to rent (and eventually buy) a house two doors from the sanctuary—where Eliceo and Emma live to this day. For some weeks I played basketball with Nelson and Carlos —an informal way for me to practice Spanish while I taught them a little English. I found it hard to believe that these childrenh ad so narrowly escaped the fate of becoming either killers or cannon fodder in a brutal war against their own countrymen.

The Sosa family let us know they did not want to go away to Canada, because they had made a host of friends in Evanston. So, we agreed to put everything we had into their fight for asylum in the U.S., against the State Department's decree. With the best legal advice and expert witnesses assembled, we demonstrated to the judge that not only the Sosa family, but thousands of others were fleeing a brutal military regime with the worst human rights records in the Western Hemisphere. The judge was moved and granted asylum—not just to the Sosa family, but to many others in their wake. It was a break in the dam, a counter-current against the Reagan-era claim that these refugees had nothing to fear but were economic opportunists and communists.

For eight years, till 1992, we ran a "railroad" out of the Clearing basement that coordinated a hundred-and-twenty host churches and communities on the route to Canada. These communities became advocates for the refugees and their experience. Not only did they support the families they hosted, but they sent contributions that kept us and the railroad running. In fact, they lent over $100,000 at 0% interest for a revolving bail fund to bond refugees out of detention in South Texas at $1,000 to $5,000 a head, money which was returned to us when we could document their departure from the U.S., and then recycle it to bond out others.

I found the Overground Railroad "good work," not because it was ever easy, but because it met a real human need, and we were a team. Each morning, we gathered to sing Taize songs, listen to each other's souls, and pray for the people we hoped to move toward refuge. Often, when we read the interview notes of the refugees and their heart-breaking losses, our work turned into a spiritual battlefield. I remember my co-worker, Mary Jude saying from time to time, "Can we take a break to sing and pray together. I'm getting really depressed." Times of prayerful contemplation were a necessity for our own healing and to make room in our souls for the painful stories of others. But just as often, we would be amazed by the faith of those who carried on through carnage and mortal danger, empowered by the solidarity they felt with a crucified Savior.

* * * * *

What was the shape of the practical wisdom gained on the Overground Railroad? When the ORR began, most of us in the network were amateurs in the work of refugee resettlement. But the main gifts needed for this work had already been forged in Christian community life. Many of the stops on the Overground Railroad were intentional Christian communities, religious orders, or congregations with an intense common life dedicated to hospitality, peace-making and justice advocacy. They knew how to rally resources of time, money and friendships for a common cause.

After a few years in the Overground Railroad ministry, I was surprised to discover that people considered me an authority in this line of work, inviting me to speak at churches, conferences, colleges, and seminaries. Whenever possible, I took along ORR hosts and Central American refugees to let them tell their stories—much like the stories of the Sosa family you've already read. Though my expertise was thin, I represented and could access the experience and wisdom of the network. I was most surprised to be invited, all expenses paid, to testify before a refugee subcommittee of the Canadian House of Parliament in Ottawa, along with Stuart Clark, from MCC Canada. The Canadian government valued our expertise and the experience of the ORR network because they valued refugees and had a heart for the oppressed of the world—perhaps because a high percentage of Canadians were only one generation removed from immigrant status themselves. The United States, by contrast, was trapped in an anti-communist narrative and rhetorically justified our funding of the military regimes and death squads that drove this refugee flood. No U.S. government agency had any interest in our work at that time except to spy on us. The FBI collected a dossier on me that I got to see a few years later under the Freedom of Information Act. But when the long-awaited envelope arrived, it was deflating— xeroxed copies of newspaper articles with my name circled in magic marker, and nothing more.

I came to realize that the practical wisdom of the Overground Railroad resided in the accumulated experience of the network itself. That is the nature of networks—the more they are used the smarter and more resilient they get. My grasp of Spanish was "*muy pobre*," but I got to know the people and the stories of a couple of thousand refugees whom we helped to find asylum in "*el norte*."

The practical wisdom of the ORR stood on a different foundation than the conventional wisdom of our world. I'm recalling a conversation that highlighted this difference for me. My best friend at Reba, Allan Howe, invited me to meet his brother, Bruce Howe, over a dinner conversation. Bruce was a shrewd and energetic capitalist whose company offered home inspections services nationwide. Allan introduced me as someone who "runs a railroad for refugees." Bruce was intrigued because he and I both were coordinators of wide-flung networks.

I explained the work of the ORR from the South Texas detention camps to 120 host groups in the U.S. connecting to eventual asylum for their refugee friends, with sponsor groups in Canada. Then Bruce asked, "What is your budget—how much do all these services cost?"

"We don't pay for any of that," I answered him. "People do all of it for free—interviewers, drivers, hosts, lawyers, lobbyists, speaker-advocates, sometimes doctors—they do it as volunteers out of the goodness of their hearts, at a personal sacrifice."

"How much do you get paid?"

"We pay our staff according to our needs—it comes to just a little more than minimum wage. You'd be surprised how motivated people are when it comes to saving lives, especially when they get to meet and welcome those same refugee families in their own homes. Our motivation is to become more like Jesus. I don't have to compel or pay anyone to do this. If I call someone and they can't do it freely right now, I call someone else who is eager and willing. So far, God has always provided. Freely you've received, freely give—that's the economy of the kingdom of God." Bruce couldn't believe it.

In the end, Bruce said he envied me. I had to admit, "Though we wade through incredible grief and pain with our refugee friends, it is good work—a totally satisfying answer to the existential question, 'Why are we here?'"

* * * * *

We never intended for the Overground Railroad to become a long-term ministry or career, but rather, it was an emergency response to a war that, we prayed daily, might soon come to an end. As the 1980's drew to a close, the civil war in El Salvador ground on with no emerging victor. The whole world was appalled by the night-time execution of six Jesuit professors and their housekeepers by the elite U.S.- trained Atlacatel Battalion at the University of Central America, in 1989. Support for the war was waning in the U.S. Congress. The United Nations began to host negotiations between the Salvadoran government centered in the cities, and the FMLN guerilla army which controlled large portions of the countryside. In 1992, it seemed timely for representatives of the Overground Railroad to organize a delegation to visit El Salvador, to assess for ourselves the prospects for peace and reconstruction of a civil society that might become a sanctuary for those who had fled. Our delegation arrived in San Salvador the day the UN-brokered peace accords were signed and the whole country erupted in celebration. But that's another story awaiting you in Chapter 15, "New Shoes for DP's: The Holy Work of Restoration after War."

CHAPTER 9

Hedgewood

Our Stubborn Roots in Kansas Soil and History

OFTEN ON WINTRY SATURDAY afternoons, brother John and I were assigned to load a farm wagon with firewood, pull it with a tractor to the backside of our house, where we'd toss it down a chute into our basement wood bin. I had ambivalent feelings about this job—I remember the cold wind biting my fingers and toes and the demands of physical effort when I would rather have been inside reading a book. Snowflakes flying through the air warned that the weather might turn nasty before we were done. But I also felt the pull of anticipated reward. Toiling in a team with my brother meant some friendly competition that hurried up the work. Tossing heavy chunks of "hedgewood," as we called it, we were "building muscles" that might impress the girls, and certainly make us stronger basketball players. And when the job was done, we had permission to join Mom in the kitchen just as fresh-baked cinnamon rolls, full of raisins and oozing with caramelized brown sugar, would rise out of the oven in a cloud of steam. I remember Saturday afternoons as three hours of all-too-familiar drudgery topped off with a satisfying mouth and tummy-filled celebration of work well done.

So where did "hedgewood" come from? The story begins more than a century earlier with the semi-nomadic Osage Indian Nation that lived on the prairies hunting bison and deer, and gardening in the river valleys. Alas, the Osage people were progressively pushed west by white settlers and the U.S. Army from what would later be called southern Missouri into southern Kansas, and eventually onto a reservation in Oklahoma where many still live. In the Osage home territory grew a tough and thorny tree that White

People called the "Osage Orange" because its fruit had a dimpled skin like oranges. But the orbs were hard, green and inedible, oozing a white sap that could irritate the skin. The Osage Indians discovered that the strongest and most supple bows were made from Osage Orange wood, bows which traded far and wide, and were worth a horse and several blankets in exchange. The early French traders named the tree "Bois D'Arc," meaning "wood of the bow."

When our Mennonite ancestors were lured by the Santa Fe and Rock Island railroads to settle the prairies of Kansas in the 1870's, the bison had already been killed off, and the era of free-range cattle grazing was coming to an end. It was hedges of Osage Orange that transformed the desolate infinite windswept prairies into habitable spaces for the earliest settlers. Hedges were easy to plant. A wannabe farmer plowed a single furrow, laid in Osage Orange cuttings, and plowed the furrow back. The little cuttings sprouted into wiry, thorny canes that grew 3–6 feet a year. In a couple of seasons, they made an impenetrable barrier that mercilessly raked the flesh of any man or beast who tried to break through. In a few years these hedgerows transformed the free-range Wild West into the boundary lines of property ownership—marking civilized spaces safe for women, children, and domestic animals. They were a force of history and of nature whose arrival evicted the free-range cowboys and other desperados with guitars, who nostalgically lamented the end of the open prairie and the arrival of womenfolk with the mournful popular song, "Don't Fence Me In." Blame it all on hedgewood!

Though hedges on the prairie tamed the landscape, make no mistake about it, Osage Orange trees were still wild and required annual maintenance to keep them from taking over the farmland. In a decade or two, these hedge rows could grow into a shoulder-to-shoulder line of sentries from 30 to 60 feet tall that sucked moisture out of the ground for as far as their shadow reached. The "hedge-apples" they dropped, and that squirrels loved to scatter, could sprout across the land and in a decade, turn a pasture into nasty, thorny woods. Prairies for grazing and haymaking had to be defended with occasional grass fires that renewed the grass and killed the little trees. It was a sign of a negligent farmer that his hedge trees were taking over a meadow.

Barbed wire was first patented in 1874, but it was a decade or two before it became the predominant way of fencing cattle on the prairies. So why didn't barbed wire eliminate the hedgerows still prevalent in the 40's and 50's of my childhood? Hedge trees, it turned out, proved both useful to leave and costly to eliminate. Hedges were still productive as windbreaks and as sources of firewood to heat homes with basement furnaces like ours, and to stoke kitchen bake ovens. Furthermore, hedgewood made the best fenceposts on which to stretch and staple barbed wire. They were rot and termite resistant, lasting a century and more. Thus, ironically, hedges as a source of fenceposts proved useful in the technology that should have eliminated them.

Osage Orange trees, while easy to plant, proved almost impossible to kill. Their roots went deep and wide and could break a plow. Cut off a tree and the stump would re-sprout new and vigorous saplings which had to be whacked off year after year. The only way to eliminate a hedgerow, farmers learned, was to hire a bulldozer operator to push out the stumps that come up looking like huge octopuses with bright orange tentacles. Most of the firewood that our family harvested in my childhood came from cleaning up after a caterpillar tractor had mauled the earth and toppled the trees. We attacked these slain giants with saws and axes. On our farm shop wall hung an antique six-foot-long rusty two person cross-cut bucksaw from another era, replaced in my day by the new gasoline-powered chain-saw.

Our Trainview's softball team framed by a spiney hedgerow.

Once a hedgerow was pushed over by the bulldozer, we trimmed the logs and branches with axes that had to be sharpened on a grinding wheel in the shop every morning. Rock-hard hedgewood was famous for dulling axes. Without a sharpened blade, you could wear yourself out with little to show for your flailing efforts. We axed the thorny twigs off of trunks and branches, and pulled the brush into piles for burning, leaving ash to scatter in the wind and fertilize the ground. Of course, we all had to wear tough elk-skin leather gloves to protect our hands from the formidable hedgewood thorns. Still, our fingers and shins were crusty with scabs by the end of the day.

My favorite times on the farm were when we made up an intergenerational, extended-family team working together as a visible community. One day when Father, us three brothers and cousin Herman were felling and trimming some tall hedge trees, one giant toppled sooner than we anticipated. At the call of "timber," I ran the wrong way and was literally pinned to the ground by thorny branches until my teammates liberated me with a few strategic cuts of the ax. That treefall could have been the end of me right there, but as it happened, I only suffered damage to my thorn-punctured jacket, and, thank God, survived to tell you the tale.

Hedge trees seldom grew straight, but rather resembled gnarly arthritic hands reaching for the sky. So, whenever Father would spot a relatively unbent section of the tree at least eight feet long, we would cut it out and set it aside for future use as a valuable fence post—three feet underground and five feet in the air. The rest of the tree was destined for firewood. We stacked the long limbs in tangled heaps onto our hayrack wagons to pull home. That's where, on various Saturdays during the winter, we would cut up the wild limbs with a 24" buzz saw mounted on the front of a tractor. Powered by belt and pulley, this unshielded spinning wheel of teeth was obviously dangerous, and little boys were warned to stay far away. We hauled logs to Father who pushed them across the table through the screeching saw, cutting off furnace-sized sections that we heaved onto a waiting wagon. Later, we would pitch those wagon loads of wood down an improvised chute through an opened basement window on the back side of our house.

Once, while tossing wood, we argued about how heavy hedgewood actually was—would it float or sink? We lugged the biggest block of Osage Orange to a stock tank and performed our scientific experiment. Indeed, the wood floated, but just barely, with a density of 60 pounds per cubic foot, compared to water at 64 pounds.

Our pile of firewood fed a cast-iron furnace in the middle of the basement that we referred to as our "fire-breathing octopus." From its red-hot belly, our pet monster delivered warm air by an array of round tin ducts to floor registers around the first floor of the house. In the mornings, however, our unheated upstairs bedrooms felt as cold as the arctic. So, we would suck up our courage, throw off the covers, grab our clothes and dash downstairs to huddle over the floor register right above the furnace where we could gratefully jump into our long-johns, shirts and overalls in more tropical weather.

When I had already left home for college and my father neared retirement, that vicious buzz-saw got its last bite. One particularly crooked piece of hedgewood with a protruding thorn hooked my father's glove and twisted it into the buzz-saw, instantly cutting off his right thumb. After an operation and a few days in the hospital, Father worked through his pain and disability with courage and eventually came to joke about his loss. He would shyly show little children his right hand and ask them to help him look for his lost thumb. I still can see Father painfully learning to write again with a pen pinched between his second and third fingers. That's when he switched to writing by hunt-and-peck on the typewriter.

That accident also marked the end of an era on our farm. The romantic tin and cast-iron fire-breathing octopus in our basement was replaced by a prosaic gas furnace fed from a propane tank in our back yard. The last practical reason for keeping hedges was gone and bulldozers upended the remaining trees that were wastefully burned in the field. However, even now as you drive through central Kansas in the 21st century, a few remnants of the miles of hedgerows remain, more out of nostalgia than usefulness. Costly fossil fuels now do all the heating rather than renewable hedgewood that used to be free—not counting unpaid child labor.

However, in our kitchen these days, in its place of honor hangs a sharp-shooter spade that Joanne's father crafted with an unbreakable hedgewood shaft, after fir and oak handles had failed. Joanne likes to brag that her hedgewood spade is so heavy she needs only to drop it in the garden, point down, and its weight alone will dig up tulip bulbs.

Our daughter, Natasha, who grew up in Kansas, got a homemade hedgewood cutting board from a cousin for her wedding. Now she lives with her family in Berlin, but she keeps alive our family's stubborn roots in Kansas soil and history with a unique e-mail address that no one else in Germany could have dug up . . . "hedgewood@*********."

CHAPTER 10

About Chicks, Imaginary Chicken Hawks

And an Inconsistent Vegetarian

WHEN MOTHER SERVED FRIED chicken to our frequent guests, father might startle them by announcing, "In this house we only eat chickens before they are born and after they are dead." It sounded a bit gruesome, but on a little reflection, the guests agreed that at their house they did the same.

So, where did those fried chickens on the table come from? As long as there were children to do chores, we had a couple hundred chickens in our chicken house, chickens whose job it was to lay eggs. And for some years it was my job to water and feed those chickens, to gather and pack those eggs. These eggs never made new chickens because they were shipped off to the Hillsboro Creamery where they turned out ice-cream and other good stuff with the eggs and the farmers' cream. In our chicken house we did sometimes have a few clucks, hens whose hormones were switched "on" to take possession of a nest full of eggs, to sit on them and brood until the eggs would hatch. But I frustrated them every day by plucking the eggs from beneath their breasts and shipping them off to make ice cream—which, in my opinion, is still the best thing that can be done with eggs and cream.

So, if hens did not hatch them, how did these chickens get here? Each spring mother would buy a couple hundred chicks that came in cute cardboard boxes from the Newton Hatchery. I say the boxes were cute because they made incessant "cheeping" noises that attracted us kids to lift the lid and peek in. There were about fifty day-old chicks in each box, milling around in the sawdust that lined their little compartments. With the lid off, Mother worried that the chicks might get cold and catch a disease, so we could admire them only a few minutes and then carried the peeping boxes to the brooder house behind the chicken house.

The brooder house was a weather-tight shed about the size of a small room in the middle of which was a low tin hood as wide as a kitchen table with a few light bulbs inside to make heat. The underside of a brooding hen where little chicks like to huddle, is about 98 degrees Fahrenheit, so the thermostat of our brooding hood was set for the same. Of course, the chicks had a part in controlling the temperature that was comfortable for them as they could come out and peck in the straw we'd spread on the brooder house floor or go back under the hood to warm up again. They had little feeder trays full of a protein-rich cereal mash and upended water bottles with saucers under them from which the chicks could dip and sip. It seems the chicks needed no mother hen to teach them the basic lunch technique. They instinctively pecked at everything in their surroundings, and soon learned what tasted good, and what satisfied their thirst.

Mother kept a close eye on the chicks in those first days to see if any got sick or were pecked on excessively. Those who got too much abuse and started to bleed might come into the kitchen and live in a cardboard box for a few days behind the kitchen stove. Early on I learned that chickens have a pecking order, a dominance hierarchy in which, inevitably, one bird was at the bottom of the list and got pecked on the most. Sometimes little chicks would die in the first days, and it was my job as undertaker to give them a proper burial. I remember feeling sorrow at the helpless forms that I'd lay on a shingle and carry to the private cemetery behind the brooder house. Sometimes I would be accompanied at the funeral by our dog and a few cats who took interest in the grave-side ceremony. They seemed to share my sadness and together we'd observe a moment of silence before I'd shovel the dirt over "our dear departed loved one."

It did not take long for our chicks to grow up and to lose their fuzz as a coat of insulating feathers appeared. They became more adventuresome and spent less time under the heated hood and more time scratching in the straw. On sunny days we'd open the little side flap door on the brooder house and watch the gangly wanna-be-chickens stream out to explore the world of grass, bugs, seeds, larger chickens, and other farm-yard animals. Sometimes a few would follow me around as if I was their mother, or perhaps they followed because, by walking through the grass, I'd scare up leafhoppers for them to chase down. We children learned to be faithful at our chores, filling the water jars and carrying buckets of mash to keep the growing chicks fed. But more exciting was protecting the flock from real and imaginary predators.

We'd heard reports of chicken hawks swooping down and stealing unsuspecting little chicks from farmyards in the neighborhood—after all, that's why they were called "chicken hawks." So, we kept an eye out for suspicious raptors in the sky. My brothers and I fashioned rubber-powered slingshots and stock-piled marble-sized stones "just in case." We practiced on targets, shooting pebbles at anything that would make a racket. Most satisfying was to shoot one of the disks on a farm plow which made a long-lasting cymbal-like "ding." I don't remember ever losing a chick to chicken hawks, or even seeing one on the farm for that matter, but the stories and rumors we got from others who knew someone who had a cousin who'd seen a hawk try such an awful deed boosted our hunter-identities to heroic proportions as we imagined how we'd seal the fate of any hawk that tried to mess with our flock.

Soon these young birds ceased to be chicks and began to visibly sexually differentiate. Some became feisty male roosters with more muscular bodies and a floppy red comb on the top of their heads. In the morning they'd let out pathetic raspy cawing sounds, but you could tell they were aiming at something like "cock a doodle doo." The other chicks turned into female pullets with more modest-sized combs, who were more interested in bugs than in combat, and who soon matured into laying hens. But both the pullets and roosters learned to run fast and fly high over the fence that circled our house, flower beds and garden. So, several times a day we'd have to open the gate and chase the critters out, and to do so before others would come in. Sometimes that was a two-child job, chasing and strategically opening the gate.

As night fell the pullets and roosters got uneasy and more-or-less voluntarily returned to the brooder house where they had safety and guaranteed food. But if they'd gotten into the garden fence, by evening they'd forgotten how to fly and had to be herded back out the gate and into their house. We couldn't leave them outside because darkness would give cover for raccoons and possums who appreciated fresh young chicken meat on the menu. So, the brooder-house side door had to be shut for the night. Often, when the whole flock was safely indoors, there'd be one last remorseful bird circling the brooder house in the dark, trying to join the others inside. Thus, the last chore of my day might be to go out and, like a good pastor, welcome that last repentant sinner home.

Eventually we moved all the pullets into the large chicken house with the older hens where they could look forward to long and productive lives as daily egg layers, incessant gossips and social climbers. But the roosters' days were numbered. By the time the first ones reached three pounds in weight, we organized a series of butchering days.

At the age of four I became fascinated by numbers and began to play the mental game of "estimating." I'd ask Father, "How tall is our tree-house tree?" He would say, "forty feet," and I'd store a picture in my memory of that tree and "forty feet." Our first windmill was thirty feet tall; our silos were forty-five feet; our farmyard with feed-lots was ten acres; and the heavy anvil in the shop weighed fifty pounds. I also learned that roosters ready for butchering weighed exactly three pounds. We pulled the big ones out of the brooder house with a leg hook, laid them on a scale, and if they weighed three pounds or more, they were ready for the big day and went into a holding cage. Soon I learned how to accurately estimate a three-pounder just by feel, and to this day I can tell you if something weighs more or less than three pounds just by remembering the heft of a butchering-day rooster.

On the big day the rooster got a new name, "fryer," because, you guessed it, he was destined for the frying pan. Butchering day often involved a few extra helpers like Aunt Ella or the Neufeldt Grandparents. We worked in something like an assembly line. One by one Father pulled the roosters out of the cage, and then later one of us boys took over as we learned by watching and doing. The rooster would fight his fate with might and main, so you had to hold his legs and wing-tips tight in your left hand as you laid his wiggling head on the chopping block. Then with the right hand you'd whack down with a hatchet and, with a little luck, cut off his head on the first try. Then you'd lay the not-quite-dead rooster down on the ground to bleed a minute or two. Some roosters however, instead of just flopping and flapping on the ground, would get on their feet and run in crazy arcs, fleeing half-way across the yard before they'd crash into a bush, and "meet their maker." That provided a lot of entertainment for us kids, chasing down errant head-less roosters. We wondered—what kind of reflexes must have resided in their nervous systems and muscles below their severed heads?

The "fryers" then went into a pot of boiling hot water for a minute which loosened the feathers enough to be pulled out by the hands-full—a rather disgusting job that we tried to avoid until the rule came down from "on high" that each one of us had to pluck our share. Once the bird was properly naked, then the last fuzz was singed off by turning the carcass over the flame of a kerosene stove. At that point the butcher knives went to work, gutting the bird, and cutting through the joints to separate the parts into drumsticks, thighs, wings, breasts, necks and that portion which Father liked most, and which he aptly named, "The piece that goes over the fence last."

The final stage of the butchering process saw Mother wrap the meaty fryer parts into butcher paper packages that one of us children would carry down to the basement freezer. And those who volunteered to help for the day would also take home a few cut up birds as thanks for their contribution.

Ah, but wait—that wasn't the last part of the day. If Grandma Neufeldt was there, she'd totally gross us out by gathering up the rooster heads and legs, and put them in her cooking pot to take home. There she would stew the heads and talons a long while, pour off the broth and frugally pluck out the last slivers of meat for her own unique version of Low-German chicken noodle soup. Everyone who didn't know what was in it said, "That was really good."

In the year that our daughter Natasha was born, I became a vegetarian. The glee with which we slaughtered roosters as a boy had a part, I believe, in my later aversion to killing animals that, on any close observation, have a conscious life of pain, joy and wonder much like our own. It may be a contradiction of my principles, but out of care for Joanne's hypoglycemic metabolism that seems to need meat, I've consented, now and then, to cut up a chicken for my love—drumsticks, thighs, wings, neck, breast and "that part that goes over the fence last."

Chapter 11

My Brief Career as a Champion Major League Rock Batter

ONE DAY WHEN I was in second grade, teacher Art Goering arrived at our one-room country school with something none of us had seen before—a portable battery-powered radio. Art announced that we would need to rush through all our day's recitations in the morning because the afternoon would be dedicated to a special educational and cultural event. That afternoon Art tuned the radio and announced that we would be listening to a Major League World Series baseball game. Most of us had only the vaguest idea of baseball since under-hand slow-pitch softball was the game we played. That way children of all ages could participate. Teacher Art explained that in baseball the pitcher threw overhand, that the game was played in a huge stadium with crowds in the thousands, and that the two best teams in baseball were facing off for the world championship—the Cleveland Indians and the Boston Braves. The fastest pitcher in baseball, Bobby Feller, was pitching for Cleveland. Immediately, he was our favorite.

    As the game went on, we were amazed at a scoreless duel where neither team could cross home plate. Whenever we played softball, our scores were in the tens and twenties because of all the errors by little kids. But in Cleveland, the Boston Braves defeated the Cleveland Indians by the miniscule score of one run to nothing. We were utterly dismayed at Bobby Feller's loss, but at the same time, totally captivated by major league baseball, and could talk of nothing else in the coming days as we followed the World Series score in the paper and on radio news at home.

    When the next baseball season came around, I had a plan: I'd sneak away from my assigned summer jobs and sit in our brand new 1948 Chevy sedan parked in the shop and turn on its radio to follow the play-by-play commentary on baseball games, getting familiar with all the teams and their starting players. During commercial breaks I'd switch over to another game and thus keep up with the American and the National league standings. Of course, if Father ever caught me listening to the car radio and running down the battery, he'd chew me out and give me another job. But he could not prevent us from playing imaginary games of baseball in our heads and with each other.

Brother John and I saved up our money, or begged it from our parents to buy gloves, a bat and a real regulation hardball so we could pretend to be Major Leaguers. However, we had one perennial problem in that there were never enough of us to make up a team, much less two teams to play a game. Sometimes Mark or Sara might join us, but the other players had to be imagined. With just a pitcher and a batter, we played in the cattle feedlot north of the horse barn so that we could use the barn door as a backstop. If I hit the ball hard back up the middle where neither the short-stop nor the second baseman could get to it, that put a man on first. Of course, every hit ball was contestable, but usually we agreed that it was an out, a single, double, or if it went over the back fence, that was a home run. Our baseballs quickly got beat up by the tin barn door and incessant use. If the cover came off, we'd stitch it back on with fish line, and finally replace the whole cover with black electrician's tape from the shop. Curve-balls were hard to throw with a ball that slick.

So, what does a baseball-obsessed farm boy do when he has no baseball and no teammates? Fortunately, our farm always had plenty of rocks to throw and bat. My delight multiplied when father brought home from the quarry a new truckload of gravel for our driveway. A six-foot high pile could be leveled out to a low mound by an evening of energetic "king-of-the-mountain" play from us siblings and a few cousins. But the gravel pile still offered me a few weeks of solitary fun. I'd scratch a home plate in the dust, station myself with an improvised bat, and slam rocks in all directions. I knew better than to use our one baseball bat on rocks since it would quickly be ruined by dents and divots. Instead, I went to the shop and knocked the iron head off a pickaxe and used the freed-up handle for my bat. Then I'd carefully replace it to its previous location when I was done. With the pickaxe handle I'd practice my line drives and home-runs by tossing a rock free-handed and then whack it as it came down.

But that was not enough excitement. I was not only the batter, I was also a radio announcer who called the game play-by-play, citing the batting averages of each player, and explaining the strategy of the moment. One afternoon when it was almost chore time, I was in the seventh game of the World Series. The home team was up to bat in the bottom of the ninth, with two outs, two runs down, with runners on second and third, and the winning run at the plate. The batter worked his way to a full count. The crowd was going wild, the pitcher fretted on the mound with the rosin bag while the batter dug in his cleats, spat on his hands, and prepared for his moment of destiny. The pitcher threw a hanging curve ball right over the plate which the batter crushed with all his might to straight-away center field, just clearing the leaping outfielder's glove and the gate in the fence next to the cowbarn. A home run! Victory! World Series champions! Everlasting glory!

But at that moment instead of glory, the day lurched into sudden disaster. I had not noticed that my brother John was letting the cows into the barn from the north feedlot with his hand on the gate just as the homerun rock caught him full on the left temple. He had no idea what hit him. He ran to the house in pain and bloody terror. I was aghast, quickly hid the bat back in the shop, and slunk my way to the kitchen where mother was treating John's wound.

At that point the story veered into further chaos and hysteria because our Aunt Helen happened to be visiting and entered the kitchen as John was wailing about his bolt from the blue. Fearing the worst, Aunt Helen believed it was Satan who had tried to kill her beloved nephew, so she went into spiritual attack mode loudly calling on God in heaven to intervene. Then she tried to gather all us children to join her in an urgent circle of prayer calling on the angels and all the heavenly hosts to beat back the Devil and his nefarious minions. Meanwhile, Mother in irritated-nurse mode, wondered how to restore order and calm to her suddenly invaded emergency room. At this point brother John, no longer the center of attention, was crying in the corner with a severe headache, holding his hands over his ears to keep out the noise, and obviously not dying anytime soon.

After Aunt Helen finally said "Amen," everyone's attention turned to John to ask him what had happened. Eventually I confessed that I'd been batting rocks and that's how he got hit. In that moment it became clear that Satan was innocent and that I was not, which made me worse than the Devil for a little while, whereupon I started to cry. My story about batting rocks was a little hard for some to believe because the rock pile and the cow barn were such a long distance apart, but all my rock batting practice had paid off in a home run farther than I'd ever hit a rock before. I was both surprised and dismayed by what I had done. I don't remember if I was ever punished for this devilish attack. Perhaps my parents felt like enough damage had been done, and besides, the cows were still waiting to be milked. Brother John was not angry at me either, and I felt greatly relieved.

But in that conscience-stricken moment, this honyak realized that now would be the right time to hang up my pick-axe handle bat and to retire from my all-too-brief career as a champion major league rock batter.

*   *   *   *   *

In the middle of this chapter, between two sports stories, I want to sandwich a little reflection on the role of athletics in my life and character development.

Though all of us children were eager participants in sports, I was the most enthusiastic and put in the longest hours of practice. John, who was three years older than I, was like a peer to me and we sharpened our skills against each other, making me increasingly competitive and little precocious among my peers. I dreamed of glory on the playing field and became known as a "scrapper," someone who turned the competition dial all the way up to the top notch.

Brother John and I worked together to mount a home-made basketball backboard and goal that projected four feet out from the south side of our horse barn, and we rigged up a light that allowed us to play at night. With this set-up we could fly in for lay-ups and not crash into the goal post, as often happened at our country grade school basketball court. We were hard core competitors, John and I, even playing at zero degrees in the winter with our mittens on. During better weather neighborhood kids would gather at our place on Sunday afternoons to scrimmage on our half-court. Us Janzen boys, of course, had the home-court advantage because we had learned how to dribble both right and left-handed on the erratic gravel surface.

My brothers, John and Mark, excelled in high school varsity basketball just like me. I went on to play a couple of years at Bethel College, and in track I set a javelin throwing record that lasted four decades. There were no heroic championships to brag about, but I enjoyed the reputation of being a jock and an intellectual at the same time according to the ideals of the classical Athenian gymnasium that included both practice fields and lecture halls.

David throwing the javelin from the Bethel College yearbook.

Others in my family hung up their gym shoes in adulthood but I persisted, majoring in basketball. Once we moved to Evanston, I kept showing up at the YMCA until at the age of fifty, my knees were so swollen and painful, I had to quit—which soon led to a puffy body and weight gain. Then, in my early sixties, when Joanne was away for two weeks to assist our daughter, Natasha, around the birth of grandson, Noah, I bought a new basketball and started showing up at the gym in our local Levy Senior Center where others my age started to play together. The rebirth of my basketball career dates from grandson Noah's birth in June of 2002.

At the Levy Center we connected to the Senior Games of America, nicknamed "Senior Olympics," which held state and national tournaments for men and women at every age level, at 55 +, 60+, 65+, etc. Senior Games rules had us playing half-court basketball with three on a side to minimize wear and tear on our older bodies. I was surprised to learn that others had had knee and hip replacement surgery and were still playing. So now, at the age of eighty-three after one back surgery, two hip replacements, and two new knees, I'm still playing and enjoying this body that God gave me.

I discovered that my childhood tendency to be a glory hog and to compete as if my ego needed to win at all costs—now is a character liability and a turn-off to my friends. The scrapper is still in me, but with the help of my Levy Center basketball buddies, I'm learning other ways to share the glory. When my opponent makes a good play, I congratulate him. When we lose, I praise the other side. Success now is not defined by victory, but by everyone sweating hard for an hour, and not breaking anything. When the game is over, we hang around and talk about other things than basketball.

I've got a growing collection of medals and ribbons in my closet which I end up sharing with younger kids in the Fellowship who can't yet read the "Senior Games of America" insignias on them.

The athletic arc of my life begins in childhood dreams of glory won in a dramatic last-second victory, securing a championship at the highest level. And that arc lands in a totally different and more satisfying kind of glory shared in the following story:

* * * * *

October 2017:

Sandford Parker seldom plays basketball with us anymore, but he is definitely on our team and shows up at every practice whenever his health allows. We're a seventy-five-and-over squad whose home court is the Levy Senior Center in Evanston, where we practice every Tuesday and Thursday noon. Sanford sits on the sidelines and settles our disputes with his unbiased judgment calls. "It sure looked like a foul to me."

Sanford used to play, but he is in his mid-80's now, on the downhill side of several bouts with cancer and a surgery that has weakened his right arm. He used to be a top-notch athlete, winning the 220-yard dash in the Alabama state Negro high school track meet back in the days of segregation.

So, Sandford got excited when he learned that the Senior Games of America would be held this year in Birmingham, Alabama, where he has many family members and friends. He joined our van ride to Birmingham and on the way, we heard more of his story.

Sanford was born to a large African American farming family near Tuskegee, Alabama. He went to black schools and excelled in both academics and sports. His strategy to escape segregation in the South was to study sciences and get an engineering degree at Tuskegee Institute, and then go into the military where opportunities were more equal. In the Air Force he became a specialist in radar maintenance and repair, taking his growing family around the Pacific to various bases. Eventually, he and his wife raised four boys and a girl. His son Ronnie, now almost fifty years old, lovingly assisted his dad on this trip, making sure he ate right and took his meds. We got many clues on this trip about how close and caring this family turned out to be.

In mid-life Sanford took early retirement from the Air Force and moved to cosmopolitan Evanston where the schools are good. He commuted daily to the Argonne National Laboratories where he negotiated and supervised grants that Argonne gave out for scientific research. Sanford's good judgment, generous spirit, and sly wit won him a lot of credibility in business, with family and with friends like us. He's a warm and interesting fellow to be around.

In Birmingham our team had its moments of humiliation (we lost five games) and our moments of glory (winning four). Sanford's extended family made up most of our cheering section. One high point for us was getting our picture taken with bronze medals won in the consolation bracket, with Sanford proudly beaming in the front row.

Our 75 + basketball team at Senior Games of America, Birmingham, 2017. Sanford Parker in black.

But the highest high point came when we were safely 20 points ahead in the waning minutes of a game. Our captain substituted Sanford onto the court and whispered to the opposition and the referees that Sanford is battling cancer, but he would very much like to participate in one more game. The opposing team played along and gave Sanford every opportunity to score but the ball just wouldn't go in. Finally, one player told the ref, "Give us a technical foul so Sanford can shoot a free throw." That's what the ref did, only he urged Sanford to step up and shoot from four feet away. Sanford heaved the ball up with all his might where it rolled round and round the rim and finally went in. The video camera was rolling. Everyone on both teams and in the stands cheered and danced like after a little league home run. It was a sublime moment of joy beyond all competition for everyone around. Sanford ambled back to his chair and sat down exhausted, totally pleased with his effort. That's the moment we'll remember most of all in Birmingham.

On the way home Sanford was in bliss, telling stories that made the miles roll by with ease. I'll close this little essay in Sanford's honor with the joke we all liked best.

There were two childhood friends who loved to play baseball, a pitcher and a catcher. In grade school, high school, and later in life whenever they could, they always played on the same team. As they got older and their bodies began to fail, they would retell the stories of their best games and often wondered together, "Will there be baseball in heaven?" They made a vow that whoever died first would try to let the other one know if they play baseball in that great by-and-by in the sky.

It so happened that the catcher died first. A few days after his funeral the pitcher got a phone call. He picked up the receiver and heard his friend's voice say, "Hey buddy, I just wanted to let you know how everything is up here. It's just like we hoped, we play baseball every day and we never get sore. It's just wonderful."

His pitcher friend replied, "That's terrific. I'm so excited to hear it."

The catcher answered, "I'm glad you're excited 'cause I just checked the roster and called to let you know, you're starting tomorrow."

* * * * *

Sanford Parker, longtime Evanston resident and sports enthusiast, joined the heavenly roster on February 3, 2018.

Mirror # 3

Seven Careers for Seven Decades

Chapter 12

Memories of Cows, a Milking Barn, and a Hobble-Dance

Practical Wisdom Is a Thing

On this dreary evening of the longest night of the year, in the seventy-third year of my life (2014), I'm feeling needy in a way that has no label. Whatever I imagine doing seems depressing. However, I did run across the opinion of Dostoevsky that even one childhood memory can save a man's soul. This evening, I want to test whether he speaks the truth.

In our apartment hallway hangs a photo that my mother had me pose for when I was about five years old. I'm standing in the midst of all the stainless-steel buckets that we used on the farm to milk cows. Because my father, sister and older brother all milked cows, this was the career that, at that age, I aspired to with all my heart.

In those days we hand-milked about five cows every morning and evening in a small dirt-floor milk barn that had no heat except for the bodies in it. Inside there was a manger with feed boxes where four cows could stand for milking at one time. But before the cows entered, I hurried to scoop a bucket into the feed barrel and dumped a portion of ground corn into each box. Then Father hoisted me up and dropped me into a wooden barrel in the corner of the cow barn right next to the door where the cows were waiting with tight, full udders, bumping against the wall to remind us it was time for milking. Inside the barrel I was safe from getting knocked over by the cows in their urgent rush to the feed boxes.

Little David with milkbuckets, hoping with all his heart to become a milker.

When we opened the west cow-barn door, the cows entered immediately in the order of their well-established social hierarchy. If two tried to enter at the same time, the top cow would butt her rival away. Usually, however, good order prevailed, and the cows would process in step with the music playing on the radio, full udders swaying, sometimes leaking and spraying as the milk was already coming down. Occasionally, as the cows filed in, one of them would sniff me in the corner and get curious, sticking her snotty muzzle in my face. Then I'd duck down and yell at the cow, making a big barrel echo until she moved on.

The first cow in the door was usually "Holstein," a large, gentle black and white bovine who was indeed of the Holstein breed. Then, came a red and brown cow that Father had named "Betty Moo." I don't remember all their names. My brother Mark recalled an explosives theme in which a series of cows were named Dynamite, TNT, and Nitroglycerine. Somewhere toward the end of the row was a shorter, tannish-colored cow named "Jersey" who gave especially creamy milk typical of her breed. Once each cow was peacefully eating her chow, a child would walk to her head end and click a chain around her neck to make sure she stayed there till the milking was done.

I pled and begged for the privilege of milking cows until one day my father allowed me to try on the gentlest and easiest-to-milk-cow of the herd, "Holstein." He gave me a cute little two-gallon bucket which I set down under Holstein's udder. By this time, she was fidgeting, stepping around, because no one was milking her. I was afraid she'd knock over the bucket or kick me in the shins. Father showed how to squat on the one-legged milking stool, making a tripod with two human legs. He demonstrated how to lean into "Holstein's" flank. "With your head in her hip," Father explained, "You can feel when she's going to move or kick. That's when you push a little harder. You have to let her know who's boss."

I leaned in as Father said, and grabbed the two hind teats while Father took the two front ones. He showed me how to pull them down, squeezing first with the thumb and index finger, and then with the rest of the fist. After a few strokes the milk started to squirt out with a ping and a squish against the bottom of the bucket. Soon I started to feel a rhythm—left, right, left, right, left. Father backed out and went to milk another cow. Frothy milk soon covered the bottom of the bucket; Holstein stopped fidgeting and settled down too. Later, Father showed me how to hold the bucket between my knees so that I could turn away with the milk rather than let the cow step in the bucket.

I kept milking at my own pace until all the other cows were done and the milkers were waiting on me. Father said, "David, step aside. I'll finish up." In a minute he'd filled another bucket, and we were ready to carry our milk home. I felt defeated, because everyone else could milk many times faster than me. But at the supper table Father announced, "We have another milker in the family. Today little David got a whole gallon all by himself. Tomorrow he'll do even better." Suddenly I felt so proud of myself that I feared it was a sin.

Until that time, I had been allowed to sleep every morning until our 6:45 breakfast, while the older children had to get up at 5:30 for chores. Now I was awakened with them and felt like a six-year-old grown-up, learning how to work hard despite fatigue until the job was done. Chores were wearisome, but along with them came the status of being treated like a real partner in the farm.

Soon I learned how to milk at almost the same pace as the others in the barn, how to carry two buckets of milk back to the house without splashing, how to run the cream separator on our back porch, an appliance every farm had in those days. We'd hoist the buckets high to pour the milk through a filter that flowed into a big steel bowl at the top of the separator machine. As one of us turned the hand crank at just the right speed, the milk would run down through the separator's spinning core which used centrifugal force to divide the lighter cream from the heavier milk. Soon the cream trickled out of one spout into a cream can for sale at the Coop in Hillsboro, and the skimmed milk streamed from another spout into the calf-feeding buckets. From there we'd take the skimmed milk to the horse barn where we bucket-fed a few calves in their holding pen.

As soon as I was dependable at these chores, Father dropped off the milking crew to give more time to feeding the larger herd of cattle in our corrals. Not long after that, Sister Sara also graduated to care for chickens and help Mother prepare the family meals. Brother John and I settled into a routine in the cow barn, paying attention to all the details that made milking as efficient and interesting as possible. Later, younger brother Mark joined me on the milking team and John moved on to other chores as well.

Each morning at 5:30 am we'd arrive at the cow-barn, turn on the lights and the radio—usually to Wichita stations KFDI or KFH. We argued about which one was the best, as did our mates at school who also milked cows while listening to the radio. Brother Mark recalled that we listened to KFDI's Bruce Beheimer with the Wichita Stock Yards report that always began with the same malapropism, "Put the coffee pot on mama."

For a few years, while milking cows, I was "up" on popular music and knew which songs were at the top of the charts. "You are my sunshine, my only sunshine, . . ." "I'm gonna sit right down and write myself a letter, and pretend it came from you. . ." "Davey, Davey Crocket, king of the wild frontier." We also caught the beginning of the Elvis Presley craze. So, milking cows from age six to seventeen marked an era of immersion in popular culture that ended when I left home for college. Since then, I've never hung around a radio, and popular music has been a cultural black hole for me.

Milking cows was not all boring. Once the cows were hooked up to their stanchions, half-a-dozen cats would swarm the place and beg for milk—and we'd oblige them. It was fun to squirt a gentle stream of milk horizontally from the cow's teat to the cat's mouth and watch her lap it up as fast as it came. The game was to see if we could get the cat to lap a steady stream, then raise that stream till she was standing tiptoe on hind legs only. At that moment we would squeeze out the last milk in a burst, so the cat's face got blasted, and she'd topple over backwards. I don't think we were cruel to them because the cats licked themselves clean and dry with lots of satisfaction. And the next day they were ready to do it again. Eventually we'd take pity on all the meowing cats, pour some milk into a grain shovel lying on the ground, and watch them shove in shoulder-to-shoulder to lap it all up.

Now comes the grossest part of this story. You might want to cover your eyes. Eventually while milking, one of the cows would poop in the cow-barn. That was the time to pull the bucket out of splashing range and let the plops fall. Then when the bowel movement was done, we'd take the shovel, scoop the crap off the dirt floor and pitch it into the barnyard corral. If we were really alert and saw the cow's tail begin to lift, we'd quickly set aside the milk bucket and grab the shovel in time to catch the brown tide just as it was ready to fall. However, in such a case you had to be careful where you stood because sometimes what came was projectile diarrhea that could splat against the opposite wall of the barn, and you did not want to be in its way.

And yep, in case you were wondering, that was the same shovel the cats drank out of with no objections. It may even be the way country cats developed strong anti-bodies and immunities to whatever germs might come after them. What they drank was no dirtier than the way they licked themselves clean from whatever they might catch, step into, or get splashed by. And "No," in case you ask, those cats did not live in the house. That is why we had springs on the screen doors.

Milk cows, at least in our era, would share the corral with a bull so that they would get pregnant and bear a calf about every 12 months. A couple of days after birth, the calf would be taken away from its Mama and raised separately. The calf bawled and the mother answered for a few days, and then the turmoil was over. The farmer's strategy recognized that cows bred for milk production give far more milk than their calves could drink. There was plenty for human consumption, cream sales, and feeding the calves skim milk with a protein supplement mixed in.

A cow that has just borne a calf is called "fresh" in the dairyman's vocabulary. This is the time when she gives the most milk. The good ones like "Holstein" would give as much as four gallons every morning and every evening. After a few months the production would taper off. About nine months after calving, we would "dry" the cow, that is, not milk her anymore. She would recover, put on weight, and give birth soon to another calf. The male calves we would raise, castrate, and put into the herd to be sent to market when fully grown at about two years of age. A female, if she looked healthy, might grow up to become a milk-cow with a decade of production in our herd.

A female calf while growing up was called a "heifer" until she had given birth to her first calf, and then she became a "milk cow." A heifer did not, of course, have any experience of being milked. When her calf was taken away, she bawled and paced the fence line looking for a way to escape and rejoin her calf. She did not know how to behave in a cow barn and panicked easily. With a newly fresh heifer, we had to take special precautions. Tied up in the cow barn, her hind end would dance away if anyone approached her with a bucket and milk-stool. Settling her down was not easy. At first, we would attach hobbles to her back legs which tied them together so she could not step away. However, she might go into what we called a "hobble dance" with her back end bouncing up and down until she wore herself out. Then she might be willing to stand while we milked her. The experience of being milked, of having an empty udder, was calming and eventually the heifer caught on that this is what happened to all the other cows and it wasn't so bad.

However, we had one famous heifer who earned the name of "Jezebel," taken from the notoriously evil, prophet-hating Old Testament queen. Our Jezebel was a leaper who, with a full udder, could clear the fences of our corral, and had to be pursued on horseback to bring her home. Her hobble dances were epic and dangerous affairs that attracted hired hands and family guests who wanted to see this bucking rodeo behavior in our own cow-barn. Once in the stanchion with back legs hobbled, she would leap so violently that often she fell on her side and the person trying to milk her had to be acrobatic to get away. After a few weeks we gave up on Jezebel. She got a one-way ticket on the next truck to the Kansas City Stock Yards where, alas, she became hamburger before her time.

Which brings up the expression, "to kick the bucket." In ordinary usage this is a euphemism for "dying." But to an old-time dairyman it meant something more specific. A cow that persistently kicked the bucket would soon meet Her Maker—with a little assistance from the farmer and the butcher. So, "What happened to that Jezebel who used to be in your herd?" "She kicked the bucket." Enough said.

The cow-barn is a space where other jokes and farmer sayings got passed along—a culture all its own. For example, "A new milker-boy was set to work on Bessie by his father, who then went off to other chores. When the father came back, he saw that the boy was holding the milk bucket under the cow's nose as she quickly drank it dry. The astonished father asked, 'What on earth are you doing, son, giving all that milk to the cow?' The son replied, "Bessie put her foot in the bucket so the milk got all dirty. I thought I'd just run it through again and let her clean it up."

So, how clean was the milk that we brought into the house from the cow-barn? Well, ours definitely wasn't a Grade A Dairy where the milking parlor is sanitary, where the cow's udders are always washed, and where machines sucked the milk from the teats into sterile hoses so that human hands never touched the liquid on the way to the refrigerator tank and the milk truck to town.

The milk we brought from the cow-barn to our back porch was processed to reasonable cleanliness. We had a sink in the back porch to wash our buckets in hot soapy water before every use. The cows were usually bedded down in straw so that they did not get muddy udders. And if the udders were dirty, we'd have a bucket of soapy water to wash them off with a rag. The milk that came into the house was strained through a paper filter and stored in gallon glass jars in the refrigerator. From there we poured a glass-full and set it before each kid at just about every meal.

We all agreed that the best thing to do with raw milk was ice cream. In the winter when snow and ice were everywhere at hand, we'd put our hand-crank ice-cream freezer to work, preparing a gallon-and-a-half at a time. We didn't need permission to mix up a batch since eggs, milk and cream were essentially free on the farm.

Milking cows by hand to support calves, cats, dogs and humans, defined a deeply rooted rural culture and an era that disappeared at our house and most of the neighbors too, when the last kid left for college. At our house that was about 1960. At that point my folks sold the cows and started to buy milk from the store—an appalling development! And not only that, once I was gone from home, they got a TV set, which is why, in my opinion, my younger brother, Mark, was corrupted by insufficient chores and unauthorized entertainment, while I turned out to be hard-working, not to mention humble, honest, and happily preserved from all self-righteousness! So, you can see how all my virtues can be traced back to hand-milking cows.

Now let us return to where we started this essay in the company of Dostoevsky who wrote,

> "You must know that there is nothing higher and stronger and more wholesome and good for life . . . than some good memory, especially a memory of childhood . . . . For if a man [sic] has only one good memory left in his heart, even that may keep him from evil. . . . And if he carries many such memories with him into life, he is safe for the end of his days."

I give thanks for a bucket-full of childhood memories in which cows, horses, chickens, cats, dogs, siblings, and parents all had a part in giving and receiving an abundant life with God's blessings poured over it like cream on strawberries. Likewise, the skills we learned in farm chores, the ability to persevere through hard tasks, and the companionship enjoyed in the cow-barn of my youth have in some way preserved me from evil and kept me safe from a too-easy life just as Dostoevsky promised. Writing up these cow-barn memories has also preserved me from wasting an evening feeling sorry for myself on the longest night of the year.

Finally, writing this story has inspired me to dish out a bowl of ice cream to share with Joanne, who is, I believe, in need of consolation for never having learned how to hand-milk a cow or host a hobble dance.

* * * * *

How close did I ever come to being a farmer?

As the picture of little David with the milk buckets suggests, there was a stage when I aspired to become a dairy farmer. In my play farm on the edge of our garden, with little tractors, home-made barns, and stick cows with nails for feet and head, I imagined upgrading to a grade-A dairy. There would be no dirt floors, but concrete pavement with gleaming stainless-steel milk tanks and modern milking machines to speed past the drudgery of milking by hand. It was no secret that hand-milking cows, like other chores at HeckuvaRanch, was designed to keep boys busy while learning the virtues of hard work the way Father had learned for himself. Our economic productivity was one bonus, but not the overriding calculation in assigning chores.

I was drawn to farming by the natural urge to gain skills, to learn how things worked in my childhood environment. My brothers and I wanted to understand the processes of efficient work, tinkering with our routines, always devising jigs and figuring out new ways to do the work more quickly. You have heard the proverb, "Necessity is the mother of invention." We disagreed. In our opinion, "Laziness is the mother of invention." The hope of getting the job done sooner with less effort was exciting for its own sake, but the hope of finishing early to gain more free time for other pursuits drove our inventions. Looking back on a lifetime of creative adaptations of my work to the pressures of curiosity, family and community needs, I would suggest a clumsier but more truthful proverb: "Skillful mastery, playfulness and reflection on the theory behind the project gives birth to fitting inventions."

The communal dimension of farm life also energized me in those early years. Farmers with their boys and hired men threshed wheat together, moved cattle together, filled silo together, and borrowed equipment freely. We ganged up to plow the fields of a farmer who was in the hospital and held a work evening to shingle the roof of the pastor's house. Together we took our trucks and chainsaws to join Mennonite Disaster Service to clean up after tornados. The same men took their turns on the local school boards and the deacons committees, which along with women's collaboration on family reunions, potlucks, and aid societies, wove a rich communal fabric of friendships and mutual care. This community was both accidental (dictated by proximity) and traditional (how it was done in farming villages of the "Old Country.") But the agrarian life I knew in the 1940's was soon swept aside in the 1950's under the pressures of run-away capitalism. The result of this community-destroying "progress" was larger equipment, larger industrial-sized farms, fewer and more aged farmers, more debt, dwindling small towns, consolidated schools, and land depleted by chemicals and erosion.

Wendell Berry has reflected in essays, novels, and poems on the virtues of that earlier era, inspiring a new agrarianism of more self-sufficient family farms where respect for the soil, local traditions, and mutual aid might lead to healthy vocations and healthy communities. The Amish have managed to preserve this way of life for another generation, although they too are running out of land and turning to other cooperative enterprises for their children like furniture building, cheese-making, and house construction while retaining their traditional communal way of life. I might have been tempted to stick around as a farmer if a communal way of life had been an option, something worth coming back home for after college.

However, that could be nostalgia speaking. Once I started wide reading to satisfy my chomping-at-the-bit curiosity (see how ranch metaphors come back to me in an instant) the rural community felt like too small a world for me to inhabit. The loneliness of field work under a hot summer sun reminded me too much of Camus' reflections on the myth of Sisyphus. (More on that in another chapter.) I had become a philosopher with manure on his boots. How was that going to play out?

Farming on a larger scale did not attract me. The economics of it were too dismal. When my grandfather Herman Janzen began farming, he could buy a new piece of land and pay it off in three or four years of production. By careful management he could set up each of his three sons with their own farms. When my father began farming it took a generation of hard work to hang onto the same acreage. Had I wanted to become a farmer, the economics would never pay off such an investment unless one began with an inheritance and held a major side-job that left no time for other soul inspiring pursuits.

Father saw those economic constraints and realized there was no way that the land of one farm split among four children could work. Instead, he wisely created the Janzen Family Farm Corporation so that each of us could hold shares, stay connected in board meetings, while someone else did the farm work. My younger brother, Mark, did manage our family farm for a couple of decades while teaching school and starting a computer technician business on the side. Later, my brother John in his retirement, has given oversight to the Janzen Family Farm Corporation, but most of the work is hired out to other area farmers.

At HeckuvaRanch I learned the novice skills of a farmer, passing the tests of the apprentice stage. I learned a few of the journey-man perspectives. But I never moved into the master stage of farming in which one becomes responsible for the year-after-year management of a successful agricultural enterprise, someone who trains others in the profession, and takes a role in wider rural community concerns like my father did.

Still, I'm grateful for the practical wisdom I learned on the farm. It gave me the foundation of confidence in having mastered a craft. My toolkit of practical farmer skills provided a head start in becoming an historian, a general contractor, a refugee-resettlement program coordinator, a developer of affordable housing, and a trouble-shooter for intentional Christian communities. Also, from my parents I learned that, while running a farm might be a profession, it is not a vocation. It is good work, but it is not worthy of a life's devotion. Other things like faith, hope and love are more important. Our ultimate loyalty and sacrifice are not to an economic enterprise, but to God's vision for shalom on this earth. That set me free to both leave the farm behind and to take it with me. Over the years I've learned that the farm is portable, the skills I learned there have come along, setting me up well for other missions that God has given me to pursue.

* * * * *

Father would occasionally assign us some difficult or even meaningless task on the farm simply because it would, as he insisted, "build character." From this flimsy starting point we kids invented a mythical system of character points that each child had to accumulate before they could graduate from home and get married. This system was akin to the medieval treasury of merit in the Catholic Church where penitents would flagellate themselves or go on pilgrimages to atone for their sins.

The quickest way to gain character points at HeckuvaRanch was to clean out the chicken house with its endless fork-loads of ammonia-laced poop pitched out the open window into a waiting manure spreader wagon. Shooting a family of skunks in the elevator pit and then retrieving them one at a time—one hand grabbing the tail and the other pinching the nose while climbing a ladder—this was another quick way to rack up merits. Of course, such feats of character had to be documented with Mother's photo camera for the eventual judgment day. The consensus of us boys was that sister Sara had graduated from home detention too soon. She was somehow allowed to marry Fremont Regier before she had gained sufficient character points, and to this day she has an "incomplete" on her record.

* * * * *

A PHILOSOPHICAL DIGRESSION ON PRACTICAL WISDOM

Most people have heard of "practical wisdom," but they do not realize that it is a "thing" worthy of theoretical attention in its own right. We usually organize and understand practical wisdom in terms of professions, although serious hobbies and other long-term personal and civic pursuits also grow and embody practical wisdom.

This chapter of cow-barn stories introduces a memoir section that tracks seven different careers I was led to pursue over approximately seven decades, each one developing its own body of practical wisdom. So, since practical wisdom is a thing, please allow me a brief introductory digression here before we move on to the six other versions of practical wisdom in my life journey.

Barry Shwartz and Ken Sharp have written a fascinating and groundbreaking book titled, guess what? *Practical Wisdom*. They memorably define this wisdom as **doing the right thing for the right reasons, at the right time, in the right amount.** This simple and essential summary highlights both the value of practical wisdom and its limits.

Theoretical philosophy can clarify concepts, examine assumptions, and compare philosophical systems by mental effort alone. But practical wisdom is gained by physical practice. For example, I began to learn the practical wisdom of a farmer as I practiced the skills and gained the experience inherent in doing farm work. I did not stick with it long enough to acquire the practical wisdom of a professional farmer at the master level. But it was the first profession I tried on.

In their book Swartz and Sharp criticize the culture and institutions of professionals in America like doctors, teachers, and judges, among others, because they neglect practical wisdom and increasingly try to make people do the right thing by rules and incentives. They point out that, the more workers are hedged in by rules, guidelines, and procedures, the dumber they get. This is because they are trained to look at the rules and not to people in their context or to draw on their own experience. In this digital age, we want to believe that everything worth doing can be reduced to an algorithm, a "tree" of instructions for which no thinking is needed. That's why doctors, for example, relate more to computers than to patients.

Similarly, the more you orient people to act according to incentives (like good grades or pay bonuses) the more they think about what it takes to pass the test or get a promotion, and the less they think about good work, good relationships, and real learning.

Practical wisdom instead, focuses on the people and the mission of a community, a business, a non-profit, or a family. Practical wisdom helps mature the character of those pursuing that mission, and to use the accumulated skills of discernment and effectiveness that can balance out competing commitments. Practical wisdom helps us find a creative path to a life of integrity and service. Instead of looking at rules and incentives, practical wisdom has us look to our work experiences, and from reflection on those examples, we can intuitively make flexible and discerning judgments that care for self, others, and get the work done in a natural and fitting way. While passing tests and gaining certificates might be involved, this depth of experience and the ability to reflect on it is what makes a "professional."

The strength of practical wisdom is apparent when we see it in operation. A wise farmer, for example, can see in a moment the right way to put up hay, can explain why to a son, do it at the right time when the hay is dry, and know how much effort it is worth—whether to leave a poor crop in the field or bail it up for fodder. The exercise of practical wisdom, whether in the home, on the job, or in community, gives real satisfaction whether it pays well or not.

However, the limits of practical wisdom become apparent when we examine more carefully the word "right" in Swartz and Sharp's definition of practical wisdom—*doing the right thing for the right reasons, at the right time, in the right amount.* Where does our sense of "rightness" come from?

For some philosophers the answer is "Aristotle," who wrote the first and most-referenced work on practical wisdom, *Nicomachean Ethics.* The virtues that Aristotle assumes and lifts up are the civic responsibilities that the Greek city-state of his day held in highest esteem.

In practice, our sense of rightness, our virtues and character, are shaped by the values of the culture around us, an ethos we pick up without noticing it—what we might call "conventional wisdom." It is a wisdom that assumes and supports the status quo. In America, "rightness" looks a lot like imperialism for the nation and the pursuit of wealth and privilege for the individual.

Some of us are lucky enough to have had good parents, teachers, or pastors who help us see conventional wisdom's flaws from the margins or from society's underside. The character of these mentors has rubbed off on us so that in the moment when we must make moral and situational judgments, we tend to channel their virtues and convictions.

For radical Christians, what we mean by "rightness" comes from the life and teachings of Jesus. But once more, we don't become like Jesus by just reading the gospels or even by memorizing the right answers from a Christian catechism. Practicing what he taught in the context of a community of disciples is the key. "Everyone then who hears these words of mine and acts on them will be like a wise man who built his house on a rock." (Matthew 7:24) The early church recognized that this transformation of character happens over time in the context of a community of shared life and resources, a free sharing of gifts and needs that monastic communities and other intentional Christian communities have tried to replicate ever since. It takes more than one hour a week in church to convert us from conventional wisdom to the wisdom of the cross.

Since this is not just a memoir but also a confession, I need to ask, on what foundation of "rightness" does my own practical wisdom stand? To that question we will return in the chapters that follow.

Chapter 13

Fighting Bookworms on the Farm
History as Science, Art and Craft

THERE WERE SEVERAL KINDS of worms on our farm. Earthworms we turned up in spades full of dirt and plunked a few into a tin can to bait fishhooks at the farm pond.

Devilish-looking green worms with yellow stripes and little horns, munched leaves day and night, stripping Mother's precious tomato plants. In an era before pesticides, or perhaps, an era when children were cheaper than pesticides, we were sent into the garden to pluck them off and stomp them underfoot, where they squirted squishy green slime on our shoes.

Colorado potato beetle larva had distinctive red bodies covered with black dots. They ate shoulder to shoulder in voracious packs which we were supposed to pinch between our fingernails. But they grabbed and pinched back, so I devised a way, without touching, to smack them in place between two blocks of wood.

Bag worms hung in finger-sized silk purses from spruce trees in our yard, after their larva had turned swaths of evergreen foliage into lifeless brown twigs. We twisted bagworms off their stems and dunked them in a can of gasoline.

Bookworms, however, were the hardest of all to track down on our farm as they could be hiding almost anywhere and were devious in the extreme. Unlike the other kinds of worms we were recruited to exterminate, children were of no help whatsoever in finding bookworms. That was a grownup job.

So, to begin at the beginning, we must ask, "How are bookworms born?" How does the egg hatch into the larva stage? Sometimes, this involves an older sister who wants to play grade school teacher, and who recruits a pre-school brother to learn the alphabet. When I was about four, my sister Sara wrote all the letters across a blackboard mounted at my height on the kitchen door right next to the refrigerator. We didn't know the "ABC Song," so we'd just race each other reciting the letters as fast as we could. Somewhere in the middle of the alphabet, I remember, was Mennonite-sounding letter pronounced "Ellemenno."

A breakthrough came for me when I grasped that each letter had a unique sound. I started pronouncing the letters and often got lucky. "Jack and Jill went up the hill. Hey," I shouted through the house, "I can read!" But then there were many times when the irregularities of the English language tripped me up, when words did not sound at all like the letters in them. So, I'd bug whoever was around to pronounce the words I couldn't decipher on my own.

Soon I fired my teacher and was off at a gallop, sounding out words and reading by myself a year before I started school. Then I tried to write original compositions on the blackboard. The first story I wrote began like many others I'd heard: "Wants upon a time. . ." Older folks corrected me and said it was spelled "O-N-C-E." I couldn't believe it. Only one letter in there sounded the way it was spelled. No fair!

Grade school for us country kids at District 85 began with first grade, not kindergarten. Since I already knew my alphabet and could read, I dove into the school library. This was stored in a cupboard on the back wall of the one-room school building, holding about 200 books for all ages. The picture books with the fewest words were at the bottom. I started at the lowest shelf, browsing upward and onward.

Morning flag salute at Trainview gradeschool.

My second-grade teacher was Art Goering—one of the best instructors I ever had. He won us over quickly because he was athletic and taught us the rules and the skills for mastering softball and basketball. He shaped us into competitive teams to play against those town folk at Elbing Grade School. Art also had an intriguing rule that, anytime of the school day, if you finished reading a library book, you could give an oral report on it to the whole school. Well, I liked that kind of attention, so I raised my hand every other day to give a report. After my sixth report in the second week of school, Art made a new rule: "Everyone has to do six book reports in the school year, and that's all."

When I was a third grader and Harold Regier was our teacher, the school board splurged and bought a *World Book Encyclopedia* set that merited its own bookshelf on the north wall. I'd race through my homework and then pull out volume *A* to read whatever interested me—which was just about everything. I devoured maps, biographies of famous people, descriptions of foreign countries, and world history in bite-sized pieces. All the knowledge of the world, I believed, was in my hands.

At the end of the school year, Teacher Harold suggested that the valuable *World Book Encyclopedia* set "might be destroyed by dangerous bookworms" if left in the empty schoolhouse over the summer. He thought the books might be safer with the Janzen family. I was all for protecting the encyclopedias from destruction and had no inkling our teacher was teasing me with his reference to "dangerous bookworms." Uncle Johnny heard about my encyclopedia reading binge and would ask from time to time, "On which letter are you now?"

In the fourth grade my reading career took to the air when mother drove brother John and me fifteen miles to Newton each Saturday morning for piano lessons with Victor Klaassen. While mother shopped for groceries, brother John had his lesson, and I read comics from the Klaassen coffee table. Now, comic books were forbidden in our home, but these were okay because they were Classic Comics—illustrated and abridged versions of *Les Miserables, The Hunchback of Notre Dame, The Three Musketeers, 20,000 Leagues Under the Sea*, and more. These comics transported me into momentous and heroic episodes of history. Having read the briefer comic book version, I aspired to read the parent books for myself.

After our music lessons, Mom picked us up and dropped us off at the Newton Carnegie Library where we were each given our own library card and the liberty to take home four fresh books each week. Seven days later I'd return for four more. I consumed books as a free-range omnivore, but I majored in adventure stories, explorers, and inventors. I read a biography of Antoine van Leeuwenhoek and spent my Christmas money to buy a microscope. I read about mountain climbers and then climbed bale piles and silos with a rope assist. I read a biography of Mozart and despaired because he was already writing concertos at my age. But George Gamow's popular *1, 2, 3 Infinity* introduced me to the excitement of mathematics by discovering that there was far more to it than just arithmetic. My teachers and school mates wondered how I could read that many books when most of their time at home, like mine, was occupied with farm chores and family activities.

I had a secret nighttime life. We children were all sent off to bed at 8:00 p.m. Then Mother or Father would "tuck us in" to assure that we'd said our prayers and were actually in bed with the lights out. Once I heard their footsteps go down the stairs, I'd tiptoe to the wall, cover the light switch with a piece of underwear to muffle the click, and read another hour or two ... or three with my head resting on an elbow-propped hand. Sometimes my wrist would cramp, and I'd change sides. Sometimes I'd wake up in the middle of the night with the light still on. Eventually, I perfected the technique of turning off the light without getting out of bed, by tossing a *Readers Digest* against the wall just above the switch.

Father figured there must be a reason why I was so slow to get up and so lethargic about my morning chores. Sometimes he would sneak upstairs, see the damning light shining under my bedroom door, and rage at me to go to sleep. He needed us fully awake for chores at 5:30 in the morning. Now, after such a warning, if I was even a little slow to get on my shoes or dragged my feet on the way to the cow barn, I got a double dose of whatever I had coming, which usually involved blisters on the back side and some derisive comment about someone turning into "a lazy book worm."

My greatest crimes, at least in Father's eyes, did not involve night-time reading, however. Saturdays were the real battleground. We were expected to be at work all day long on something productive for the farm. Father would give us jobs—sweeping the shop, hauling and stacking hay bales, pulling nails out of old boards, or throwing a load of firewood down the basement chute for furnace fodder. Once we were busy at work, Father would go on to other tasks in the shop, the field, or off to town on some errand. Just like the Second Coming, we had no warning about when he would show up again and inspect our work.

After slaving dutifully for a while, my mind would wander back to the book I had been reading, and soon I'd actually be reading it someplace comfortable and out of sight. I turned into an escape artist who, however creative I might be, eventually I got nabbed. Here is a partial list of places where I was tracked down and arrested for illicit self-education.

—On the third-story treehouse of the big elm in our front yard

—In the basement wood pile behind the furnace

—On top of the silage in an almost full silo

—In the outhouse

—Sitting on a pile of mash sacks in the feed bin of our chicken house.

—Upstairs in the horse barn on top of the hay bale pile

—In a cave within the bale pile reading with a flashlight

The result of getting nabbed was that I'd be led back to the work site by a pinched ear, receive a few whacks on the behind, and have to finish the job under Father's watchful eye. Then I'd get another job.

Sometimes I used a simpler strategy, which was to smuggle a book along with me to the work site, and when Father was out of view, I'd start to read. Of course, I'd work now and then to give the impression of some progress. When Father's pickup truck arrived back from town in a cloud of dust, I'd hide the book and look like real busy. But "woe was me" if Father found a book tucked in my jacket pocket or under a pile of shingles that we were tearing off the roof! That book was gone—gone until I returned another day and apologized, meekly asking for it back lest I'd have to pay a growing library fine.

My brothers and I took this kind of treatment in stride as if it were normal for kids growing up on a farm. Our peers and cousins were treated the same, and it was no big deal. We reasoned that if we'd finish a job and Father found out, we'd just get another one. So, it was up to us to schedule the breaks that we thought we needed in order to become well-rounded in our educational and work experience. In fact, our wide-ranging reading habits stood us in good stead. I felt like I had a head start in any course I took, or any job I held because I had already boned up on it in my own time. The benefit of a self-directed course of readings that included the classics of intellectual history, has been a blessed continuing life-long liberal arts education.

* * * * *

As a child I found creative ways to insert book-wormish digressions into whatever project my father had assigned me. Later on, as I began to read bigger books, I noticed a few classical writers who had a similar habit of inserting intriguing philosophical digressions into their main projects as well. In other words, as an amateur philosopher, I'm inviting you to digress with me for a moment from the theme of lazy book worms into a digression about digressions.

While plowing wheat stubble one long summer in my college years, and pondering whether I should become an historian, I remember enjoying Tolstoy's many digressions in his novel, *War and Peace*, inserting rambling observations about the philosophy and meaning of history. There Tolstoy observes that the outcome of Napoleon's 1812 invasion of Russia did not turn on his tactical brilliance, nor upon the blunders of the Russian generals. Instead, Napoleon's army was defeated by the character of the Russian people in their limitless capacity for suffering, and in the blind contingency of Russia's brutal winter which had the final say in that historic disaster.

A few years later, I was captivated by the digressions of Polybius, the Greek historian of Rome's unlikely rise from a small republic to imperial conquest of the Mediterranean world in his work, *The Histories*. Between narrative sections, Polybius inserts essays concerning the emerging craft of the professional historian.

The freedom of these great writers to indulge in wisdom-seeking digressions from their main historical project has given me courage to do the same in this and other chapters.

* * * * *

I didn't get a history major while in college because, at that time, there was no full-time historian on the faculty. So, I took as many courses in the history of philosophy as I could.

I lucked out and got a Rockefeller Foundation scholarship to attend Harvard Divinity School so that I could test my calling to become a pastor. Though I found a good spiritual home in the Cambridge Mennonite Fellowship, I soon realized I was not becoming a pastor. By my second year at Harvard, I was convinced that the study of history interested me more, so I began cross-registering for courses in the Harvard History Department. At Harvard, with my feet on the first rungs of a ladder to elite professional success and status, I pondered the dedication it might take to make a name for myself like so many other powerful and well-placed Harvard graduates?

But, as it turned out, my heart was not sufficiently drawn to that kind of elite and demanding career. Instead, I was attracted to Joanne Zerger (back at Bethel College) who was deeply drawn to a radical vision of discipleship and community as her mentor, Al Meyer explored this future in a small, committed circle of students and faculty. From Cambridge and North Newton, we wrote each other daily and schemed where we could land for a life together pursuing God's calling. Joanne got a graduate scholarship to study English Literature at the University of Kansas, and that's where I set my sights for further graduate work in History.

Immediately after our wedding on September 4, 1964, we indulged in a one-night honeymoon campout in a Janzen Flint Hills pasture. The next day we carted all our wedding gifts in a cute VW Bug with a yellow plastic flower at the top of our antenna, to a duplex apartment on New Jersey Street, in Lawrence, Kansas, a fifteen-minute walk east of campus. On Labor Day we prowled city parks to find water because H2O had not yet been turned on in our apartment. In those days we blissfully believed that a newly wed couple could live just fine on love and fresh air. In retrospect, the adjustments of a big wedding, a quick honeymoon, a major move, both of us jumping into graduate school, and learning how to keep house together, all in one weekend—not advisable. But we had our consolations. Every time we felt discouraged, we'd open one more wedding gift, admire it, write a thank-you card, appreciate the gift of each other, and return to life with a little more joy.

In two years at the University of Kansas I completed the course work for a M.A. degree majoring in modern European history. I researched and wrote my thesis on August Bebel, a pre-World War I German Democratic Socialist leader who was a protégé of Engels, in an era when the working class was anti-war, and creating networks of practical solidarity under intense persecution. It fascinated me that Bebel, who had no higher education, used his prison experiences to educate himself and to write books that stirred the masses to believe in their own genius and destiny.

However, it was a course on "History as a Profession" that intrigued me the most, perhaps because it drew on my philosophical background and involved reflection on the actual work experience of the historian—a perfect example of practical wisdom. There I was intrigued to learn that the historian looks at his work simultaneously as science, art, and craft.

The study of history is not scientific in the sense that you can predict the future like you can predict the trajectory of cannon balls in physics. In human history there are continuities of cause and effect that allow some rough estimates of the future, but the course of human history on every scale from local to global, is also greatly impacted by contingencies like the brutal Russian Winter that destroyed Napoleon's army in 1812.

But the work of the historian can be somewhat scientific in that s/he can posit a thesis and test whether the evidence bears it out. The historian tries to get as close to the truth of what happened as you can by accessing primary sources, first-hand accounts, documents and artifacts of the events themselves, trying to get behind hearsay, rumors, and propaganda.

History as art recognizes that intuition, imagination and empathy are important in understanding historical characters and movements. The farmer-boy stories that I tell are history writing. They tell about things that really happened. Truth matters. At the same time, the interpretation of these events can be taken in a million different directions. How I write these stories has a lot of similarity with fiction—not that the events are made up, but in the way the moods, themes, general impression are created. I am not just telling the facts of a story, but I am creating a world in the imagination of the readers allowing them to enter into another person's viewpoint and experience.

History writing, like teaching, is also a craft. The writer develops work habits, refreshes memory with appropriate reading, discovers certain hours of the day that work best for creativity, others that are best for proofreading. The historian develops a workshop that is outfitted according to the tools and the equipment needed. I think I had an advantage over other history majors by growing up on a farm where we had free access to the tools and machinery of a workshop in a family where we learned from each other how to get useful things done. For the history writer now-a-days a lot of that craftsmanship comes down to a word-processor and google search, with visits to the library as well as treks to other countries and other centers of documentation where you can dig up primary sources. The historian also needs conversations with other experts where one's theses can be tested and revised by good counsel. In the process, the historian discovers that ideas are not just data that by accumulation will add up to insight. Ideas are more like tools by which you can collaborate with others and rework our understanding of how our world came to be.

So, when and where did I practice my craft as an historian? I was a teaching assistant in the History of Western Civilization class that every liberal arts major had to take at the University of Kansas. There I conducted book discussion groups, wrote and graded exams as part of a team of about fifteen other assistants. This was enough experience for me to realize that I enjoyed teaching history and sharing the excitement of learning with students up close.

But as the Vietnam war heated up and the military draft was breathing down my neck, I chose the path of a conscientious objector to war. So, before I could defend my almost-completed thesis, Joanne and I were off on a three-year stint with the Mennonite Central Committee to perform my alternative to military service. First, we spent a year in French language study in Brussels and Paris, and then taught two years at the Secondary School level in the newly independent Democratic Republic of the Congo. I taught world history, African history, and Congolese history alongside whatever other subjects the school needed of me in a time of teacher shortage. I also compiled a sourcebook of primary documents for teachers of Congolese history, something that did not yet exist seven years after independence. This experience gave me the idea that I should prepare myself for a life-time career in African history.

However, before we returned to the U.S., I was invited to teach two school years at Bethel College, my alma mater, as adjunct professor of history, filling in for a couple of professors on sabbatical. Once again, I really enjoyed my work in preparing lectures and coaching students in both life and academic issues. I had a roll of toilet paper in my desk drawer that I would pull out and hand to students every time they cried in my office—something I discovered, happened quite often. It was a time of existential crisis for many students who felt the anguish of a foolish and genocidal war our country was waging, and that snatched many away to kill and die in Vietnam. I had both theological and personal reasons to be active in the peace movement alongside my students.

I had applied for Ph.D. studies in African History, but by that time my heart and calling led to intentional Christian community and peacemaking rather than climbing the academic ladder, wherever that might take me. I realized that African history would probably be done better by Africans. America needed peacemakers more than any other place in the world. Joanne and I were called to put down roots with other young families who felt the same vocation to seek first the kingdom of God in intentional community and peacemaking.

So, in one sense, my career as a professional historian was brief, but in reality, it has turned out to be life-long. Just as the wisdom of the farm accompanies the adult farm boy wherever he goes, so the trained historian has followed me into community activism and has been of service as a writer in nearly everything I've done. I end up researching, writing, and mentoring others much like an historian would do. I'm grateful to look back and see that my ambitions as an historian were tamed and refocused to make me a useful servant of family, community, and the kingdom mission rather than sacrificing them on the altar of a personal professional career according to the conventional wisdom of our age.

* * * * *

In conclusion, if the bookworm is the larval stage, what might the chrysalis be? A dissertation, an article in *The Mennonite*, the first book contract, a career as a teacher? All of that has come my way in some degree, but now

I'm asking the ultimate bookworm question—what does the mature bookworm-turned-into-a-butterfly look like?

When my parents Louis and Hilda were in their eighties, they each relished the opportunity to write their memoirs. That is when Father admitted to me that he was a little bit proud of what I'd done with my incessant reading habits. He acknowledged that, even while on the farm, he usually was reading several books at once on the side, and now he had the freedom to read as much as he liked. He was also glad to see that I hadn't turned into a lazy bookworm incapable of doing a good day's work.

Here and there, I suppose, I've occasionally done a full day's work. But most days have also involved pushing ahead, usually late at night, on several books in a wide range of subjects that I'm eager to talk about with anyone willing to listen—a character trait that, I observe, just about every Janzen in our clan has inherited, for better or worse, from Father Louie.

Chapter 14

Building the ALCAN Highway
What Goes into Good Work?

Did I ever tell you about the summer when brothers John, Mark, and I worked on the dangerous and heroic construction of the Alaskan-Canadian-Highway? We bulldozed and blasted our way through impenetrable forests, bridged raging mountain streams, and tamed steep snow-packed slopes where avalanches threatened at any moment to wipe us out? Yessiree! Let me tell you, those were the days!

We had read about death and survival in the Alaskan wilderness from stories by Jack London in our school library. *Boys Life* and *Popular Mechanics* put illustrated tales of heroic adventures before our eyes. But we had one problem to solve: How could we commute from our home at HeckuvaRanch at Rural Route 3, Newton, Kansas, to the border of the Alaskan wilderness? Our problem was that we did not have enough wilderness on the farm to build a truly heroic highway.

But then we discovered the overgrown ditch on the north side of the country road going west from our farm driveway. There we found a serious incline with rocks and rubble to clear, overrun by pigweeds and sunflowers taller than a man. On the scale of our toy tractors, home-made bulldozers, and steam shovels, these weeds amounted to a serious forest of tall pines and tangled underbrush, prowled by wild moose, grizzlies and nasty packs of wolves. At the bottom of the ditch ran a stream of water after every rain, so of course, we needed to build bridges with huge earth-work ramps and 1 x 8 board spans. A really stubborn rock or weed that resisted our bulldozers, had to be blasted out with "dynamite" that came from our 4th of July firecracker stash. So, you see, it was only a minute's walk from our front door to the wilds of Alaska.

Of course, in the summertime on the farm we were occupied all day by chores in the cow-barn and chicken-house, by hay-making, and garden work. There was no chance to build the Alaska-Canadian-Highway (ALCAN) until after supper when the late summer sun gave us free time until dark. In Alaska, of course, the light lasted almost till midnight, so we gallantly and urgently worked over-time to push our road westward toward the setting sun.

Another problem we faced, however, was that we didn't want to lug our earth-moving machines home every night and break the spell of our imagined world, so we'd hide them in the weeds near the construction site. Alas, one day tragedy struck when brother Mark's wonderfully realistic Tonka road-grader (bought with Christmas money) was stolen by someone in a passing car. That piece of bad news, however, was woven into our story as the dastardly work of a Japanese invasion—remember, we were only a few years from World War II.

But no adversity could deter us. On Sunday afternoons we'd recruit cousins and visiting friends to help with our highway-building project, and they'd get excited too. With indomitable spirit we pushed onward in our quest to tame the wilderness for the cause of civilization. Our vital road linked America with our last western frontier, with gold mining towns on the Yukon, and Indian fishing villages. Our road would deliver medicines and missionaries to indigenous tribes. The fact that white-people diseases and imperialism traveled on that road too, did not bother our consciences. In those days we were unapologetically on the side of progress painted in the glowing colors and myths of white supremacy.

But all that excitement faded at summer's end when brother John got too old to care about toys and imaginary road building, and all our construction equipment moved back home. Still, the seeds of real-life grown-up construction projects had been planted.

* * * * *

Growing up on the farm gave us boys a wide range of project management experience, especially in the area of construction and carpentry skills—first of all by observation, then by play, and finally by actively working alongside older mentors.

When I was in the second grade Father hired Jake Klassen, a local carpenter, to complete the construction of our grain elevator after all the concrete foundation work was done. That year I'd come home from school and check in with Jake's progress each day until chore time. He took me on as an informal apprentice, patiently answering my endless questions as he continued to work. Jake allowed me to hold one end of the many boards that we carried to the work site. I watched while he explained how to frame a wall, lay tongue-and-groove flooring, and nail on ship-lap siding to shed the rain. He let me use his light-weight finish hammer to practice with and even to nail a row of shingles. I saw Jake consult the architect's blueprints and understood how they carried the design and the measurements that the carpenter translated into reality. For many years, I assumed Jake's gentle and thoughtful spirit automatically went with the craft of carpentry, that is until twenty-five years later when I led a construction crew of my own.

Inspired by Jake Klassen's work, brother John and I also built toy barns, grain elevators, and hay sheds out of salvaged fruit boxes on our basement workbench, with our little vise and hand tools. Looking back, it seems to me that this combination of hanging around adult craftsmen and playing at the same work with peers might be the ideal way for children to begin their life course in practical wisdom. One benefit of this upbringing on the farm was that we automatically assumed if something needed building, we could build it; and if it broke, we could fix it. What an empowering and meaningful simplification of life!

* * * * *

As a young adult embarking on my 30's, I eased by several stages into the responsibilities of heading a construction crew as a licensed general contractor. My two-year stint with Bethel College as an adjunct history professor came to an end in 1971 when the other professors returned from their sabbaticals.

At that point our newly formed intentional community needed me to bring home more income, so I worked for a while in a dismal and exploitative factory job cutting plywood panels for camper trailers, ten hours a day. After the first shift I learned nothing new, no one there cared about me—only my production, and I never saw the finished results of my labors. My work matched up perfectly with Karl Marx's analysis of "alienated labor" in the Capitalistic system. But I saw no revolution coming because the energy of resentment by workers at their very real oppression was bled off in weekend binges and violent entertainment which left them exhausted, poor, and fated to face another meaningless Monday morning with a hangover. Meanwhile, this chastened intellectual stuck it out at the trailer factory for four months because I sensed God wanted to teach me experientially how *not* to organize work and how *not* to treat workers, as if this knowledge might be useful one day.

At that point I escaped the working class for a while and landed a proposal with the Mennonite Central Committee to cover my expenses as a writer and community organizer on the theme of alternatives to incarceration. I edited a newsletter called *Liberty to the* Captives taken from Jesus' Jubilee proclamation in Luke 4:18. This was meaningful ground-breaking peace and justice work. But its demands, and my ambitions, often took me away from home and community to attend weekend conferences, to visit innovative programs, and to join meetings where we developed an area prison visitation ministry.

Meanwhile, Joanne was sinking under the load of two toddlers underfoot—one home-made (Natasha, born in October 1970) and the other ready-made (James, born January, 1972) who came to us by adoption at the age of fifteen months. Our community, New Creation Fellowship had the wisdom to see a crisis coming. They made it clear that I needed to return home and find work that fit our family's needs. They asked a younger member, Bernard Regier, to move in with us as an "instant uncle" and frequent baby-sitter. For a year, Jake and Irene Pauls met with Joanne and me every Thursday night for marriage counseling, and the community covered our Friday night baby-sitting needs so we could have a couple's night out. The love and gifts of community saved our sanity and our marriage.

After I wrapped up my work with MCC, I was hired as a carpenter with a local construction company building an apartment complex. This work allowed me to be home every evening and weekend. The work was more meaningful than factory work because I was learning new skills and observing the management needed to develop a large-scale construction project. But there was no sense of solidarity on the job as the other workers were either too self-absorbed or too foul-mouthed for me to connect. To ease my feeling of exile and to connect more with community, Jake Pauls, leader of New Creation Fellowship at the time, shared one lunch a week with me on the job site, offering spiritual companionship in a mentoring relationship.

* * * * *

This seems like a fitting place to share a theological reflection on the nature of "bad work" and "good work."

Because of sin, according to Genesis 3, God cursed the tempting serpent and the woman, Eve. But for Adam and his seed he added,

"Cursed is the ground because of you,
In toil you shall eat of it all the days of your life. . . .
You are dust,

And to dust you shall return."

In peasant times, this was an honest description of work—soul-crushing toil, an uncertain hope of survival, and fated to do it all over again another year. In the mammon economy of our day, where everything of value is measured in terms of money and Gross (sic.) National Product, some people can escape the grind and find more meaningful and higher paid work, but usually at the expense of others who do the hard labor at the bottom of the social hierarchy—most often women.

But with the inbreaking Kingdom of God that Jesus called together in a concrete community with his disciple band, another world of justice and peace opened up that did not have to wait for the next political revolution. The Apostle Paul's manifesto gives this new reality a name: "So, if anyone is in Christ, there is a new creation; Everything old has passed away; see everything has become new. All this is from God who has given us the ministry of reconciliation. (2 Cor. 5:17) From this verse our community took its name, "New Creation Fellowship," and with the name came the courage to imagine that among ourselves we might play with our own internal economy, like little kids playing farm or playing house, we could explore what "good work" might look like.

I began to research answers that other communities had come up with like the Bruderhof, Koinonia Farm, and the Amish. But the most inspiring resource I found at the time was the work of Lanza del Vasto, a philosopher and disciple of Gandhi, who founded a community (The Ark) in France that explored more self-sufficient and non-violent ways of working and living together. "In the practice of any craft," he wrote, "we are less concerned with the quantity of the product than with its quality, and less concerned with the product than with the artisan." Del Vasto asked, "You want a better, more fraternal, more just world? Well, then start building it: Who is stopping you? Build it inside yourself and around you, build it with those who want it. Build it small and it will grow."

With all this encouragement, I developed a teaching with a five-point outline of what good work might look like.

1. **It is creative,** participating in the creativity of God that seeks to embody the teachings of Jesus in the New Creation. It can begin now and does not need to wait for an uprising in the larger society.

2. **It provides a useful service,** meeting essential human needs. However, for this to work we must simplify our desires, to be content with meeting our basic needs rather than multiplying our wants according to the latest market inventions.

3. **It supports a balanced life** with room for Sabbath contemplation. Sabbath is both a gift and a command. God knows what is good for us—both to work hard and to rest well. The Sabbath is given so that we might reflect on and give thanks for the gifts of life—alone, with God, and with one another in the beloved community.
4. **It grows everyone's capacity, skill, and wisdom.** This is a stronger motivation than "making money," to discover and to grow in the capacity to effectively love and serve others. In and through work we discover who God made us and what God made us for.
5. **The work itself is communal and builds community.** We wanted work we could engage in together in fellowship and daily service to the local Body of Christ.

Note that none of these five principles have any reference to "making money." Money, in terms of a nation's GNP, is an empty abstraction. Money spent on health care counts just as much as money spent on addictions. Money spent on war and destruction counts the same as money spent to resettle refugees from war. Money, as Jesus reminded us, is a terrible measure of value. Jesus instead teaches us to see the kingdom of God at work within and among us.

In more recent times, Wendell Berry has been a prophet of what he calls The Great Economy. This is the realm of nature (sunshine, rain, soil, plants and animals, natural resources, beauty) which was given to sustain life before there was money. Similarly, families are a cash-free zone where goods are exchanged because of love according to the motto, "freely you have received, freely give." This Great Economy is fundamental to survival, the Mammon economy is not. In intentional Christian community with a common purse, we discovered the opportunity to participate in the economy of God's forgiveness and generosity and to see how far we could promote it in the world. "Good Work" in the context of the Great Economy cares for many needs simultaneously without cash exchanged. It trusts that if we seek first the kingdom of God, all these other things (including the money we need) will be added to us. It does not idolize careers that take people away to wherever the highest paying job might beckon.

We had no hope of undoing the Capitalistic system on the world's scale, but we could defeat this system within us and around us on the scale of community. We shared the excitement of imagining what an integrated life of common work, common meals, common celebrations, etc. might look like when we applied the radical teachings of Jesus. On the human-sized scale of our internal economy and relationships, we could play with community structures to undo the oppression and alienation of the Mammon Economy. It was like "playing farm" as a child, where we could change the layout of buildings, equipment, feed bunks, and roads three times in a morning. Only now we were grow-ups playing with the structures of work, celebrations, community, and family life. Rather than becoming slaves of institutions, schedules, and traditions, we discovered their malleability, the way they could become servants of the kingdom and of a satisfying common life. New wine skins for new wine.

Though the Mammon Economy of GNP is measured in trillions of dollars, it is actually far smaller than The Great Economy which is nature's way. What if we had to pay for sunshine, air, rain, the beauty of nature, the love of family, the respect that we are accorded every time we walk outside and are not assaulted? Once we see The Great Economy everywhere around us and within us, we begin to experience ourselves infinitely in debt to it and infinitely rich in possibilities.

* * * * *

5-4-20

As Joanne and I ate supper last night on the back porch, overlooking signs of spring in every direction, our talk was constantly interrupted by the singing of a persistent cardinal and an equally insistent flicker, often overlapping each other's calls. Of course, birds sing like that to attract a mate or to mark their territories, but this went on way beyond any utilitarian needs. Such a long and sustained performance only makes sense because they sing for the sheer joy of it all. Even now as I write in my journal, I feel loved just remembering the time.

JC: "David, I hoped you'd notice how loved you and all the critters are by the Father. The birds of the air and the lilies of the field overwhelmed me with joy too. You are just dipping your little finger into the vast abundance of the Great Economy, the Kingdom of God."

* * * * *

In the mid-1970's, after a year of journeyman work in construction, the Fellowship discerned that I was ready to lead a crew that eventually took the name New Creation Builders. We were an unlikely bunch of under-employed liberal arts majors with a widening range of skills, such that I could line up one job after another to make us a decent living. We started out as painters, then house remodelers, then as solar collector installers when that was cutting edge technology. Eventually, I took and passed the City of

Newton Permit Office's general contractor's exam and was licensed to take out permits for larger projects. With the help of sub-contractors, we took on building additions, building out attics, moving houses to places where they were more needed, and jacking up houses to put in basements and better foundations.

Our crew was flexible, including our community's teachers and students during summer vacation. We included an aspiring writer until he landed an editing job on *The Mennonite*. We supported an ethnomusicologist with steady work and occasional vacations while he assisted Cheyenne Mennonites to gather an indigenous collection of hymns. With the support of steady earning work, I could give some leadership in the local peace-movement and sit on the New Creation Fellowship leadership team meetings. Of course, when Joanne urgently needed my help in the family zone, I had the flexibility to be there. On occasions, we could provide meaningful work in times of transition for persons coming out of prison or struggling with mental illness. The size of our crew varied from as few as three to as many as twelve.

Our crew not only completed outside jobs, but also took care of the maintenance and remodeling needs of our own dwellings. We organized memorable community workdays where we'd work Amish-style to build and erect trusses, make home improvements, catch up on garden work and landscape our neighborhood. In one day, using the energy of children, men, and women, we erected a one-and-a-half story garage/shop in our back yard as large as the city would allow on a residential plot. Soon, this workshop became a hangout for parents and kids building Christmas presents and assembling furniture according to family needs.

Each morning around the shop's wood-burning stove, our crew would assemble. We'd take half an hour to hear about each other's lives, review the work before us and our client's needs, and conclude in prayer. These morning meetings also gave us a chance to talk out our tensions, learn from our mistakes, forgive one another, and reconnect around our common mission. As a close-knit brotherhood (and sometimes sisterhood) of common work, we discovered that God had given us the blessing of "Good Work" that carried our souls and built community. The work was wholesome for our families and beginning to look like the redeemed economy of God's kingdom on earth as it is in heaven. We were active intellectuals exercising a variety of gifts, with sawdust on our shoes and callouses on our hands. We found something deeply satisfying for body and soul to be so integrated in community life and ministry.

In New Creation Builders, we never succeeded in putting everyone in the community to work in common businesses, but the persons who had professional jobs in the mammon economy were enfolded for most of the hours of the week in community life and decision making, participating in a wide family zone where singles, married couples and children all had a vital place. For a decade we experienced a vibrant village life within a block radius, nestled in the small town of Newton, Kansas.

* * * * *

This seems like as good a place as any to recycle a few old carpenters jokes:

As we shingle a roof, a bird flies overhead and bombs me with poop. While I'm wiping it out of my hair, Fred remarks, "Aren't you glad cows can't fly?!"

A carpenter's apprentice is sent to the lumber yard with the following shopping list: "A dozen post holes, a box of one-inch thumb screws, a gallon of striped paint, and an eight-foot stud-stretcher."

A hick carpenter goes to the lumberyard and announces, "We need a dozen two-by-fours six inches wide." The salesperson asks, "Do you mean two-by-sixes?" "Yeah, two-by-sixes will do." "How long?" "Oh, a long time. We're building a garage."

A guy on our crew (who will not be named) finished a task and announced, "That's good enough for who it's for"—just as the owner walks in.

A carpenter catches his apprentice throwing about half the nails away as he tacks on siding. "What you doin,' throwin' them nails away?" he yells. The apprentice answered, "A lot of them have the head on the wrong end." "You dummy," the carpenter screams, "Don't you know, we use those on the other side of the house?!"

Did you hear about the blind carpenter who picked up his hammer and saw?

* * * * *

Well then, if New Creation Builders was such a groovy gig, how come it came to an end? In God's economy, preserving a particular institution is never an end in itself. Its life span should be according to its usefulness to a higher purpose. In the last year of the crew's existence, a few members transitioned to work with a better long-term fit for their gifts.

Though community life was a joy for us, Joanne and I also lived in close proximity to most of our relatives, and in the same town as many of our college friends. We felt a growing need for a sabbatical from the long and growing list of other people's expectations upon our time and attention. We felt like a plant whose roots had completely filled the pot with no room left to grow. Our roots either needed a larger pot, or to be pruned. We left New Creation on a one-year sabbatical, in which others would take over our responsibilities. Then we expected to return and see what we felt was a clear call to pick up again. Also, as an interracial family, we wanted to find a setting where James did not feel so much like the odd one out.

We moved to Reba Place Fellowship for a year, which then turned out to be a permanent (forty years and counting) move. Joanne found her dream library job and a good counselor. I became the househusband and grew into a director role of a refugee resettlement ministry that you'll read about in the next chapter. While we were away, New Creation Fellowship dismantled the common purse community and became a community-oriented congregation that was no longer neighborhood centered.

After our departure, two young men continued the business of New Creation Builders, but after a few months they closed up shop and found work where they felt more room to grow in their gifts. The community celebrated the gift that New Creation Builders had been, and with an auction dispersed our equipment and supplies. From a distance, I felt some regret over those developments, but the demise of New Creation Builders could not erase the memories we made of good work that served our families, our community and the ministry of the community so well for so long.

The management skills I'd learned have proven portable, useful and durable. God and community taught me how to bring together the gifts of owners, workers, and professionals to build a collaborative team where cash-flows, supplies and a common schedule complete a project such that everyone is blessed and would want to do it again.

Since New Creation Builders, I've landed in other forms of satisfying good work that sustains family and community, using and growing our people gifts in other expressions of the justice and peace of the Kingdom of God. Long live "Good Work!"

Chapter 15

New Shoes for DP's

The Holy Work of Restoration after War

ONE EVENING IN 1946, when I would have been five years old, Father took me along on a mysterious evening errand to Peabody, Kansas, a small town five miles north from our farm. Peabody only had one block of stores lining Main Street, and all of them were closed except for Keller's Shoe Store where one light burned and the owner awaited us.

Mr. Keller was a genial fellow who knew how to give his customers the royal treatment. His store smelled of fresh leather and he didn't mind that kids touched and sniffed the new shoes on display. Whenever my shoes grew too tight or wore out, this is where our parents brought us for new footwear. Mr. Keller would sit me in the high-backed cushioned chair, raise my foot onto his angled stool, and measure me heel to toe with his sliding gage. Soon he'd return from back shelves with boxes of shoes under each elbow that he thought might fit and please me. Our parents allowed us children to choose our own shoes so long as they were durable and not too fancy. With new shoes I looked forward to the next Sunday when I'd make my squeaky entrance into church, and all the kids would look my way and whisper, "David has new shoes."

But we had not come to Keller's store to buy new shoes. Father had persuaded Mr. Keller to unload a couple dozen pairs of outmoded styles that were not moving off his shelves. We were going to donate them to the Mennonite Central Committee for displaced persons who flooded Western Europe in the aftermath of World War II. So, my job was to tie shoe-pairs together by their laces and drop them into a couple of large boxes that we then hauled to the car. On the way out of town we made a conspiratorial detour past the ice cream shop for two nickel cones which we licked while looking at each other on the drive home. Father reminded me to wipe my face clean so that my brothers and sister wouldn't ask why they didn't get ice cream too.

The next morning mother and I wrapped these big shoe boxes in stiff Kraft paper, bound them up with twine, and drove them to the tiny Elbing Post Office where they were sent on to MCC distribution centers in Germany, Netherlands, and other countries overrun with "DP's." It took me a while to figure out that DP's were "Displaced Persons" or what we would now call refugees.

I was born in the year of Pearl Harbor, so my first memories had overtones of a distant war. I only had a vague idea of where the fighting was taking place—it must have been somewhere beyond Buhler, Kansas, the farthest trip we made to visit grandparents and cousins. I understood that God did not want Mennonites to fight in wars, but that most other people did anyway. I was puzzled by Father's friendship with Mr. Keller since Peabody was a super patriotic town and the Kellers were not Mennonites but Methodists.

One day in 1945, I remember our family took a picnic to our Flint Hills pasture where we children splashed in the spring while father counted cattle and checked the fences. On the way home we passed through the small town of Burns and overheard church bells ringing, celebratory gunshots, and a few drunks shouting in the streets, "The War is over." We quietly thanked God and moved on without joining in the festivities.

Mennonites were taught to love and pray for our enemies because that's what Jesus did. If we kids wanted to play cowboys and Indians with pretend guns, we did it out of parental view and hearing. We heard about Mennonite young men who were away doing alternative service as conscientious objectors to war—working in mental institutions, building trails in public parks, and caring for DP's who had fled the war's devastation. But with World War II's end, the work of peacemaking and restoration fell to all of us, and I was eager to put my hands to the task. Mennonite Central Committee speakers like Peter Dyck circulated through the churches with movies of the war's devastation and of the massive relief effort of Mennonites and other agencies to aid in the work of reconstruction.

Christmas bundles for MCC were a big deal in our family, and in all the families of our church. Early in the fall we children each prepared a package for a child our own age—underwear, clothes, warm socks, toiletries, and one toy—all neatly wrapped and safety-pinned in a big towel with a personal letter enclosed. Sometime after Christmas we got back a letter in German, expressing lavish thanks. We heard about desperate families struggling to survive and prayed for them. Some of these contacts became pen-pals for years.

I remember getting sent half-a-mile down the road to Grandma Janzen where her whole living room was organized into a large-scale production line making up CARE packages of dried foodstuffs like coffee, raisins, and powdered milk. I was not much help until it came time to wrap and bind the packages with twine. I knew how to hold my index finger on the first half of the square knot while grandma slipped the last loop into place and pulled it tight. These boxes went to relatives Grandma knew in Germany, and to strangers she would later come to know and correspond with. My job was also to carry the boxes into Aunt Ella's Chevy Coupe for a ride to the Elbing Post Office.

One Saturday afternoon mother called all us children to the radio to hear an announcer tell about a whole trainload of wheat flour departing from Newton, flour ground from grain donated by Kansas Mennonite farmers to feed the survivors of the war in Europe. No doubt, a truck load or two from our farm was included in the shipment. We were surprised to hear Father's cousin, Reverend Walter Dyck, offer the prayer of dedication before the locomotive blew its whistle and the train pulled out for the east coast and freighter shipment across the ocean.

In 1948, when I was seven years old, Bethel College, only a dozen miles from our home, co-hosted an historic Mennonite World Conference. Of course, our family attended. The most dramatic moment came when Mennonite delegates from Germany tearfully asked forgiveness for the loss of their pacifist stand, for getting pulled into Hitler's Nazi regime, and for adding their efforts to fight the war. However, after the war's end they were astonished by the Mennonites of the United States who rescued many of them from starvation and helped them find new homes by their generosity. American and German Mennonite leaders embraced on the stage to long applause from the audience.

At that point my father leaned forward and pointed my attention to one of the German delegate's feet. Father whispered in my ear, "It looks to me like he is wearing a pair of Mr. Keller's shoes." I took a deep breath and felt as much pride as a little Mennonite boy is allowed to feel when participating in the enemy-restoring work of reconciliation.

* * * * *

I see the wisdom of my parents and grandma Janzen involving us children in the Gospel calling to resist war and to love our enemies in whatever creative and constructive ways could be found. The continuities between this upbringing and our later life are easy to discern. This relief work for victims of war was a part of our heritage that we never thought to question. We only thought of new ways to apply this legacy to the changing world in which we arrived as adults.

This ministry of reconciliation, of course, goes back to Jesus in his Sermon on the Mount, and other sayings urging his disciples to a radical love that extends even to enemies, because God is like that, sending his rain on the just and the unjust alike. With the Apostle Paul we trace our lineage to the vision of a new creation making us ambassadors of a new nation called "Reconciliation." (2 Cor. 5:17–18). Our lineage goes back to the Radical Reformation, to a persecuted band of Anabaptists who refused the work of soldiering and participation in a state church that was married to warring nation states. Our home remembered that era in the thick volume of *The Martyrs Mirror* memorializing men and women who would rather die than betray their non-violent Jesus.

In my childhood, the memory was still alive of my grandparents who, as children, had come over from "the old country," Russia and Prussia, in the 1870's fleeing the nationalistic fervor and forceable recruitment of young men to serve in imperial armies. Many families, often entire churches, emigrated to America where cheap land and greater religious freedom beckoned. They did not flee as refugees who had lost everything. But they saw the war clouds coming and fled with a strong appreciation for the plight of others who did not escape. Like many Jews, they took to heart the commandment of Exodus 23:9: "You shall not oppress a resident alien; you know the heart of an alien, for you were aliens in the land of Egypt."

* * * * *

Our parents totally supported my "conscientious objector to war" claim in a time when young men were drafted to fight in Vietnam. Instead, in 1966, I was approved to do my alternative to military service with the Mennonite Central Committee in their Teachers Abroad Program in the Democratic Republic of the Congo. MCC got a two-for-one deal since Joanne and I went together. In the Congo we were following on the heels of my sister, Sara and her husband, Fremont Regier, as MCC agricultural development workers, and my brother John as an earlier MCC volunteer and later as a cultural anthropologist. After a year of French language study in Belgium and France, we landed among Tshiluba-speaking people in a village called Bibanga of the Eastern Kasai province, in a Southern Presbyterian mission school, where Joanne taught English, and I taught whatever gaps needed filling in a time of teacher shortage. This was only seven years after independence when the country still had few home-grown teachers. The line-up of subjects I taught included math, physics, history, philosophy, and geography, not to mention filling in as basketball coach, assistant principal, and faculty advisor to the student court.

I'm a player/coach on the Bibanga highschool basketball team.

Despite primitive circumstances and times of utter exhaustion, we were also totally welcomed and blessed by smart and highly motivated students—only the top five percent made the cut into secondary school. Many of these students came from families that had been refugees from a civil war that divided the country after Independence. Helping them live and study at peace on campus with their war-time rivals, was a challenge that almost everyone took on with Christian charity.

I recall my first encounter with our local pastor, Joseph Mukuna, a bright new seminary graduate, who inquired about my pacifist convictions. He had gone to a Presbyterian seminary where his pacifist reading of Jesus' message was put down. I loaned him a couple of books in French by Andre Trocme, a pacifist pastor and champion of the Jews during World War II. The next Sunday pastor Mukuna began to preach Christian non-violence from the pulpit. He too had risked his life as an ambassador of reconciliation in the throes of a recent civil war. At the same time, we often went to pastor Mukuna for coaching in cultural sensitivity in our role as servants of Jesus in a time and place when, as white teachers, we were honored way beyond our deserving as elite members of the local class system.

* * * * *

In El Salvador, in the 1970's, there was a spiritual revival among campesinos who gathered into study groups led by lay catechists in the Catholic Church. There they learned how to read and discuss the Bible in a new way, discovering that their oppression and poverty was not God's will. In the book of Exodus, and in Jesus' parables they learned that the justice and peace of God's rule was meant to be practiced here in this life, not just in heaven. Their cause was taken up and voiced in weekly radio broadcasts by Archbishop Romero.

In the U.S. most of us awoke to their plight when on March 24, 1980, Romero was assassinated while celebrating mass. Not only was he gunned down, but leaders among the campesinos and city workers who drew hope from his message met a similar fate at the hands of death squads and massive military repression. For many of us in the Churches of North America, this news hit home when we heard the riveting testimony of Yvonne Dilling, this Church of the Brethren volunteer in her mid-twenties, who happened to be at the edge of the Lempa River, border between El Salvador and Honduras, just as thousands of campesinos fled their homeland before a massive military sweep.

Yvonne tells the story *In Search of Refuge* (Herald Press, 1984) of a miraculous deliverance (fifty died while three-thousand and more fled into Honduras) on March 18, 1981, in their own exodus from Egypt into a wilderness, utterly dependent upon God and the good will of the Honduran people. In the UN sponsored refugee camps, miserable as they were, the Salvadoran refugees learned how to organize and become one people, launching their own schools and learning to form grass-roots committees for every need. And more importantly, they became a new kind of church that could meet under a mango tree—not needing a building of stone to which only the priest had a key.

Up to this point our network of Overground Railroad communities assisting Central American refugees toward asylum, had not heard of Valle Nuevo. At a 1991 conference of radical Christian communities in Grand Rapids, Michigan, Yvonne Dilling sought me out. We walked and talked the whole night through. In her soft yet passionate voice, Yvonne told me about a bold initiative on the part of Salvadorans in the Mesa Grande refugee camp who had refused to be helpless victims, forever refugees in an endless war. They determined to organize themselves into villages of peace that would be defended by the means of peace back in El Salvador. With the solidarity and support of international friends, they had taken down their refugee camp barracks, put the boards and tin on trucks, and made the long trek back to their homeland, to establish their own communities of solidarity, insisting that they would begin now the future that was going to happen when the armies laid down their weapons and the people would be allowed to create their own future.

The faith of these returned refugees inspired Yvonne and through the night, as she told about the hardships and courage of her refugee friends, God was talking to me as well. A vision was coming together. Could the Overground Railroad become, not just an organization to help refugees find asylum in a strange land, but could we support communities of refugees to find sanctuary on their own soil?

Yvonne's plea focused on one particular village of about 900 souls, 150 families, who had settled just across the road from the first two encampments of returnees in Cabanas Province. I returned home and arranged for a delegation of adults and teens from Plow Creek Fellowship and from Reba to make a first visit to Valle Nuevo.

Meanwhile the struggle in El Salvador that began as a religious awakening among the poor, was seized upon by the U.S. and the Soviet Union as a show-down between superpowers.

The arrival of our delegation in January of 1992 had been set for weeks, hoping to cross enemy lines during a stand-off war between the Salvadoran Army and the FMLN guerilla forces. However, on the day of our arrival, the United Nations-brokered Peace Accords were signed and the whole country, it seemed, erupted into celebration. We joined a jubilant crowd of half-a-million persons thronging into San Salvador's central *Plaza Nationale*. Every tree and statue was covered with bodies climbing high into the air, cheering, shouting speeches and singing songs of solidarity far into the night. Politicians speaking from an improvised stage celebrated the Peace Accords that promised a national police force created out of demobilized members of the army and the FMLN troops. The army would be downsized, no longer to control and harass civilian populations.

The next day we arrived for the first time in Valle Nuevo, part of the larger Santa Marta municipality. The approach of our mini bus was greeted by barking dogs, hordes of excited children, and a wide banner over the entrance to the soccer field proclaiming, "Vivan los hermanos que se solidarizan con nuestra communidad." (Long live the brothers and sisters in solidarity with our community.) We were regaled with songs of solidarity. Lydia and Tomasa read poems they had composed for the occasion, and Pastor, as member of the Directiva (Leadership Council) held the megaphone.

An improvised banner at Valle Nuevo welcomes us—"Long live the brethren in solidarity with our community." A mural of the martyr, Archbishop Romero, in the background.

But the biggest drama was still to unfold. Our first morning in Valle Nuevo we woke to roosters crowing, the discovery of fleabites in the night, and the "put-put" sound of communal masa grinders. We heard mothers firing up griddles to bake our breakfast tortillas with hot beans and sweet campesino coffee of ground toasted corn. Excited children came to drag us by the hand to the *"cancha"* (soccer field) where something really big was about to happen. Hundreds had already gathered and were waiting.

Soon we saw what the hubbub was about. Out of the mountains came a single file of FMLN soldiers with red bandannas around their brows, men and women, carrying their guns, forming smart lines on the soccer field, about two hundred in all. Blue United Nations Landrovers arrived and international observers stepped out to make sure this important event went right. Over the horizon came a white helicopter that descended in a huge cloud of dust onto the soccer field, and out stepped one of the FMLN generals along with a UN Peacekeeping Forces Commander to the general applause and cheers of the crowd.

A United Nations helicopter descends on the Valle Nuevo soccer field to demobilize guerilla troups.

The FMLN General and the UN Commander made speeches announcing that as of this day the FMLN troops were no longer soldiers but civilians. They could lay down their weapons in exchange for promises of job training and subsidies to build their own homes.

Later that day, in a communal gathering, we expressed our apology that it was our government who had funded their killers, and our tax dollars that had oppressed them and sent them into exile. Could they forgive us?

"Of course," their leaders replied without a moment's hesitation. "Isn't that what our Lord has taught us to do if we want to be forgiven for our own sins." It surprised us to hear the *Directiva* and a woman's group thank us profusely and emotionally for being with them because if their enemies knew they had international solidarity—sister communities in *El Norte*—it would add to their safety. And if anything happened to them, they could trust that we would let Washington know... and then they wept with relief. And we cried too. We hugged each other all around the circle. We had no idea that our brief friendship could have such power. Somehow, in that moment we knew that God had bonded us together, that we were one people, called to walk a common path of solidarity, come what may.

A few months later we received a message from the Valle Nuevo *Directiva* saying that a large plot of land (about a square kilometer) had become available for sale on the mountain of El Picacho, just north, adjacent to their community. If they could buy this steep mountain (northern Cabanas is nothing but steep mountains) it would be enough, in good years, to grow the corn and beans they needed to feed their families. Without this land, in the long run, their men would have to migrate to other countries for work in order to survive, and they would be no better off than before the war. To buy the land they would need $25,000 down and another $25,000 within a year. Could we help?

I took a few days of retreat in prayer at the Plow Creek cabin and asked God for a word. I could see that the time had come to close down the Overground Railroad network because the Peace Accords had slowed the flow of refugees, refugees who now had hope for security and peace back home. I proposed that the network which had grown up caring for refugees fleeing north, had one last task, to secure a sanctuary for the village of Valle Nuevo in El Salvador. There was general assent. We set a goal of raising $25,000 this year, trusting that other groups would come together to raise the rest the following year. And that is what happened.

Closing the deal had some typical Salvadoran twists and delays. The lawyers of the seller of the land insisted on cash, and they openly doubted that simple campesinos could come up with that much money. But a few weeks later I wired $25,000 to a bank in Sensuntepeque (the capital of Cabanas Province). The folks of Valle Nuevo wondered how do we get that much money across a town rife with bandits? With typical campesino daring, a couple of Valle Nuevo women put the mounds of bills into two baskets, covered them with towels as if they were tortillas for the market, and marched with the money on their heads across a town (their version of an armored vehicle), delivering the two bushels of cash to an amazed circle of lawyers, realtors and land owners. They counted out the money and it was all there. They signed papers, took pictures, shook hands and the dream began to seem real.

El Picacho, the mountain Valle Nuevo purchased to aportion between 160 families for basic subsistence.

* * * * *

That was in 1992, and now it is 2024. Almost every year there has been a delegation from Shalom Mission Communities in the north to our sister community in the south, Valle Nuevo. A new generation of leaders, both north and south, have claimed this relationship as God-given and worthy of investment.

The first years we came expecting to help build something or assist in some project, but our hosts insisted, instead, on us hearing their stories of incredible hardship and loss from the years of war, so that we could know the pain in their hearts and pray for their healing. Instead of building stuff—at which we would be hopelessly inept—we played with their children, studied scripture together, visited classrooms learning English, stood in as election observers, went on walking tours to see what they had done with the land, taught each other our songs—in short, we became family. Each delegation was a mix of old-timers and folks new to the relationship. They and we realized, that if we came as missionaries or service workers, as "haves" giving to the "have nots" the relationship would go sour. But if God wanted us to be family, then we needed to be honest about the great chasm that imperialism and racism had created between us as we read about and discussed in Jesus's parable about the "Rich Man and Lazarus," in Luke 16:22 ff. Indeed, we recognized that someone had been raised from the dead and come to us, brothers and sisters of the rich man, to warn us of our impending judgment. We needed their forgiveness again and again to make this relationship work.

Often our group included teens for whom the trip was something of a rite of passage, and also a wake-up call. After returning home I heard them say, "I'm done complaining about the things I don't have." "I want to study Spanish and become a teacher in a place like this." "I want to be baptized. Now I know what faith is for." They were impressed by the leadership roles that teens exercised in the community and how highly these campesinos valued education, not for personal gain but for community service. God knew this is how it was supposed to go. helping them to heal and to be assured that someone cared. We studied scripture together in the manner of base Christian Communities, like they'd formed in the refugee camp, discovering the good news of Jesus and the kingdom, not just for heaven, but for a life of peace and justice here and now.

Some years we've been able to get visas for folks from the south to come north to visit our communities, but more often the U.S. State Department has denied them. Over the years we've helped fund hydroponic gardens, build Habitat houses, bore wells to upgrade their water system, and fund a host of other projects in Valle Nuevo. But relationships have always come first, and projects have followed according to Valle Nuevo's suggestions.

The book, *Companeros: Two Communities in a Trans-national Communion* (by Joe and Nancy Gatlin, and Joel Scott) tells the stories of exodus and redemption in the experience of our Valle Nuevo friends, and of our decades-long relationship, which I commend to you.

CHAPTER 16

Section Hands in the Garden
From Model Railroading to Affordable Housing

EVERY SPRING MOTHER GOT the idea that we boys should get our destructive energies out of the house and into the garden where there were thousands of clods to break up and some tractor-dump loads of cow manure to spread. So, with hoes, shovels, and rakes, we made the dust fly. However, just being gardeners was not dramatic enough for my brother John and me; we needed bigger and more manly roles. We became "section hands."

Now-a-days, no one knows about section hands, but in our childhood, we were mesmerized by railroads, trains, steam locomotives, and crews of brawny men responsible to maintain a section of ten or twenty miles of that railroad track. The section hands traveled out to their task for the day on a little railroad cart, powered by a "put-put engine." At the worksite the guys heaved the cart off the tracks to let the trains pass by. There they set to work with their manly equipment to maintain and repair the tracks, signals, crossings, and bridges. Section hands impressed us with their bulging biceps, vivid cusswords, and their ability to accurately spit an arc of tobacco juice wherever they wished. But we were especially impressed by their skill in raising pickaxes above their heads to drive them down with grunts and gusto to break up the gravel between the railroad ties.

So, we became section hands in the garden, strutting our muscles, talking in railroad voices, and raising our hoes above our heads to smash them down on every cowering clod within sight. We practiced hawking our throats and gathering saliva to spit a glob between each sentence. In our new-found roles we worked at top speed to fix the tracks before the next train came through—an urgent matter of success or train-wreck, of life or death on the main line. As a five-year-old, I was carried away with enthusiasm in my manly role, attacking clods with a vengeance until—uh oh, you guessed it—my hoe came down smack on top of my brother's head. John let out a yell, reached under his cap and brought before his face a hand covered with blood, whereupon he began to cry and ran to the house.

Our mother had been through nurses training, so accidents like this were no cause for panic. She quickly assessed the situation. Since the cut was on John's scalp, there was no need to go to the doctor for stitches because the scar would never show under all that hair. So instead, mother washed out his wound under the kitchen faucet, applied some sterilizing ointment, and wrapped a few ice-cubes in a rag for John to hold on his throbbing head.

Then mother turned to me and declared, "David, you need to tell John you are sorry and ask his forgiveness." I protested, "It was an accident." Mother summarily disqualified my defense. "You hurt him; you need to say you're sorry."

The longer I looked at my brother slumped there on a stool holding a rag on his head and with tears still in his eyes, the worse I felt for him. Finally, I squeezed out the necessary word, "Sorry." John looked at me and dutifully replied, "I forgive you." At that I was suddenly overwhelmed with remorse and relief and broke down crying. In that moment I made a solemn vow, and though I have broken many other promises, this is one that I have kept. Never, ever since that fateful day, have I ever, not even once, raised a hoe above my head pretending to be a section hand.

However, in writing down this story, I have felt a curious urge rising, compelling me to visualize the next time I visit my brother John—I want to check his scalp to see if there is still a scar on the crown of his head that remembers the brief thrill of playing mighty "section hands" in a garden of clods where a railroad ran through it more than seventy years ago.

* * * * *

We Janzen boys were fascinated every-which-way by the passenger and freight trains that steamed by on our western horizon several times a day on the Rock Island line. Often, at our Uncle Johnny's farm that bordered the tracks, we'd stand as close to the onrushing trains as we dared and threw clods, watching them explode against the on-rushing cars. It felt like we were taunting a fire-breathing dragon in some primeval mythological drama.

I drew innumerable steam locomotives like this, whose smoke filled the whole sky.

One time at the Elbing grain elevator, we lingered to watch a locomotive switch grain-cars onto the siding. Then the engineer, who had some idle time on his hands as other cars were filled with grain, invited me to climb up into the cab where he patiently answered my questions about all the gauges and levers that helped him manage the mighty steam engine. He even allowed me to pull the whistle cord that blasted its scream into the air for miles around. Wow! For months to come, in art class I would draw nothing but locomotives that filled the sky with their powerful billows of smoke.

Our fascination with railroads was amplified by a major wreck and derailment three miles down the track when a passenger train ran into a truck with a bulldozer on it, cutting the truck in half, knocking the train on its side, killing one person and sending forty others to the hospital in ambulances. Of course, everyone in the area swarmed the scene and then speculated on how long it would take the railroad to repair the track and haul away the damaged equipment.

Brother John and I began to build our own model railroad in the basement. Our parents allowed us to take over a cellar guest room for our railroad layout because, in their words, it might "keep the boys out of trouble."

Soon we learned that toy trains were not just a children's enterprise, but there was a magazine called *Model Railroading*" to which we eagerly subscribed, illustrating incredibly detailed and realistic layouts. Model railroading, we learned was a serious hobby that grown men pursued with big money and thousands of hours of dedicated time. For several years we invested every bit of spare change, our Christmas money, our allowances, and all our earnings into an HO gauge (1/8" = 1 foot) railroad growing in the basement. Our finished layout included 120 feet of track; paper-mache mountains and tunnels; miniature trees, and a lake; a village with houses, cars, and pedestrians; stockyards with miniature cattle and cattlemen—the works. My specialty was to build scale model houses, a depot, factories, passenger cars, cattle pens—all with an Exacto knife, balsa wood, airplane glue, and hobby paints. My brother, John, excelled in laying the track, tending to the rolling stock, and rigging up the wiring to control the train engines. Our basement became a magnet for friends and cousins, especially in the winter when the cold drove us all indoors. We didn't just play with toys, but we created and developed a hub of imagined activity for a village of people with a railroad that served as its economic life blood and connection to a larger world. We became what grow-ups might call "project developers."

Did this childhood railroad-building obsession carry over into adulthood as it did for so many other grown-ups in the *Model Railroading* magazine? Not really. One reason had to do with our lack of enthusiasm for more modern railroad technology. Sometime in our grade school years, the railroads began replacing steam locomotives with diesel-electric engines, which though safer and more economical to operate, proved too prosaic to be interesting to us children. They had less fire, less smoke, no steam, less drama or danger.

Diesel engines and a steam locomotive stream past onlooking Trainview school mates.

These diesel engines were lamentably devoid of soul and mystique. Eventually, our model railroad languished under a cover of basement dust, and never made the transition into the diesel-engine era.

At the time I did not know it, but my introduction to larger-scale project development was launched. It arced, like a brawny section-hand's projectile of tobacco juice, from our farm-house basement in the 1950s to New Creation Builders in the 1970's, and then bounced to land with a splat in 1995 in Evanston Illinois, where my attention turned to an enterprise called Reba Place Development Corporation. Stick around and you'll hear stories of prowling dragons and a team of heroes urgently engaged in the life-and-death drama of turning distressed and crime-ridden buildings into more peaceable communities of housing affordable for our low-income neighbors and friends.

* * * * *

The work of developing affordable housing preceded us in Rebaland, but our arrival marked a new phase of that work. Reba Place Fellowship began in a large house at 727 Reba Place in Evanston, in 1957. As the community grew it purchased a few other old mansions in the neighborhood as communal living spaces for its members. Then, in the 1970's an opportunity arose to take up the property-management business. An investigative journalist exposed a prominent candidate for mayor who turned out to be an absentee slumlord in the Reba neighborhood, i.e. a fire-breathing predatory dragon. This would-be mayor moved to clean up his reputation by quickly dumping two apartment buildings (39 units) between Reba Place and Monroe, on Sherman St. The Fellowship purchased these buildings to improve our environment, give employment to a few young men, preserve diversity, and to provide housing options for our members. Our ministry was to offer housing affordable to our low-income neighbors with rents set at the level of our costs. At the time the housing market was depressed, so the Fellowship could finance the purchase of other apartment buildings with conventional mortgages. Over time, our pattern of local management progressively improved the peace and safety of our neighborhood, producing a village effect for people who knew and trusted each other. This permitted many informal ways of sharing life to grow up—like free-food distributions, a price-free thrift store, a food coop, baby-sitting collectives, and more.

However, all was not peace and light in Rebaland. There were other "fire-breathing dragons" prowling the neighborhood in the form of negligent and absentee slumlords, racial discrimination, and a criminal sub-culture of alienated youth with no meaningful work or elders to take them on.

By the 1990's, however, property values had risen to the point where we needed to access larger grants and government funding to keep growing this kind of redemptive housing ministry. So, my mentor, Julius Belser, launched Reba Place Development Corporation, standing on a wider ecumenical and civic base. In 1995, he asked me to become its Executive Director. Just like the Overground Railroad era before it, Julius was the chairman of the board, and I was the director of operations. My construction background commended me for the job. We had a strong oversight team which included Julius's son, Nevin Belser, who was in charge of the Reba Place Fellowship housing operation with a work crew that eventually included our son, James Janzen.

RPDC's first project at 700–02 Monroe, was another distressed building, the source of more than a hundred "911" calls in a year. Young men were dealing drugs on the street, a threatening presence that police could not keep up with. When someone was shot in front of the building our alderman approached Julius and said, "The police can't handle this menace. If the city helped Reba buy this building, could you turn it around?" With down-payment funds lent by the city at no-interest for 40 years, RPDC bought the building and Julius prophetically named it "House of Peace," which it certainly was not at the time.

So how do you "turn around" a run-down, crime-ridden building that is a terror to the neighborhood? Our plan, to use a basketball analogy, was to launch a "full-court press" that engaged the whole community. We interviewed the residents and decided to not renew the leases of two families whose sons opened the door to other gang members, using the basement as their base of operations. The other tenants agreed to a development plan that would eventually put the building into their hands as a limited-equity housing cooperative. They embraced the name "House of Peace" as the goal of a two-year transformation scheme.

My job as developer was to line up the funding and a professional team including lawyer, architect, city housing planner, general contractor, and neighbors in support of an ambitious renovation plan. But even more importantly, we needed the buy-in of the alienated young men in the neighborhood. And that recruitment began on the Reba Park basketball court. Since I liked to shoot hoops, had a three-point shot, and I was the only white guy on the court, they hung on me the nickname, "Larry Bird."

I explained to the guys that on up-coming Saturdays, we would need to hire young men for renovations. How about if we paid them $10.00 an hour and hired their mothers to make a meal to feed the Saturday work crews?

$10.00 an hour was double the minimum wage at the time and they were all for it. So, on a series of Saturday work days we made a line of teenage guys interspersed with a few Reba adults, and moved trash hand-to-hand from the basement to the dumpster trucks on the curb. And then we helped residents to box up their stuff and move their furniture up and down stairs to vacate one three-apartment stack at a time for renovations. I chose one of those teens to be my foreman to assemble supplies, set up a snack station, and to organize the payout line at the end of the day. The general contractor also agreed to hire a few of the young men as laborers on his crew. As a result, the guys from the basketball court united to claim this project as their own and would let no one mess it up with graffiti or vandalism. The fire-breathing dragon was tamed and became a defender of the neighborhood. Our motto was coming to life—"RPDC: Renewing housing, persons, and community."

The House of Peace Coop at Custer and Monroe, home base for twelve Evanston families one step up from homelessness

The "full court press" became more tangible when a couple of twenty-something Reba basketball stars organized an annual tournament in the park that gathered teams from the whole area and turned the event into a block party, pizza festival, featuring half-court three-on-three games with referees and trophies at the end. An actively engaged community was turning the neighborhood around.

In 1999 we tackled a larger 25-unit building on our block in similar need of redemption. It had three pages of code violations—drug dealing was rampant from the front sidewalk as soon as the police went around the corner. The city again helped us buy this distressed building, and with a series of Saturday workdays, we put the neighborhood youth to work, facilitating the renovations of six units at a time till the whole building was upgraded with new kitchens and bathrooms. The contractor again hired some of the youth onto his crew. Soon peace had returned to the building, and we could outfit a common laundry facility and bike-storage area in the basement. People were learning how to be good neighbors.

Then we took on an abandoned antique mall across the street from the Reba Church Meeting House where plate glass windows were falling out onto the sidewalk. We turned it into a classy suite of offices and a center for music lessons and recitals called, The Musical Offering. Again, we recruited a mob of young men to fill a dozen dumpster truckloads of trash and junky antiques. We worked like "section hands" with crowbars and shovels, demolishing crumbling walls and sagging ceilings. And this time no one got smashed on the head because we all wore hard hats. Over fifteen years we tackled eight projects renovating one commercial building and producing sixty-seven units of affordable housing.

* * * * *

Following the housing crash of 2008, RPDC was treading water, not launching any new projects, just keeping up with property management and peace-making in the buildings we owned or managed. This allowed me to make frequent trips to advise and consult with a wide range of Christian intentional communities in what came to be called the Nurturing Communities Network. (More on that in chapter 17.) So, like the Apostle Paul's tent-making work, RPDC allowed me to earn a part-time salary for Reba Place Fellowship, while ministering to younger Christian communities for free.

In the 1990's one young teenager on our Saturday workday crews, caught my attention for his steady good cheer and hardy work ethic. The contractor hired him. Eventually he married and moved into the House of Peace Coop where he was elected president of the Coop. He was a joy to work with—good humored, full of constructive ideas, a natural community organizer. He finished college and worked for a decade in the corporate world, but then circled back to volunteer with us at RPDC. We elected him to the board, and I took him on as my assistant. Adrian was a Jesus-follower who wanted his life to count for more than just making money. He met with Julius and me in our weekly planning meetings where Adrian would talk about his dreams to become an advocate in the city for affordable housing, giving to others the head-start he had received as a teen. Adrian learned the ropes as my assistant, then I suggested we trade roles, so he became the

RPDC Director, and I became his assistant. He eagerly picked up all the practical wisdom I could offer.

Adrian Willoughby, my protégé at Reba Place Development Corp.

In 2015, Adrian began to make a name for himself as an affordable housing advocate in the northern Chicago suburbs, giving presentations to clubs, civic groups, and the Evanston Housing Commission. He won a couple of grants from the Evanston Community Foundation and the local Rotary Club to help build up our organization with the goal of developing new affordable housing projects. Meanwhile, our mentor, Julius Belser was in serious decline, and passed away in December of 2018. What Julius had given to me I was passing on to Adrian. It felt like life was coming full circle and I could soon retire.

One month later I got an hysterical call from Adrian's wife crying, "Adrian is dead." He died during a polar vortex of a heart-attack after snow-blowing a neighbor's sidewalk. Four hundred people, including the mayor of Evanston, showed up for his funeral. The *Chicago Tribune* wrote a loving tribute to this promising young man who died at the age of 39. Thus, began the hardest year of my life—in the space of a few months I'd lost my best friend (Allan Howe), my mentor and father figure (Julius Belser), and now a "son" and protégé (Adrian Willoughby).

What would we do with Adrian's dream of revitalizing RPDC, recruiting a new generation of board members and inviting a wide circle of donors to build more housing for the seventy-plus people on our waiting list? A few days after Adrian's death, Keith Banks, an African American financial advisor on our board stepped forward and offered to carry on with Adrian's dream. Knocked down but not out, we felt this was God's call and we pushed ahead together. So, here I was once more, an assistant and senior advisor to someone who is taking the role of RPDC Director. Relaunching RPDC with a new cast of characters was a hard slog, but God has provided a new team that is gaining experience and adding new partners to take on an expanded housing development mission. As new staff came on board I tried to pass on my practical wisdom and watch them grow. I began again to enjoy my work because, like model railroading, and every other kind of work that I've been given to do—eventually it becomes more like play. I forget myself and enjoy the people I'm working with and for. I enjoy turning out flow-charts of our tasks for the coming year, scanning web-sites and learning how we might do our jobs even better. This is good work because it grows our gifts, builds community, engages creativity, all while supplying a basic human need.

On December 8, 2022, the RPDC Board and Staff conspired to throw me a glorious retirement party attended by more than fifty friends and affordable housing peers. They told me to get a haircut and write a speech. Conspiring with Joanne, they created a slide show of my work history going back to milking cows and raising sheep on "Heck of a Ranch" till my RPDC retirement. My speech lifted up the Jubilee vision of Moses and Jesus, to give each generation a level playing field of assets and opportunities as a cure for oppression and domination politics. I expressed my gratitude for Keith Banks (Exec. Dir.), Martha Burns (Property Manager), and Pam Tingley (Administrative Coordinator) who endured my training sessions and now have taken over.

A diverse group of RPDC staff, board, and residents throw me a retirement party iat the end of 2022.

Chapter 17

When the Ruts Get Too Deep

From Family Trips to the Nurturing Communities Network

Our 1951 summer family vacation trip was an urgently needed getaway from a farm in shambles. The wheat harvest went way past the usual Fourth-of-July wrap-up because of incessant rains and historic flooding. Countless times the combine got stuck in the wheat fields and needed to be pulled out by our biggest tractor with a long chain. Everything broke down that could, and had to be tediously repaired. We escaped on our annual family vacation trip two weeks behind schedule, leaving behind our hired man, Leroy Hiebert, with lots of chores and a rutted mess of fields too wet to plow.

Our family of six made our get-away in a 1948 Chevy sedan and got as far as Kansas City for the first night. There we toured thousands of devastated houses, factories, and railroad yards left behind by epic floods. It was the first time I'd seen houses and cars filled with mud three feet deep. We saw where the raging floodwaters had swept away bridges and tumbled trains on their sides like an angry child who abuses his toys. All the photos we took turned out the color of mud.

The next day we got as far as Detroit where we visited the home of someone who had been a hired hand in the Janzen family, but who had long since escaped to live in the big city. Our hosts, trying to be gracious, asked, "Would anyone like a beer?" That was a memorable and awkward moment for us children because no one to our knowledge drank beer except for a few derelicts that we children imitated in their drunkenness. We watched our hosts drink beer and get a little jolly, but to our amazement, they did not get drunk. We didn't know that ordinary respectable people might drink beer and not get staggeringly sloshed, the way our teetotaling Grandma Janzen had warned us. Our first culture shock of the trip!

In Detroit we toured the Ford Museum, a sprawling village set in an older era dramatizing all the inventions that had, supposedly, improved our civilization. It included a replica of the earliest auto factory assembly line—a celebration of the genius behind the industry that had launched automobility. We children all came away inspired to become inventors like Henry Ford and Thomas Edison.

Next stop on our sightseeing tour was Niagara Falls. Our first look came at night when multi-colored floodlights lit up the breath-taking ever-changing panorama. I remember us children laughing at the tourists who were taking flash pictures from a mile away. We knew better. Though mother was in charge of our new "Kodak" slide camera with flash-bulb attachment, she allowed us older children to take pictures from time to time, giving us artistic hints on how to frame a good shot.

The next morning, we got to see the falls up close where the cataract plunged to its chaotic landing on the boulders a hundred-and-sixty-seven-feet below, causing huge plumes of fog to rise up way higher than our viewpoint at the water's edge. How did that work, we wondered until a tour guide explained that the visible water pulled even more invisible air down with it, and that air had to escape back up again, taking water vapor with it. If one cascade came down and another had to go up. We were excited by the physics of our first major waterfall. Every wonder on our trip was stored away in memory to brag about to our friends and playmates upon our return to Kansas.

The next day we drove from Buffalo to New York City, a much longer and more tedious drive than we anticipated. This was in an era before the interstate highway system, so we had to drive through the middle of every city and town on the way. We three older kids in the back seat would get restless and pick fights about imaginary boundary lines between your space and mine, just to break the monotony of the boring miles. Mother suggested we play the ABC game, looking for letters on signs and license plates to complete the alphabet. But we always got stuck on "Q" and then would start picking on one another again. How about following our progress in a road atlas, mother commended? That was fascinating for a minute, but our car didn't move along fast enough to make that game interesting, either.

At lunchtime we'd stop at a road-side park with a picnic table, and mother would bring the picnic basket out of the trunk with premade sandwiches, fruit, and hard-boiled eggs. In fact, mother had thought ahead to bring a half a crate of boiled farm eggs, enough for each of us to eat one a day on the whole two-week trip. We were frugal at mealtime, but in the middle of the afternoon we'd usually persuade Father to stop at an ice-cream shop for cones all around. The long, boring, muscle-cramping drive was slowed by more traffic jams as we approached New York City. I fell asleep the last couple of hours and woke up groggy but happy to land at Mother's cousin's place, the home of Carl Neufeldt, in Mt. Vernon, NY. where they were eagerly awaiting us even if the night was half gone.

The Neufeldt home was our first encounter with television. We begged to watch any hour of the day or night. I remember getting up in the morning just to look at the test pattern. Late at night we watched wrestling matches with great interest until our cousin, Max, let us know from his superior knowledge, that these matches were staged to appear violent and outrageous, but in reality, it was all acting. What a let-down! The next day both families went sightseeing in down-town New York, were we visited an exhibition of the latest technology, where tourists could stand in front of a TV camera and see themselves on the screen. Now that was something to brag about back home! "We went to New York City, and I was on TV." I didn't mention I was "on" only ten seconds, and then it was the next person's turn.

For three days we stayed with the Carl Neufeldt family and toured the biggest sights of the biggest city in the USA. Soon we wearied of hearing tour guides brag about how everything in New York City was the biggest in the world—the Empire State Building, the George Washington suspension bridge, the American Museum of Natural History, the Bronx Zoo, Central Park, the Cathedral of St. John the Divine, etc., etc. America was, by implication, the greatest nation in the world, and New York City was the epitome of this young empire. Each time we heard the phrase, "biggest in the world," we'd look at each other and roll our eyes.

I also remember a drive-by tour of the Traphagen Elementary School in Mr. Vernon where Carl Neufeldt was the principal. He impressed us with his dignified demeanor that could command good behavior from children, just with a glance.

Our glorious time in New York City had an even more glorious wrap-up in a glorious three-hour boat tour around Manhattan Island, narrated by an invisible voice on the P.A. system that recounted the history of each building on the skyline as we chased our cousins around on the upper deck.

From New York we drove to Washington, D.C. I don't remember us expressing much patriotism, just amazement at the size and grandeur of the capitol buildings that we had seen so often in pictures. I remember climbing a lot of steps and looking up a lot at the Washington Monument, the capitol dome, and other landmarks. By this time, we were travel weary. We had a running argument with Father about how to plan our family trips. He was always eager to see one more impressive sight that he believed would be an educational experience for us all. We wanted less time in a car seat and more time to hike in some scenic spot or to play with new-found friends where we could stay for a while.

We were happier when we got to the home of Father's cousin, Arthur Regier, in Newport News, Virginia. He and his wife had a son about John's age, and two older daughters who doted on us. Arthur lived next to a golf course where he was a member. Us boys borrowed his golf clubs (without permission), snuck onto the golf course and shot a few rounds until we had lost two balls in the water. Then we hurried back home before someone found out about our misdeeds. That was my first experience playing golf. It did not impress me enough that I ever wanted to pursue the sport on my own.

Father's cousin, Arthur, was an interesting fellow who left the Regier farm for a science education at Kansas State University, and then ended up an aeronautical engineer at Langley Research Center. He enjoyed philosophical discussions and engaged us boys with interesting questions both ethical and technological. At one point he worked on the problem of noise pollution at airports.

Arthur asked Father, "How can you afford to leave the farm and take a long vacation trip like this?"

"Actually, it's cheaper to take a vacation," Father said with a laugh. "When we're on the road, the kids aren't breaking any farm implements." That twisted logic would only have occurred to Father because the flimsiest excuse would suffice for him to make a trip to see the wider world beyond the farm.

After two weeks, we returned home and were welcomed by all our cats, but our beloved dog, Jiggers, was missing. During our long absence, we later learned, he started making tours of other farms around, to sample their food and affection. But when Jiggers showed up the next day, he was overjoyed, as were we—bouncing and yipping and wrestling till our bodies and souls were thoroughly reunited. While we were gone the land had dried out and Leroy had finished most of the plowing. He was glad to return our chores to their rightful owners. Our world was back together again.

However, the culmination of our trip came a week or two later. By that time all our photos were developed, which allowed us to invite anyone and everyone in the area to join us for an evening feast of watermelon and trip pictures. Farm families, in those days, were starved for social events and news of the wider world. We set up our slide projector and screen outside where there was room for everyone in a chair, on the grass, or walking around with another piece of watermelon. That's when we could tell our stories, narrating the highlights of every day on the road. We showed every single slide, even the blurry shots where the camera slipped. This was the moment we kids had been waiting for, to deliver all the bragging we had stored up from the wonders of the far away world we had seen.

Now, when I reflect back on those annual post-harvest vacation trips our family took, one theme keeps repeating itself. Mother and Father felt something of a calling to connect with the "fallen away" members of the Mennonite tribe in diaspora. They visited their some-what-alienated cousins both out of curiosity to learn about their different worlds, but also from a mission to help those who had "flown the Mennonite coop" to use a chicken-house analogy, to nevertheless, stay connected to their spiritual and familial roots.

In some ways, Hilda and Louis were at their best and most alive when they offered hospitality to strangers and when they traveled to strange places. What accounted for this confidence and curiosity that was so unusual in the context of their more insular Mennonite farming enclave? In some ironic ways, my parents' security and unity with each other about their particular ethnic and spiritual roots allowed them to engage with a much wider world in a curious and constructive way. They loved to take us children along to church conferences where they were constantly meeting old friends and making new. They loved to visit and invest in Mennonite camps because they had met in such a gathering as young adults. In their many travels they stayed with Mennonites whenever possible, and then with their newly made "Yankee" friends when there were no Mennonite landing places. They gladly extended hospitality to all these friends in return. The list of contacts on their annual Christmas letters grew into the hundreds as they seemed to never alienate anyone, and their network of connections grew to connect the dots around the world.

I see that my siblings too inherited this knack for making friends around the world. So, where did that confidence, that lack of anxiety about people who are different, come from? Where was it rooted? I never heard my parents talk about this explicitly, but now I see how they were part of a Biblical people with a heritage as immigrants, exiles, and sojourners somehow immune to patriotic idolatry or imperial ambitions of the society around them. Rather, they were connected to a people rooted in God's faithfulness across the ages and continents. In this way the Mennonites are much like the Jews, rooted in the Bible—not in a fragile literalist or fundamentalist kind of way, but in a wider world view with a spiritual foundation, and that allowed them to listen to other people and points of view without feeling threatened. They gave us both roots and wings, and for this inheritance, I am most grateful.

So, what did I do with that inheritance? Where did that arc from childhood land in the most recent chapter of my life? That story follows after these five asterisks:

* * * * *

Since 1971, Joanne and I have lived in Christian intentional community, a way of gathering with other disciples of Jesus to create a culture where the Sermon on the Mount become normative rather than viewed idealistically from a distance. That doesn't mean we always succeed, but as John Alexander (Church of the Sojourners) described it, "we're not playing tiddleywinks, we're playing baseball." Christian discipleship in community is the game we're playing and if we fail, that's the game we're failing at.

Since this kind of semi-monastic life is out of synch with the dominant culture, we're not going to get much support by reading the self-help books of conventional wisdom, or even conventional denominational church leadership. We're looking to other similar communities for outside support and accountability. One important tradition in maintaining connection and support has been **visitations**—something like community health check-ups from outsiders who share the same values and commitments, who are playing the same game. Over the years I have been invited, on many occasions, to visit other communities to help them review their life, leadership functions, and to set goals for the coming years.

However, what had been an occasional ministry, in 2008, became my main work for a decade. In that era, two young maverick prophets, Shane Claiborne and Jonathan Wilson Hartgrove, launched what they called the New Monasticism Movement. Shane's book, *The Irresistible Revolution*, and Jonathan's *Seven Marks of a New Monasticism*, along with their speaking tours on campuses and youth conferences, inspired a new wave of local attempts to begin intentional Christian communities, many of which were floundering for lack of experience and practical wisdom in the art of communal living.

About that time my work in developing affordable housing came to a pause as the housing bubble burst. My community mates suggested I take a retreat and listen to the Lord about what else I might give my attention to. It seemed the Spirit was recalling for me the joyful struggles of founding New Creation Fellowship (Newton, KS), back in the 1970's, with lots of support from Reba Place Fellowship and the Shalom Association of Communities. Was God asking me to become a pastor and apostle to this new wave of communities? When I asked this question of Shane and Jonathan, they were excited and each threw $5,000 into the pot for me to begin offering visitations in what Jonathan dubbed, "The Nurturing Communities Project."

As I went around on these visits, I'd write up trip reports that circulated in a widening list of contacts across the U.S. and Canada. Typically, I'd make a trip every month or two, often visiting a handful of communities in one metropolitan area. Those trip reports now are available online at Report Archive—Nurturing Communities Network.

In that decade of community visits, the Nurturing Communities Project grew into the Nurturing Communities Network with its own Steering Committee of community leaders. We sponsored regional conferences, leadership training workshops, and developed other resources for communities on a similar radical discipleship path. In 2013 we published *The Intentional Christian Community Handbook: For Idealists, Hypocrites, and Wannabe Disciples of Jesus*.

A 2013 Nurturing Communities gathering hosted by the Benedictines at St. John's Abby in Collegeville, MN.

It seemed to me that every line of work I'd ever pursued until then, came together in the ministry of listening to and counseling new communities. However, by 2018, it seemed right for me to pass on the leadership of this movement to a younger and more energetic team.

Here's my last trip report as the Nurturing Communities Director.

* * * * *

FALL, 2018, NURTURING COMMUNITIES NETWORK REPORT

Dearly Beloved in the NCN,

This is a goodbye letter of sorts since I've been officially "retired" as coordinator of the NCN since Sunday evening, October 21, at about 8:00 pm. I'm pondering what metaphors might describe how I feel about it all. Am I like an old horse put out to pasture? No, it's not that, because I'm still going to keep on doing what I've been doing, visiting communities. Only now I'm free to do that at a slower pace, while others do more of it—which would allow me to, Lord willing, to finish a few half-written books in the coming years.

Someone suggested that I'm the bride who tossed a bouquet that was caught by three hopeful people who now have to figure out between them what to do with it. Good luck with that! At other times I feel like a runner who has passed a baton forward to others with fresher legs, eager for several more laps around the track.

In any case a younger three-some has taken that baton—Nancy and Joe Gatlin (Hope Fellowship, Waco TX), and Elizabeth Turman Bryant (Spring Water Community, Portland OR)—ready to carry on the calling of nurturing a network of communities in the power and guidance of the Holy Spirit. Halleluia.

September 28–30: Bloomington (Indiana) Catholic Worker Community Visitation

The Bloomington Catholic Worker Community, made up of three families offering hospitality for formerly homeless guests, has been in a season of turmoil. The six adults, however, easily agreed on one thing—to ask two local friends, Virginia and Forest, to join me, coming from a distance, to conduct a community review. Earlier in the year, the BCW had said farewell to another family, releasing them to explore a farming community with a more interfaith spiritual base. However, the way that decision was processed in BCW left two brothers estranged, and the community somewhat paralyzed regarding long-term planning and commitments.

Virginia, Forest, and I went through the motions of reading the Bloomington CW questionnaires, conducting personal interviews, eating in different homes, playing with children, and enjoying a "lack of talent" show, but the essential work of reconciliation, the turning of hearts, was something we could only pray for. And indeed, in answer to everyone's prayers, during a session of "listening patiently to one another with accurate empathy" the two estranged brothers began to confess how hard is their inner work of facing trauma from the past, and trying to control patterns of anger stemming from families of origin. These were, it turns out, some of the triggers that kept exploding in their conversations now. But in that holy moment confessing their brokenness, God also worked to reveal their love for one another. Instead of landmines being triggered when they came close, tears of regret led to a spontaneous embrace. When love is confessed like that, the demons have to flee—they just can't take it.

However, in the few minutes that remained in our visitation, there was a sober realization that a house where an evil spirit has been cast out, cannot long remain empty, or others will return. According to the parable of Jesus (Matt. 12:43–45) the end might be worse than the beginning. So, what would it mean to not just try to control one's feelings of anger and rejection, but to do one's homework, to seek healing from Jesus for these memories at their root? What changes in community decision-making might do a better job next time they face a crisis, if someone is discerning whether to stay or leave the community? We gave some suggestions and blessed the community as we went on our way back home.

Now, even as we are apart, we've remained connected through several rounds of e-mails and other conversations that continue the work of visitation. In the midst of such honest struggles, we have become dear to one another and bonded in the love of Christ.

October 19–22: NCN Retreat at Englewood Christian Church (Indianapolis)

We were about fifty persons representing eighteen communities from Vancouver, New York, Texas and points in between, who met for a leadership retreat October 19-22. Englewood Christian Community bunked us in guest rooms, fed us lavish meals and bed-time snacks, and lovingly cared for our every need. This freed us to explore the theme, "Empowering a New Generation for Community Leadership." Many discipleship pairs, older and younger, shared what they're learning about growing in maturity in the work of community across the differences of the generations. The social, theological, and personal issues that need to be resolved in order to make authentic commitments to Jesus and to community, seem increasingly complex for each generation in this corrupt and corrupting society. Thus, the work of discipleship, we learned, is a long-term task, and the good news is that we will all be changed, mentors and protégés, into the likeness of Christ.

The really good stuff of retreats like this happens before, between and after the sessions. We were brave enough to eat burgers in the childcare center's "garden" despite a chilly, windy, sunny fall day. We got a walking tour of the Englewood neighborhood, traipsing through the yards of houses that two decades of community workdays have salvaged from urban blight to allow for the proximity that builds community. We hung out to make music, tell stories, and pass around the latest communal baby—Maggie DeLaurel. We also made some calendar decisions, launching a three-year cycle of meetings. In 2019 our leadership team hopes to encourage and facilitate regional gatherings of intentional Christian communities so that you don't have to drive more than a few hours to meet your cousins in the network. In 2020, we plan for a continent-wide "Y'All Come" kind of gathering at a place to be announced. And in 2021, we look forward to another leadership retreat. In the meantime, we're building a map of communities who know each other well and are eager for more visits. . . .

CHAPTER 18

Career Number Seven
*Si Dios Quiere**

WE BEGAN THIS MEMOIR section under the title "Seven Careers for Seven Decades." If you've kept count, we have told the story of only six careers thus far. Conventional wisdom tells me that I should now retire and take my ease. However, I remember the quip of theologian Stanley Hauerwas, who claimed, "There is no Florida in the kingdom of God." By that, I believe, he means as followers of Jesus, we don't look ahead to a bucket list of extravagant trips or a shuffle-board retirement in a gated community far from the woes and ills of the world.

At the age of eighty-three, I do feel the freedom of not worrying about the daily operations of Reba Place Development Corp., or the Nurturing Communities Network, but rather I respond occasionally when they ask for my advice. I am feeling the freedom to read late into the night if I want to, take naps when I have to, and listen to the Spirit with journal in hand each day. I have more freedom to attend demonstrations sponsored by Mennonite Action in favor of Israel's security and Palestine's liberation.. Persons going through life crises and vocational changes keep finding me. Each week I'm listening to the woes and dreams of a few younger prophetic mentees. I hope to finish this memoir, of course and then help a few of my friends write theirs as well. Basketball still keeps me young. But mainly, these days, I'm learning the practical wisdom needed for my seventh career as outlined in Joanne's ever-ready "Honey Do List"—which, * God willing, should be enough to keep us connected and me out of trouble in my old age.

Mirror # 4

Family Ties that Bind and Loose

CHAPTER 19

Thanksgiving Blizzard of 1952

Through the Snow to Sudan and Back

YOU THINK YOU KNOW about snowstorms? Well, let me tell you about the November 26 blizzard of nineteen hundred and fifty-two when I was eleven years old. After all, what's the point of enduring all the misery and hard work of growing up on a farm in the "good old days" if you can't brag about it once in a while to your wimpy, pampered city-slicker descendants?

Back in the day, brother Mark and I daily walked a mile-and-a-half to "Trainview," our one-room grade school next to the Rock Island railroad tracks. Radio weather forecasts were guesstimates in those days. Anyway, it was only November, not really winter. We knew it could start snowing later in the day, but no one expected anything like the epic blizzard that slammed us without warning. By mid-afternoon the wind picked up from the north and snow started flying at us thick and horizontal. Looking out the upwind school windows all we could see and hear was howling white calamity coming at us straight from the North Pole. The schoolhouse had no telephone to call our parents. Our teacher knew better than to send us children home in this blizzard. We would wait out this storm and let our elders figure out how best to rescue us. About two hours after the snowstorm began Robert Regier, all bundled up with thick coat, cap, mittens and scarf, appeared on a farm tractor which carried a kid-hauling lumber box he'd built and attached to the rear hydraulic lift. We young'uns who went home in an eastward direction crawled in. It must have taken him two trips because he hauled off ten children from two Regier families, the Ewerts and us Janzens. Later, we learned that the eleven west-bound children—the Dycks, Busenitzes, and the Ed/Edna Janzen families—got home by piling into the teacher's car which was pulled by a chain through the wild snow drifts by a bundled-up farmer on his tractor.

With us children boxed in the back, the tractor plunged steadily through the drifts that were piling up especially deep across the east-west roads. The kid box had some straw in it for insulation, but I remember it doing us little good as our toes and fingers soon screamed with pain and then, more worryingly, went numb. We had not dressed that morning for a blizzard like this. At the Walt Ewert farm we all crawled out and scrambled into the house. I wanted to warm up my fingers under the hot water faucet, but someone screamed at me, "Don't turn on the hot, it will scald you. Start with cold water," which I did. Eventually blood returned to our fingers and toes, a painful feeling that made us dance and cry until we could finally rejoice in digits restored. By that time the electric lights flickered and died in the Ewert house, so candles and kerosene lanterns were set out. Surprisingly, the phones lines still worked. Parents were calling back and forth, sharing the latest news and devising child-rescue plans.

Word got to us that sister Sara and brother John had been dismissed early from Berean Academy in Elbing and had driven home as far as half a mile east of town where their car was hopelessly stuck in a drift on the edge of the road. (And that's where it sat completely covered in for a week until a snowplow came through, narrowly missing it.) From their stalled car, John and Sara trudged a quarter mile north with faces into the howling wind and took refuge in the William and Elisabeth Regier home. We wondered, would we ever get home that night or would we have to wait out the storm where we all were stuck? Actually, a sleepover with lots of kids in a candle-lit house eating someone else's food didn't sound too bad.

It turned out, however, that the north-south roads were not drifted as deep as the east-west roads, so our father unhitched the International Harvester truck tractor from our cattle trailer and set out to rescue us. He managed to bust through the drifts with lots of backing up and plunging forward, until he picked up John and Sara from the Regier's. Then on the way back, he picked up Mark and me from the Ewert farm. It was kind of cozy with four kids and Father crammed into the truck cab, and the heater blowing on high. We prayed, however, that the tracks Father had made coming south would not blow shut before we got home. By the time we reached "HeckuvaRanch," it was already dark, but the cows still waited to be milked, the cattle fed, and eggs had to be gathered before they froze.

The storm dumped about a foot of snow on level ground, but on the many open fields the snow blew horizontally until it met a hedgerow, the kind that flanked most country roads, and there the snow piled up in drifts six feet deep and more. This was not the biggest snowstorm ever, but it had the deepest drifts which shut down roads and downed power lines longer than any storm since. This made farm chores a lot harder but not impossible. We stomped paths through the snow to the chicken house and cow barn, lifting our buckets high enough to get through. The horse-drawn fodder wagon had a hard time reaching the cattle feed bunks, so our F-30 Farmall tractor with a hydraulic-powered bucket on the front, plowed out the path for the feed wagon. We had to shovel snow out of the feed bunks to make room for the cattle fodder on which a herd of steers anxiously waited. We had to chop ice in the stock tanks so the cattle could drink. Each time the ax came out of the water it was heavier with ice. Stomping feet and clapping our mittened hands only worked for a while: then we'd have to duck back inside the house to revive our fingers and toes. Father trumped us complaining kids and claimed, "There are four extremities I can't keep warm—nose, toes, fingers and belly."

The next morning dawned clear and bitterly cold. The world was a wind-sculpted wonderland. I remember Mother going out with the new family slide camera, taking pictures of our row of ten-foot-tall cedar trees east of the round-top shed, snow-loaded up to their crowns. The cattle truck had swales of sharp-edged wind-driven snow that curled around it in fantastical shapes like desert dunes. And all the trees were stark studies in black and white, plastered to the top on the windward side. In later months we projected those pictures whenever out-of-state friends or relatives visited, to impress them with what we'd been through.

At the time of the blizzard, Mother already had a modern kitchen which meant we had to improvise when electric power failed. The refrigerator contents could just be stored in the back porch if we kept the cats out. The electric stovetop and oven, however, were useless, so the old kerosene kitchen stove was brought up from the basement and put back to work. Our house stayed warm as it was heated with a wood-stoked furnace in the basement. Mom experimented with baking her own bread on coals in the furnace. I remember how the loaves came out burned on one side, but they still tasted pretty good to us hungry kids.

School was canceled for a couple of days, so we had plenty of time to do the extra work that went with chores after a snowstorm, and still to improvise some snow play. We had two sleds, one a light-weight store-bought Red Flyer that Cousin Herman had lent us, and a heavy home-made sled that brother John had welded out of rigid angle-irons with runners that could not be steered. We organized ourselves for some serious sledding. Sara drove the tractor, John was in the light sled roped behind the tractor, and I was in the heavy beast-of-a-sled roped behind John. John zigzagged to make the ride more fun, and then he toppled off his sled. Sara wasn't looking back or listening to us. We both screamed at her to stop, but she kept on going long enough for me to run over my brother, tumbling him in the snow a couple of times before my sled and I passed on.

Then Sara heard us and stopped the tractor. She insisted that I should apologize to my groaning brother, but I claimed innocence because I had no way to steer my sled and miss him. I suppose I could have rolled off my sled to lessen the impact, but that had not occurred to me. Instead, I was yelling at my sister who failed to stop the tractor, and whose fault it really was for not listening. So, there we were, yelling at each other rather than caring for our brother who limped off to Mother in search of medical attention and some real sympathy. Apparently, John survived since he is still with us. In case he has forgotten it, this could be one more traumatic story of farm-life survival he can brag about to his grandchildren.

On Thanksgiving Day, which fell two days after the storm, our plan was to eat at Grandma Janzen's table, which was in her bungalow half a mile west of our farm. But mother was short a few ingredients for our share of the meal. So, father saddled up our riding horse, Dieck, rode across the fields and along the high and snow-free Rock Island Railroad track to Elbing. The telephone gossip line informed us that Klassen's Grocery store in Elbing was re-supplied by a truck that made it through from Wichita. Father came home with a sack-full of groceries over his shoulder and a far-out story of a pop truck that was stuck in Elbing because of the blizzard. All the pop bottles had frozen and cracked. Anyone who wanted could bust off the glass and enjoy a free "popsicle." Mom said she was glad we didn't live in Elbing, where we'd be cutting our lips and tongues with invisible glass shards. I still wince when I think about how tempting those popsicles were, and that I missed out on them.

On Thanksgiving the road going west from the farm was still closed with gigantic drifts. Instead, we made our way to Grandma's place in a farm wagon drawn by a team of work horses. We set out across the fields where the snow was generally un-drifted. When we got to a fence, Father cut the barbed wires, drove the wagon through, and twisted the strands back again behind us. I think we had to do that twice until we got close enough to Grandma's house that we could walk ourselves and the baskets of food to her table.

Mother holds the horses at Grandma Janzen's house.

So, what did we give thanks for? God's gift of a beautiful snowstorm plus a little ingenuity that allowed us all to sit around one table and celebrate a year of blessings together.

It took a full week for the snowplows to get to our country roads, and only then could the REA (Rural Electric Association) line repair trucks get through to hook up the busted wires and restore power. By that time, however, we'd been back in school already a couple of days. We walked across the fields and along the wind-cleared railroad tracks. The teacher could drive as close as Elbing and walk the last mile along the railroad tracks from the south. The propane tank still had gas, so the furnace worked, and we were warm. No problem.

Our favorite recess game was Fox and Geese. We tramped out two concentric circles in the snow and then added spokes like a wagon wheel. A few foxes tried to catch the rest of us geese who had to stay on the paths. If we were tagged, we had to wait in the center until some goose dashed in without getting touched and set us all free. Then when the snow started to melt, we'd roll balls and stack them up to make snow men—which activity quickly degenerated into snow-ball fights.

Then one afternoon while school was in session, we heard a distant clanking and roaring sound approaching from the west. As the noise got closer, we all went to the windows, so the teacher had no choice but to declare a recess. We all lumbered through the snow to watch a caterpillar tractor with a big bulldozer push its way down the road, lunging to the right and the left to clear a path through the drifts. If the snow drifts were six feet deep, then the ridges the plow piled up on both sides of the road were like mountains to us Kansas kids. As the caterpillar driver roared past, we cheered him on, and he waved back to us like royalty in a parade.

By that time the snow had begun to soften up, which allowed us to make perfect snowballs to throw at each other. Quickly we organized into two teams ranked behind these two high ridges of snow and started to pelt one another across the road-way gap. And then to our incredulous delight, we saw the first car making its way down the newly plowed lane. Without a word, we all hid behind the ridges and eagerly stockpiled as many snowballs as we could make. When the unsuspecting driver and his car came by, we emerged as one from the heights above and, kapow-pow-pow, we let him have it from every direction. Our teacher futilely pleaded with us, "Now children, be nice."

Later on, the driver, whoever he was we don't remember, complained to one of the school fathers and insisted that those awful kids must be punished. "They could have broken my windshield." But what can you do with all the high-tension electricity of twenty-one kids cooped up for a week by a monster snowstorm, and suddenly given release with a common project way more satisfying than fighting one another? I remember a board member coming to school the next day and giving us a tongue lashing that we hardly heard or remembered. We looked at each other and ached with the effort not to smirk or laugh out loud. Ah, that snowstorm was such glorious and memorable fun!

Oh, no, wait. That Thanksgiving blizzard was a misery we barely survived, which is what gives us the right to brag and exaggerate about it even now, seventy years later.

* * * * *

We grew up in a family with "accordion pleats" that easily expanded to include persons of other tribes, tongues, and nations. Though we were snowbound in 1952 and had to improvise a Thanksgiving meal with Grandma Janzen, often, we had holiday guests in our home from beyond the circle of kith and kin. Our farmer father who never graduated from high school, was, for many years, on the board of Bethel College, personally recruited by the College President, Ed. G. Kaufman, to represent the Prussian Mennonites of our area. Father took this assignment seriously, taking our family to nearly every play, opera, concert, outside speaker, or conference that the college might host. This amounted to a broad liberal arts education for all ages.

Other cultural exchange opportunities also came our way in that foreign students often ended up at our table at Thanksgiving and Christmas times as well. That was an opportunity for us children to lead our guests on farm tours and to invite them to join in our play. Ours was, you might say, a family without borders.

When Joanne and I joined intentional community in Newton (New Creation Fellowship, 1971), and later, in Evanston Illinois (Reba Place Fellowship, 1984), instead of lamenting our new family, my Janzen parents "came along for the ride," making friends with all our friends who were eager to meet them in turn.

In Matthew 19:48, we read about an awkward encounter between Jesus with his disciples, and his blood family who, apparently, believed he was going crazy and had come to take him home. At this, Jesus replied, "Who is my mother, and who are my brothers?" And pointing to his disciples, he said, "Here are my mother and my brothers. For whoever does the will of my Father in heaven is my brother and sister and mother."

I grew up in a family where this kind of tension did not exist, because my parents eagerly made friends with the communities we joined, not out of some strategy, but because we continued with many of the values of the home in which they had raised us.

* * * * *

WINTER, 2016: THROUGH A BLIZZARD TO SUDAN AND BACK

This evening Joanne and I took to the streets because the sidewalks were buried in fifteen inches of swirling snow. We leaned into the blizzard winds for three blocks to arrive at the country of Sudan, that is, to Habiba's apartment on Monroe Street in South Evanston, Illinois.

Forty days earlier our friend, Habiba, heard the sad news of her brother's death back in Sudan. Habiba is a Sudanese refugee from Darfur who lost her husband and many other close relatives to the genocide in her homeland. Through incredible courage and some unlikely miracles, she arrived in our neighborhood and was "adopted" by a few resourceful friends in Reba Place Church.

This evening, Habiba and a host of Sudanese friends, were celebrating the end of mourning, forty days since the death of her brother in Darfur. The apartment was filled with about thirty people, including lots of kids who overflowed into a friend's apartment downstairs.

After taking off our shoes and coats, and hugging Habiba, I was ushered into the living room where a dozen men were simultaneously praying the Koran. Habiba gave me an English translation to read as I saw fit. Meanwhile, Joanne was with the women and babies in the bedroom and kitchen where countless platters of food were cooking, baking, and assembling as if by magic. There was pungent air from burnt oil on the stove with several smoke alarms beeping unnoticed as part of the general celebratory hubbub.

I hung around respectfully for about thirty minutes in the prayer room where each one read aloud in Arabic at their own pace in a sing-song kind of voice. Occasionally one of the men would bow down, touching the floor with his forehead. I could see the prayer book was thick and everyone still seemed to be in the middle of the tome. So, I tiptoed out to ask Joanne what was happening to her plans to only be there for a token fifteen-minute appearance. Joanne was sitting on a bed talking with Habiba. Joanne assured me that she was having a great time. The women had already eaten first.

Habiba jumped up to fix me a plate of food. I was the non-Muslim white guy who could, apparently, eat whenever I wanted, prayers finished or not. She remembered I was vegetarian, so I got a plate with cooked rice, delicious baked vegetables, a stew of sweet oily eggplant mush and a bottle of water. I ate as much as I could and then we got up to leave. Habiba pressed on us a bag of fried bread balls, something like fritters. It was obvious that the period of mourning was over, and everyone was free to have a good time. Soon the men would finish praying and eat as well. Then the women would pray, Habiba explained, "But not as long as the men, because women have many other things to do." So, full of spicy food and lavish good wishes, fortified with many hugs from friends and strangers alike, we stumbled out of Africa, through the time-warp of culture shock, and back into the roaring Illinois blizzard, with the wind behind us, stomping across the swirling arctic snow back home.

Chapter 20

Lost, But Not Really Lost

One day, the year before I started grade school, I gave my family a tremendous scare, and all our neighbors too. The story begins a little after four pm, the time when my older siblings, Sara and John, would have been walking home from school. I must have annoyed mother enough that she conceived of an errand to get me out of her hair. "David, go meet John and Sara who are walking home from school." I was old enough that Mother trusted me, and the neighbors were trustworthy enough that I had permission to walk the country roads.

The usual route to our one-room grade school was a mile south and half a mile west, so I set off in that direction. I was a little surprised that I did not see Sara and John on the road, but I just trudged onward, expecting to meet them soon. I walked south past the huge half-mile cottonwood tree that the road had to bend around, past the Zion church cemetery on my right, past a ravine on the left where our neighbors dumped trash. At the mile intersection I turned west past Walt Ewert's farm: But still no brother or sister on the road. I strode on toward the schoolhouse next to the railroad tracks where I saw the teacher's car pull out and drive away in the opposite direction. On the school yard I wandered around, peered into the locked windows and verified that there was, indeed, no one "at home." So, what was I to do?

It did not occur to me to be afraid, nor did I imagine that people back home were missing me and calling the telephone party-line, alerting all the neighbors that "David is lost."

By that time, darkness was falling and I wanted to get home as soon as I could, which meant walking diagonally across the fields toward our farm yard where the house and yard lights were already shining. The hike across the fields was slow going at first since the ground had been ploughed and clods in the shadows were tripping me up. After I crawled under a barbed-wire fence, progress was easier with pasture turf under my feet. I skirted Uncle Johnny's pond on my left and saw a herd of cattle up ahead who also saw me. Out of curiosity they came to check me out. They caused me no fear because I knew there was no bull in the herd. So, I walked between them, and they graciously parted, soon following along behind me like an escort till the next fence where I bid them adieu.

From there I set my sights on a gap in the hedge row which led to our farm's driveway. I noticed cars driving slowly along the road with people shining flashlights into the ditches, but it did not occur to me that they might be looking for a "lost David." I walked through the hedge gap, down our driveway, and opened the gate to the fence around our house. Upon hearing the gate clatter, sister Sara saw me and shrieked my name. "David, you're home. Where have you been?" Soon the word got around by phone that David had come back safe and sound. A few neighbors dropped by to verify with their own eyes that "the lost" was indeed "found." I wondered what all the fuss was about, since, as I insisted, I'd never been lost at all. I always knew where I was, and the path back home was never in doubt.

I was puzzled, however, by the fact that I never did meet up with my sister and brother. It turns out that they decided to walk home north along the railroad tracks with cousins Herman, Edna and Doris, and then a half-mile east to our ranch. Who knew?

I remember sitting at supper, which the family ate late because they had been out looking for me. They peppered me with questions about where I had been and why I did not consider the fright I had put everyone through. I could identify with the twelve-year-old Jesus who hung out safely in the temple, communing with the elders the way I had been communing with our local geography, and all the while our families were frantically looking for the lost boy, who was never lost at all.

After supper my mother, who was still trembling with fear, asked me to come sit with her in her recliner chair, and there she wrapped both of us up in the same blanket. Perhaps she remembered sending me on this perilous errand. With tears in her eyes and sobbing in her voice she said, "David, I thought I'd lost you. It is so good to have you back." Together we soaked up the comforting warmth of a long and snuggly moment together.

My impression of Mother from those years is that she was often upset with me because I was a lot of restless energy for her to handle in a season of life when she already had two older kids to manage, a toddler to run after, and an endless list of urgent chores to keep our household and garden running. But this one memory lets me know that I was beloved and that I too had a deep place in Mother's heart.

Now in my old age I take naps wrapped in a patchwork afghan handstitched by my mother—something like she gave to all her children. And if I'm feeling emotionally needy, I can still wrap up in her blanket and hear her say, "David, I thought I'd lost you. It's so good to have you back."

Chapter 21

Lessons our Piano Taught Us

About Pride, Humility, and Solidarity

Mother took my older sister Sara and me to our first piano lessons with Victor Klaassen. It was at Berean Academy where Sara was a freshman at the time, and where Victor had been hired to shape a few miscellaneous instrument players into a fledgling band. Mother wanted all her children to attain competency at the keyboard so we could play piano in church, accompanying hymn singing, something she had found meaningful in her youth and early adult years. I must have been about eight years old at this time, only beginning to read music. Sara's trial lesson was scheduled first to see if Mother felt confident to enroll her three oldest children under Victor's tutelage. Victor began by citing his credentials, including that he was proficient in half a dozen instruments and was just a few hours short of completing a master's degree in music. Victor had Sara play a standard hymn, which she did—adequately.

At that point Victor took the keyboard and played the same hymn with all the flourishes thrown in, swelling to a prodigious crescendo that could have filled an auditorium.

Victor turned to mother and triumphantly announced, "I can teach your daughter how to play like that!" In that moment Victor noticed how Mother's physique had turned rigid and her demeanor icy cold. After a long pause she announced, "We don't believe in showing off like that, not in church or anywhere else." Suddenly a cultural and theological chasm had opened up between us, down which someone was about to plunge headlong.

Though Victor Klassen had a Mennonite-sounding name, we knew he attended the Assemblies of God Church in Newton, whose sign listed the pastor right next to Victor as music director. On the other hand, we were General Conference Mennonites, who worshipped with a deliberate simplicity and reserve. After a moment, both Victor and Mother began to apologize profusely to each other. Neither one wanted to lose the opportunity for us children to have a personal teacher who could help us grow in musical proficiency.

Our family had always benefited from a piano in the house which Mother loved to play on the few occasions when she had the time. It was a sturdy upright Gulbransen originally built as a player piano. But those player-piano guts had long ago been eviscerated, leaving behind two sliding doors that we could open to observe the live action of hammers and strings any time we wished. My assignment was to practice piano a half-hour every day, either before evening farm chores or after supper. I was supposed to play each piece ten times so I hurried through them as fast as I could.

Saturdays, oh my, that's when I was supposed to practice a whole hour. I remember hurrying through my pieces twenty times, and then every five minutes I would rush outside to move the garden hose to water another one of our newly planted Austrian Pine trees, happily knocking out two tasks at once. That probably explains why I turned out to be an efficiency expert rather than a musician.

Eventually, Sara continued with weekly lessons from Mr. Klaassen at Berean Academy. while older brother John and I rode with mother to Newton on Saturday mornings. We took our lessons at a grand piano in Victor's parlor while mother went shopping. Each Saturday morning, tucked in our lesson book there would be a $15.00 check from Father to Victor Klaassen for these three lessons. Five dollars for a half-hour lesson seemed absolutely extravagant to me in those days. I doubted that I could ever make enough progress to be worth it. But taking piano lessons had other fringe benefits.

I could read classic comic books from Victor's coffee table while John took his lesson. Then Mother would drop us off at the Newton Carnegie Library where we'd pick up four new books each week to take home, adding some adventure into our work-a-day routine of chores on the farm. I made slow progress at the piano, never getting beyond John Thompson's third level book. Each year we prepared recital pieces and practiced them *ad nauseum*—and Mother professed to enjoy them all!

Eventually our family acquired a used church reed organ that was powered by push pedals. We moved it into the parlor beside the piano. I was surprised to learn that my farmer father could play that organ. Then he showed me an old photograph of himself taking lessons on the Bethel College chapel pipe-organ from the esteemed Bethel choir director, Walter Hohmann. Who knew? So, on the occasional rainy Saturday when father had to stay inside, he played the organ and I played the piano, as we worked our way through the hymn book in a rough duet.

Soon Sara also took up the cello and John picked up the French Horn, which instruments we purchased from Dickie's Music Store in Newton, according to Victor Klaassen's recommendation. Father innocently asked Victor if he got a commission for referring us to Dickie's. Victor was greatly offended at the suggestion that any sordid kickbacks might have been involved.

Years later, Father showed me a letter from Victor, whose conscience had stricken him to the point of confessing that, yes indeed, he had been given a commission from Dickie's from the sale of John and Sara's instruments. I was a little surprised that Father included me in this little morality play. I think he wanted me to be wise to the way the world sometimes works, that people can't always be trusted to tell the truth, but even so, they can be forgiven.

My progress as a pianist stalled out after about four years of lessons. I never was good enough to play hymns for the Sunday school opening service at church the way Sara and John had done before me. When I asked Mother if I could quit taking lessons, she reluctantly agreed. I think I redeemed myself in her eyes some years later by marrying Joanne, a pianist who could accompany church singing whenever needed. Between the two of us, our average ability was quite respectable.

Joanne at the piano, bringing up the family average, leading singing with granddaughter (Jaden) and friend (Carol Richardson.)

Now I'm pondering the lessons Mother tried to teach our family about not using music or any other skill to "show off. Taming young egos to be respectfully aware of others was, of course, Mother's goal. She taught us humility, to never gloat over our triumphs. In my childhood, I remember hearing more than once the German proverb, *"Eigenlob stinkt"*—"Self-praise stinks."

At the same time, Mother felt deeply the glory of music well performed, and was transported to seventh heaven by hearing the Bethel College Chorale under the direction of Walter Hohmann, or Madrigal singers led by Elvira Voth. I remember our whole family, trooping to Lindsburg, Kansas, to hear the Swedish Lutherans at Bethany College sing the whole Messiah. We followed the music in a thick volume that displayed all the orchestral and vocal parts in a score that mother treasured from the days when she sang in such a choir. She coached us to all to stand up when we got to the *"Halleluia Chorus."*

I observe that in our family, there was a gradual decline in musical talent from Sara on down to my younger brother, Mark.

Once I quit music lessons, Mother stopped those Saturday trips to town. Mark eventually was persuaded to take some piano lessons from Thelma Andres in Elbing, driving himself three miles to town in the farm pickup, even though he was only twelve years old. Then one day, well before he got a driver's license, Mark skidded off an icy patch in the rutted road, ran the right front wheel up a fence post which gently laid the pickup truck over onto the driver's side in the ditch. Mark had to push the heavy passenger door up and out to escape. Shaken up, he ran to the home of his teacher who called the farm to announce the accident. With farm tractor and chain, we tipped the pickup back on its wheels and drove it home. Not long after, Mark's teacher unselfishly advised our parents that with Mark they were not getting their money's worth, which marked the sorry end of piano lessons in the Hilda and Louis Janzen family.

Somehow, when our parents' possessions were dispersed, the piano ended up in our home. As an adult I am grateful for the lessons I got and the pleasure it has given me to sit at the piano from time to time, playing some of the works within my range. I think the high point of my piano career may have come when twelve-year-old Natasha and I worked up a father-daughter duet for her piano recital. My part ended with a glissando that stopped on the highest C of the piano. Many generous people commended me after that performance. Their praise was a bit like marveling at dancing elephants at the circus. It's not that they dance so well, rather, the wonder is that they can be trained to dance at all.

James and Natasha had both taken lessons, so when we moved from Newton, Kansas, to Evanston, Illinois, to join Reba Place Fellowship in 1984, the piano came with us in a U-Haul truck. Before the move I had carefully measured all the passageways and determined that the piano could indeed make it into our second-floor apartment dining room—but just barely. So, with the help of a huge crew of Reba Place Fellowship volunteers, we took off the handrail to the stairs, and slid the piano over a bed of planks making a smooth incline up the steps. To keep the piano from sliding back down between pushes, we used a hefty rope that was wrapped around the kitchen radiator and held taut by two mighty anchor-women, Joanne Janzen and Char Oda. At the top of the stairs, we had to take the house door off its hinges, somersault the piano on its end, swivel it 90 degrees, and catch it as it fell through the entryway.

After all those years our piano and its movers taught us one last lesson—it was never, never, never, ever going to leave our dining room at 726 Seward again—which is one reason why we have enjoyed its company right here in the Reba Place Fellowship neighborhood, without a single thought of moving for the last forty years.

* * * * *

This seems like a fitting place for a wisdom-seeking digression into the topic of ambition with its intimate connections to humility and pride. James K. A. Smith, in *On the Road with Augustine: A Real-World Spirituality for Restless Hearts*, takes a robust view of ambition, claiming that the opposite of ambition isn't humility, it is laziness, failure to exercise one's gifts, doing inferior work rather than the best we can, poor stewardship of the influence that people naturally accord us, fear of leadership when that is what others need of us. Jesus observes that to those whom much is given, much will be required. We are accountable for what we do with the gifts God has given us.

Is that all Jesus has to say about ambition? Actually, Jesus does not bless all ambition as virtue. It depends on the end for which it is exercised. "You know that those who are considered rulers of the Gentiles lord it over them, and their great ones exercise authority over them. But it shall not be so among you. Whoever would be great among you must be your servant, and whoever would be first among you must be slave of all." (Mark 10:42–44)

The disciples were arguing about who among them was the greatest. In an ironic twist, Jesus does urge them toward greatness—not the greatness of conventional wisdom that amasses power to lord it over others. Rather, they are to compete for greatness in the direction of servanthood. Otherwise, ambition serves self and reinforces the status quo of privilege and injustice.

From 2008 to 2018 my work was primarily visiting intentional Christian communities as a trouble-shooter and a mentor of community leaders. In this ministry I was surprised by how often I was thanked and praised for my wisdom. It's what polite folks apparently say to people with grey hair who spend most of their time listening. But it bothered me that their attempts to honor me, and my awkward response, drove a subtle wedge of unacknowledged feelings between us rather than bring us together in thanksgiving. By that time in life, I had curbed my impulses to brag, or to dangle my accomplishments for others to admire. But, in some more subtle ways, I was like my mother, and what I resented in her turned out to be a lot like my own struggles and temptations.

How, I wondered, did Jesus deal with praise? As I studied the matter, I saw two strategies. "A certain ruler asked him; 'Good Teacher, what must I do to inherit eternal life?' Jesus said, 'Why do you call me good? No one is good but God alone.'" (Luke 18:18-19) Jesus, too, was uneasy with praise because he knew that the gifts he exercised had their origin in God and not in himself. Thus, praise did not stick to him, but was passed on to God, something, it turns out, people could agree with him on.

Jesus' second strategy was revealed in his encounter with the woman who touched the hem of his garment and was healed. "'Daughter,' said Jesus, your faith has healed you. Go in peace.'" (Luke 8:48) Jesus is careful to show how this healing was an exchange of God's power and the woman's faith—something everyone could humbly celebrate.

Though people mean well, there is something alienating about being put on a pedestal. In visiting other communities and listening to their troubles, I learned that when people praised me for my wisdom, I did not need to deny that something wonderful had happened between us. But I could reframe the moment the way Jesus did, acknowledging that this holy and liberating moment we shared was the fruit of God's spirit hovering over a conversation where everyone's gifts and experiences came into play, and by reflecting on that exchange, wisdom emerged. I had just provided the summary. That was something we could celebrate together in spirit and in truth.

The fulfillment of ambition that our hearts long for does not come from basking in others' praise—that actually increases the distance. Rather, it comes from recognizing that the goodness of this holy moment is a collaboration of God, you, and me. It was meant by God to bring us all together for a shared joy. And in that space, we can confess our needs and brokenness in simple honesty; and in that moment the Spirit shows us a common way forward to greater maturity and joy. Joy comes, not from victory over someone else, but from being real with each other, and then God shows up with the wisdom we need. This is what I've been learning, and it is good news.

* * * * *

Did we ever resolve this tension between Mother's wish to be proud of us, her children, and our awkwardness at playing that game? You decide. Here's an extended excerpt from an e-mail I sent to our daughter, Natasha, and her husband, Ingo Ulbricht, from September 25, 1999:

> "I'm in Kansas for a week, hoping to visit mother each day around 4:00 pm in the Kidron-Bethel Nursing Home when the aides suggested she would be most alert, right after her nap.
> Thursday (9–16–99) I found her sleeping in her wheelchair. The only words I got out of her were a mumbled, "Good morning." I rolled mother outside hoping the fresh air would stimulate her. She opened her eyes a few times, but I don't think she recognized me. Later, back in her room I read to her from the first chapter of her autobiography, *Madame Queen*, and a few phrases caused her to smile with recognition. I just held Mother's hand for a long time and reflected back to her my memories of all the kitchen work, gardening, children bathing, music and art these hands had produced, now gnarled with arthritis and trembling with Parkinson's Disease. I gave mother a few kisses and said goodbye. It seemed like her ability to communicate was almost gone. Perhaps a little more goes in than comes out. Last Christmas Mother was grieving the loss of her ability to read, that her world was getting so small. Now, I think, Mother is more at peace. I'm glad I have a few more opportunities to be with her.
> On Friday Mother's eyes lit up with recognition when I said, "This is your son, David." I rolled her outside again and she peered toward the light. I asked if she enjoyed the sun. She said, "The sun never shines here in Russia." It seems her memories, stories from childhood, imagination and dreams all can run together. Back in the room I gave Mother a piece of chocolate and told her it came from Natasha in Germany.
> Later I sat right in front of Mother's wheelchair and she got playful, touching my nose and stroking my face as she giggled a little. I felt as if she were playing with a two-year old child. Then I asked if she still served corn candy. Her face lit up and she remembered, "They served corn candy at Natasha's wedding."
> Monday brother John and I went for a visit with Mother who was most stimulated to have two of her sons there at once. John asked to take some photos, which pleased Mother up to a point. After about six flashes she said, "That's too much attention."

I tried to tell Mother about her grandchildren, James and Natasha, but she looked past me without comment. Then she announced, "Let's go parade in the corridor." So, two sons and their mother rolled through the building, passing through doors without punching in the codes, and setting off alarm bells as we rolled on, causing people to look at us as mother, no doubt, hoped they would. When we stopped to talk with the new CEO of the retirement complex Mother interrupted to tell us about her arts and crafts items in the Kidron residents show case. Soon she said, "Let's go back."

Back in Mother's room John read a poem Mother had written in 1984 on the "Aura" of a tomato plant in her garden. Mother smiled several times in recognition of a phrase or image. At the end she said, "That's when I was at my best." Soon mother's eyes began to droop, and she fell silent. We rolled her to the supper table where the residents were beginning to gather, and an attendant took over.

John and I talked about how a person's senses gradually fail in old age, but character persists. Mother's pride in her children used to irk us—having her leave our books and dissertations on the coffee table so that her friends would have to bring up the subject. Now her wish that we "Parade the corridor" doesn't bother us as much. In fact, we were a little proud of our mother at 92 years. God has forgiven us a lot by now and we can forgive our mother, too.

Mother is declining in her strength and ability to communicate, though her basic health seems steady. Tomorrow, I have to return to Evanston. This may be the last time I'll see her in this life.

Mother doesn't talk much about God or the afterlife the way our Grandmother Janzen used to do at every occasion. But with Mother there is a lot of gratitude for the family she was given and for the chance she had to put a couple of decades into art and other forms of creative expression after her children left home. Her trust in God is assumed, received, nothing to be anxious about. She is in good hands.

* * * * *

Hilda Gertrude Neufeldt Janzen made it into the new Millennium, passing into glory during her sleep at the Kidron Bethel Nursing Home on March 13, 2000, at the ripe age of ninety-two.

CHAPTER 22

Climbing, Jumping, and an Unforgettable Pain in the Butt

AT THE AGE OF four my farm-boy peers and I entered into a joyfully obsessive climbing and jumping phase of life. We liked to hoist ourselves up fences, hay racks, and trees to view the world from on high, and then to jump down on the other side. The front steps of our church were an ideal place for boys to dare each other to jump from "higher than thou," and then land squat on the sidewalk below. Our parents, of course, forbade us, warned us that we could hurt ourselves, and they threatened to spank us if they ever caught us doing it again—which meant we returned to the site with spies posted at the corners of the building to warn us of any parental appearances. Their dire warnings also meant that if we sprained an ankle, skinned our hands or banged our knees, we would never admit it. So far in my young life, the exhilarating flight of zero gravity was more than worth any bad landing that followed. In any case, the painful landings taught us how high was too high, unless, of course, someone dared us, and then more pain was still worth a higher climb and a longer flight to glory.

Then one day my parents noticed that I was walking with my left leg pointing outward at a funny angle, so they took me to a chiropractor who pulled on my thigh and manipulated my hip until I walked straight again. Both the chiropractor and my parents warned me against jumping off high places, which I took that to mean "Don't do it when they are watching."

Late one afternoon on the farm I noticed for the first time how the east wall of our shop made a potential ladder up to the ceiling. That's where Father had built ranks of storage bins for nails and bolts of different sizes along with other assorted supplies, which, of course, I had to climb and explore. Each row of bins had a facing board nailed across the bottom that

I could easily grab to pull myself up another level higher. Hand over hand, step by step I climbed to the top where I discovered a moment too late that the top ledge was covered with an accumulated layer of dust which my hand grabbed and then slowly slipped off, toppling me backwards through the air to the concrete floor below, where I impaled my right buttock on the corner of a one-inch angle iron that formed the base of a grinding wheel.

"Yeeaauuww!" I screamed and ran crying to the house, where Mother pulled down my pants and examined my punctured and bleeding butt. She washed the wound clean, put on a temporary bandage to stop the flow. Then from the back door she called Father in from his chores to take me to see Doctor Tate six miles away in Peabody. We had all heard about the funeral of another Mennonite boy near Newton who had recently died of tetanus poisoning from a scratch by a rusty nail, so Mother was taking no chances.

By the time we got to Peabody, Doctor Tate's clinic was closed for the day, but he consented to leave his family supper table and meet us downtown anyway. In those days small town doctors would still do favors like that. I don't remember what all the Doctor did to my behind because, well, it was behind me, and I couldn't see any of it while lying face down on the leather-covered examining table. I supposed from the poking and pinching on my rear end that the Doctor gave me a tetanus shot and sewed up my most recent posterior body opening.

By that time my heinie was so inflamed I could barely walk, so Father carried me down the stairs to the car. On the drive home I waited for Father to reprimand me, or to spank the other buttock when we got to the back porch where a paddling stick sometimes leaned against the wall. I was, after all, the cause of a most inconvenient and embarrassing trip to town. But none of that happened. Instead, when we got home, Father carried me over his shoulder into the house. We noticed that supper was put away, the house was dark, and everyone else had gone to bed. Father surveyed the scene and suggested, "Why don't we eat some corn flakes," his favorite box cereal. When I sat down on the hardwood kitchen chair, I cried out in pain. So, Father found me a pillow from the living room and carefully lifted me onto it, which made everything all better. When the corn flakes box was empty Father continued, "I'm still hungry. How about you? Would you like some ice cream?" Of course, I would.

Then Father brought up the topic I'd been dreading. "You know, David, you weren't supposed to climb like you did. That was a bad fall. You could have smashed your head. You had Mother really worried. Do you think you've learned your lesson?" Eagerly I nodded "Yes," and felt a wave of relief wash over my body followed by a sudden love for my merciful Father. Then he lifted me onto his shoulder and carried me upstairs to the bedroom, helped me carefully pull down my pants and put on my pajamas so that nothing touched my bandage. He tucked me under the covers, listened to my prayer, and said goodnight. I drifted off to sleep fondly remembering the intimate hours I'd shared with my father rather than trauma as the dominant experience of the day.

I told this story recently to our housemate, Eric Colbert, who grew up in a single-parent family on Chicago's Southside. He said, "If that had happened to me, when we got back from the emergency room my mom would have whipped me to an inch of my life just to make sure I'd never do such a thing again. That's the way us kids on the Southside were raised."

I asked Eric, "Would a whipping like that have prevented you from climbing and jumping again?" "No," he acknowledged, "It would only make me more rebellious. We did things way more stupid than that."

I reported that my father had whipped me for many other things—some of which I deserved. But mostly I don't remember them. It's this one time when I didn't get spanked that I remember most, along with a few times when Father apologized to me for losing his temper and whacking me in public. I suppose those moments are why I remember my father with love and forgiveness.

I asked Eric, "Do you remember your mother with love?" "No," he answered. She had me when she was only seventeen. I think she felt too oppressed by life to have time to love me."

At that time, Eric had a seven-year-old daughter named Angel. She lives with her maternal grandma where Eric often visits. I asked Eric, "If Angel ever comes to live with you, will you give her whippings when she misbehaves?" "No," he said, "She adores me too much right now to misbehave. But when she is older and if she ever gets into trouble, I'll for sure . . . ." Then he paused and added, "You know, there was one time when my mom didn't punish me. When I was a teenager, before I knew how to drive, I snuck into our car with the keys and went for a joy ride which ended in a really bad crash. My mom was going to beat the daylights out of me until she saw the car which was totally destroyed. At that moment all the fight went out of her, and she melted down because she saw she had almost lost me. I think that's how I'd want to treat Angel if she ever does something bad. Maybe I'm learning a different manner of doing things than the way I was raised." Later Eric passed on a bit of folk wisdom he'd heard: "Holding onto anger is like drinking poison and expecting the other person to die."

It's amazing to me now how a small act of mercy from my father, and grace from Eric's mother, could make waves big enough to lift our boats out of the muddy and angry river of life and onto the dry shore of forgiveness even now, thirty and seventy years down-stream.

CHAPTER 23

Father Teaches Me to Survey Terraces

And Join the Fifth Agricultural Revolution

ONE DAY WHEN I was about ten years old, Father recruited me to help survey a field for plowing terraces. I was excited because surveying involved math, geometry, and engineering—subjects I hoped to master one day.

You may have heard that Kansas is as flat as a pancake. True, some places in Western Kansas are so flat you can look down a railroad track and see the curvature of the earth as grain elevators progressively sink out of sight over the horizon. But in middle eastern Kansas where we lived, the landscape had a gentle roll that could quickly erode if a "gully-washer" rain fell on fresh plowed land. Father explained that we were sending tons of fertile soil each year down muddy rivers all the way to the Gulf of Mexico. Most farmers didn't worry about that because the topsoil was still deep enough to grow another crop. But Father had a longer-range view as a steward of God's good creation, and for that reason was one of the first farmers in our area to terrace fields. The whole idea of terraces, Father explained, was to slow the rain runoff enough that it dropped its sediment, and the water left our land running clear. I felt privileged to learn both the spiritual and practical wisdom of the farming profession as stewardship from my father.

But before we could survey the land, I needed a little training. This wasn't precise surveying like laying out legal property lines or setting building foundations. Janzen standards for this task were "good enough." Father had me practice a manly stride of exactly three feet per step alongside a tape measure. Then he handed me the surveyor's measuring rod, something like an eight-foot ruler. He taught me how to hold the measuring rod exactly vertical, making sure I placed it on an average plane of dirt—not on a clod or in a hole. After that, father set up his surveyor's transit on a tripod on the uphill edge of the field. The transit was something like a telescope that could be calibrated to exactly on the level, and with the crosshairs of the scope he could read the marks on a measuring rod up to quarter of a mile away.

Now we were ready to begin. First, we took a siting of the measuring rod right next to the transit. Father wrote down the height and we pounded in a stake. That was our starting number. Father set me up with a canvas bag of stakes slung over my shoulder, a mallet, and the measuring rod. With this outfit he had me step off one hundred feet and hold the measuring rod straight up. Then Father took a sighting of it. If the ground was too low, he'd signal me to walk uphill in an imaginary 100-foot arc with the transit at the center. Eventually we'd find a spot at the right level and Father would give me a thumbs-down sign, and there I'd pound in a stake. Our goal was to set a line of stakes across the field such that each stake was 100 feet farther and 3 inches lower than the previous one. So, guided by hand signals from Father, I marched across the field laying out the contours of one terrace after another. In a few days Father would plow the contours of the stakes into sinuous terraces that let the water flow gently downhill to a grassy waterway where the tight turf could handle an occasional flood of water without erosion. In fact, these grassy waterways caught the soil runoff from our neighbors upstream at each big rain. Father used to look at those wide slabs of freshly arrived dirt and marvel at the short-sightedness of our neighbor and of the poor stewardship of the land that God had entrusted to him. Father's soil conservation ethic has stuck with me ever since.

*   *   *   *   *

So why didn't I make farming my profession as Father had hoped? The moments of hanging out with my father and learning from his integration of spiritual and practical values, as conveyed in this surveying story, were rare, and not the dominant theme of my growing up years. I think Father's main concern was to make sure I behaved and would turn into a responsible adult. I did not have the sense that my own spiritual journey—what went on in my own soul, was of interest to him or the other adults I knew as a child. Though Father and I had a bond, it was not a soul connection. I decided early on that I would need to learn about life as a self-directed independent study with occasional conversation with my peers. I felt an early need for what some people call emancipation.

I remember working on the farm during one college summer break. By then, I'd learned how to plow a field while reading a book, guiding the tractor by the feel of the steering wheel as the right front tire followed the furrow. And as I drove endlessly back and forth under the hot summer sun, I happened to be reading *The Myth of Sisyphus* by the French philosopher, Camus, who contends that life is inherently devoid of meaning, and yet, we are fated to keep searching for it. Camus compares the absurdity of human life with Sisyphus in Greek mythology, who was doomed to repeat forever the same meaningless task of pushing a boulder up a mountain, only to see it roll down again. That's what lonely farm-work had come to mean for this melodramatic philosophy major in his existentialist phase of life.

What happened to move me beyond Camus' conclusion that life is absurd? Here, in short form is the short answer I came to in my college years. I can acknowledge that the world as a given does not have any meaning in it. It is just so much data. But faith is to life what a good hypothesis is to science. Faith is like an action plan that when you try it on, it reveals an order and a meaning that the data of life confirms, but never would have suggested on its own. The truth is that we never have enough data to make life decisions in a timely way. We usually operate on spiritual intuitions that come to us, mostly from the more credible people around us whose lives abound with joy and meaning, especially if they have taken an interest in us.

In college I did find a few mentors whose lives were bright with joy and meaning, and who took an interest in my own spiritual development, which is a story already told in Chapter 4, on mentors in my life. But to answer the question Camus posed—his thesis about the absurdity of life—this was refuted for me by the presence of mentors whose lives were full of joy and meaning, and by a spiritual encounter with Jesus that ignited a conversation that has continued to this day. Logically speaking, one fully alive person refutes the argument that life is absurd and meaningless.

* * * * *

But the farm was still in me, as was my interest in farming more generally. I recall visiting the farm after I'd moved to Chicago, and feeling pangs of regret that one by one, the old landmarks were disappearing. First the old breezy cow barn was gone, then the horse barn with the basketball goal on the south side, then the spruce trees that I had watered as child were dying of blight. Now, in recent months, the windmill and the silos have come down. How could "they" do this to me, obliterate the anchors of my childhood memories? The pain I feel at the disappearance of childhood landmarks tells me how deeply they were rooted in my soul.

But what did I expect? That others would preserve our farm as some kind of museum for an occasional nostalgic visitor from the city? I find comfort in writing and reading all these farmer-boy stories to my city friends, which they applaud at our community variety shows. The rural childhood I shared with half the world in my early days, is now exotic, ancient, even legendary in the retelling, and somehow deemed more authentic than the memories of those who grew up in town.

Maybe, since I cannot live on HeckuvaRanch and tend its landmarks, it is my job to write up these stories and make them as true as I can remember. Thank you, dear readers who by your kind attention, console me in the slow, painful, and inevitable loss of my childhood farm.

* * * * *

Father, I have learned, was taking our farm through its first steps into the fifth agricultural revolution that is gaining the name of "Regenerative Agriculture." I've been reading about it in a book by a popular geologist from Oregon, David Montgomery called *Growing a Revolution: Bringing our Soil Back to Life* (Norton & Co, NY, 2017). Montgomery champions the profitability of soil regeneration as a viable future for the world's farms and farmers. Montgomery reviews the history of farming revolutions on this planet. The stages go something like this:

1. **The Neolithic revolution** began about 7000 years ago in multiple river valleys around the world—China, India, the Fertile Crescent, and the Nile of Egypt. Humans left behind the precarious life of hunter-gatherers and began growing their own grub by hand and with animal power, which created the food surplus that gave rise to cities, diversified professions, and empires. This way of producing food spread to the rest of the world and continued largely unchanged in Europe and America through to early modern times.

2. **Scientific Farming:** In line with the Enlightenment, revolution number two began in England in the 18th century, leading to improved techniques with university-based farm experiments and academic training of agricultural experts.

3. **Mechanical farming** using steam, and later diesel-powered equipment, this constituted revolution number three. Our farm completed this transition in my childhood as the use of tractors gradually replaced horses for draft power. Tractor powered threshing machines had been in our family line already a hundred years, by then.

4. **The Green Revolution:** This fourth phase gave us enhanced seeds and chemical fertilizers that have doubled food production around the

world. One result of these revolutions has been the steady erosion of soil and impoverishment of the lands that remain. Vast areas of the earth that used to support farming have turned into deserts. With conventional farming, farmers have little control over the inputs of agri-business—GMO seed, fossil fuels, chemical fertilizers, and an increasing need for pesticides. Then, when farmers want to market their products, again they have no control of the prices at which they sell their goods. Industrial-scale farming is taking over; the food we eat is increasingly synthetic and unhealthy. It is a dead-end business of soil and farmer depletion.

5. **Regenerative Agriculture:** The fifth revolution is what Montgomery's book is about. It's a grass-roots farmer's movement that is learning how to increase carbon storage in the soil by no-till agriculture, working with the underground sources of microbial fertility using cover crops, manure recycling, and minimal outside inputs. Regenerative farming improves the soil as well as crop production with local inputs, and gives farmers more control of their bottom line.

Since we all must eat, the wider society has a stake in this fifth revolution because it sequesters more carbon, slows global warming, and reduces the use of fossil fuels. The author maintains that the amount of food produced by conservation farming increases as soil fertility improves and can match the productivity of the Green Revolution.

I like this approach because it is not righteously dogmatic like some permaculture zealots who aim for zero fossil fuels, for example. The goal of conservation farming is to improve the quantity and quality of the soil, and improve the lot of farmers, on which all food production of the earth ultimately depends.

I see a spectrum of ways to feed the world. On the right are the huge corporations of agri-business with their monopolies on GMO seeds and petrochemical inputs that have the power to maximize crop yield this year, but the consumer does not pay for all the real long-term costs. They are heedless of durable soil fertility, sustainable quality of life for the family farm, environmental impact, or global climate change.

On the left end of the spectrum is the permaculture movement of idealists and purists who visualize a pesticide and herbicide-free, post-fossil fuel way of farming. They promise that mobile chicken pens, animal traction, underground microbial-fertility networks, or some other magic bullet will result in a good life for farmers and their families. Someday it will feed the world, restore the watersheds, slow climate change, and build community—in other words, be a permanent solution to all our farmer problems.

But I've noticed that few of these idealists are actually making a sustainable living from farming apart from niche products, educational grants, book sales, or outside jobs.

In the middle of this spectrum are the actual farmers whom David Montgomery is interviewing and who are, in the overview of his book, pioneering a way to survive both this year and long-term, who care about building up soil fertility for the next generation, who aren't purists but who are moved by a conservation ethic, who care about the environment and are willing to make experiments with minimal tillage, drip irrigation, targeted fertilizer inputs, etc. But what they are not willing to do is to bet the whole farm on one new radical innovation that could fail. These farmers benefit from both the right and the left-hand sides of this spectrum in different ways.

I think the idealists need to let go of their self-righteous purism and make friends with farmers in the middle of this spectrum for a journey of mutual learning and blessing. In this regard, the local churches, made up of actual farmers, and intellectuals only a generation or two removed from the land, can support a new kind of venture that connects with farmer's markets, schools, urban congregations, and people generally who are hungry for a wholesome and sustainable way of life that honors God and creation, of whom we are all dependent children.

* * * * *

What difference does it make that this nostalgic farm boy in the city, this weekend gardener, this intellectual who reads Wendell Berry and David Montgomery—what difference does it make what a city-dweller like me dreams about the fifth agricultural revolution? I've had the privilege of being on the board of Koinonia Farms for twelve years as the spiritual descendants of that famous theologian in overalls, Clarence Jordan, moved their pecan orchards away from chemical pesticides toward organic production. They have turned their exhausted plowed-up soil into pastures with rotational grazing. Their extensive organic gardens are feeding a multitude of visitors. All these transformations have made Koinonia Farms an area leader and teacher of this fifth agricultural revolution.

Koinonia Farms begins the day with prayers and communal work for members, volunteers, and short-term guests.

Likewise, I was on the committee that supported Plow Creek Fellowship as an older generation folded their communal life and gave their houses and lands on to Hungry World Farm, a new non-profit that is extending the Plow Creek vision of sustainable farming and education about healthy food to another generation in the region.

Meanwhile, at the Janzen Family Farm Corporation, of which Joanne and I are stock holders, my brother John, in his semi-retirement years has led our family farm into organic certification, production of grass-fed beef, and independent marketing.

Though it is from a distance, I have had a hand in three boards that moved three farms into the fifth agricultural revolution. Though I have made some contingent changes away from the farm, the continuity of values has been strong. I believe my father would be proud of what his son has done with a day of surveying lessons back in 1951.

Chapter 24

Driving Cattle to the Kansas City Stock Yards

and Proposing with Manure on My Boots

For weeks I looked forward to the day, bragged about it to my school mates, and reminded my teacher that I'd be missing school because I had to drive a herd of cattle with my dad to Kansas City Stock Yards. Of course, this wasn't a 19th century overland cattle drive with lonely cowboys moving a thousand longhorns, followed by a chuck wagon and a cloud of dust. We drove these cattle in a semi-trailer truck, 1950's style. I was probably a third grader the first time I went.

On the night of our departure, I hardly slept at all, waking at every noise in the house until 3:00 am. That's when I heard the distinct sound of my father's farmer boots hitting the floor and then his quiet call up the stairs so as not to wake my siblings, "David, it's time to get up. I need your help to load the cattle." It took me less than no time to get dressed, pull on my coat, and step out into the sharp winter air. Jiggers, our farm dog, was eager and ready for a familiar cattle-moving routine.

Next to our cattle pens a semi-trailer was already backed against the inclined loading dock, ready for a score of fattened beef cattle to walk up the plank to their final destination. It seemed like the cattle could smell the scent of death in the air and would not move toward the truck until Father and Jiggers began to yell and bark, driving the herd, a few at a time, up the chute. My job was to urge them up the last steps onto the truck with an electrified prod called a "hot shot," and then to prevent them from coming back out. Jiggers and Father persuaded one group after another to get on the truck. Finally, father looked at the load from above the cattle rack and discerned, there's room for one more. With Jiggers nipping at his heels, father twisted the last animal's tail until he squeezed in, and I dropped the gate. I wonder now if this scene of panic-stricken, bellowing pandemonium had anything to do with my decision some twenty years later to become a vegetarian, a way to honor the souls of every living creature.

Solemnly father and I climbed into the truck cab and bade Jiggers goodbye. Father looked at his watch and announced, "It's 3:30—five hours to Kansas City, unless you get hungry for breakfast." He stared up the big engine in the International Harvester tractor, whose heavy rumble drowned out the noise of cattle complaining behind us, and shifted into first gear. I was intensely curious about everything mechanical, and father was eager to help me learn what this truck could do. One day, he hoped out loud, I'd be ready to drive cattle to the stockyards myself.

In first gear we pulled away from the loading chute. In second gear we drove across the farmyard. In third gear we hit the township dirt road and picked up speed. Once we got onto the black-top highway to Peabody, we ventured into fourth and fifth gears, galloping across the plains and down the hills. But fourth and third gears were needed to climb the grades without lugging down the engine. The five gears forward and one in reverse, could be doubled, father showed me, by pulling out the red over-drive button on the side of the gear shift lever. Ten speeds forward, and two in reverse—wow! That stuck in my mind as something worth bragging about when I'd get back to my school mates.

This cattle truck and trailer belonged to my father and his brother, Uncle Johnny, who together made at least dozen trips a year to the Kansas City stock yards, plus many other local runs for gravel, sand, lumber, grain, and hay bales. The thirty-foot trailer was as big as any on the highway in those days, though now most are at the 58' maximum allowed.

At that time there was no inter-state highway system, so Kansas Highway # 50 ran down the main street of most cities we passed. Peabody, Florence, Strong City, Emporia, Ottawa, Gardner, Olathe—a string of towns each with their own character and stories which father told me as we rolled though in the dawning light. Outside Emporia we halted at a truck stop alongside other semi-trailers. Father got out, whacked all the tires with his cattle herding cane to check the air pressure. Then we climbed up the stock racks to see if the cattle had organized themselves into a peaceable array and that everyone was standing. We used the restroom. Then, passing the pop machine I begged Father for a soda, but he thought that was a ridiculous idea for 5:00 in the morning.

Soon we hit the highway again. My job, Father reminded me, was to keep the driver awake. So, I talked until I ran out of topics, and began to ask questions. Where were the Flint Hills? Between Florence and Ottawa, Father explained, we were in Flint Hills territory, a swath of stony land that ran north and south across the state of Kansas where the rock was too near the surface to admit a plow. Thus, by default, the original prairie grass was preserved much like the Indians and the buffalo had known it. These hills were ideal now for grazing cattle in one-mile-square plots bounded by barbed wire fence. The land rolled between tree-lined valleys, up long hills that required lots of gear shifting, and then high plateaus where the truck could gallop at top speed.

For many miles the highway ran parallel to the Santa Fe railroad tracks. I was startled to see a passenger train passing us, its rotating Mars light slicing through the night, followed by a couple of diesel engines and passenger cars with half-lit windows, mocking our fifty miles an hour as it sped on ahead. Then half an hour later the same train passed us again having stopped to let off passengers in the town between.

Father showed me the wordless language of signals that other truckers understood. You were supposed to dim your headlights to greet an oncoming driver and to not cast glare into his eyes. When you passed a slower truck, the other driver would blink his headlights to let you know it was safe to return to the right lane. If an oncoming truck repeatedly blinked its lights, beware! A highway patrol car was waiting just over the hill. I was excited to learn about the trucker's subculture, in which, it turns out, my father was at home.

By the time we approached the small towns surrounding Kansas City it was already full daylight. Father asked, "Are you hungry for breakfast?" "Sure enough," I said. So, he pulled the cattle truck with its bellowing cargo alongside a diner in the little town of Gardner. Inside, a grizzled cook behind the counter named "Mister Morris" greeted father by name and asked, "Now who is the little truck driver with you?" Mr. Morris slapped a menu before me, which I scanned until I saw "pancakes," and made my order. Father and I proudly sat side-by-side on the swivel stools, two truck drivers waiting for breakfast. Impulsively, I tested my stool with a body spin. Father reminded me, "Truck drivers don't do that."

Soon a stack of steaming pancakes landed in front of me. Father put a hand on my shoulder, leaned forward with eyes closed, and offered a whispered prayer, giving thanks to God for safety on the road and for the good food before us. Between tending to other clients "Mr. Morris" teased me about playing hooky from school and about eating a lumberjack's share of pancakes. He joked to me in parting, "Don't let those big mean stock-yards cattle eat you up." I swelled with pride when he added, "Mr. Janzen, you've got a fine boy there." Every year, I begged that we stop for breakfast again at Mr. Morris's diner in Gardner, Kansas.

Coming into Kansas City, Father told me to pay attention to the route, passing over viaducts and under railroad tracks in a bewildering series of turns. "One day," he reminded me, "You'll be driving cattle to the stockyards, and you'll need to remember the way." And then we were there, facing a row of unloading chutes just like the one we had at home, only here there was a score of them with a host of trucks maneuvering for position. Father picked a vacant spot and told me to stand exactly three feet over from the chute so he could line up the truck trailer through his side mirror. Then he expertly jockeyed the truck into position on the first try. (Back at home on my toy farm I practiced the same moves with my miniature cattle truck until I knew the backup routine by heart.)

We lifted the tail gate and the cattle eagerly bolted into the relative freedom of a maze of alleys in a vast city of wooden fences and stock pens sufficient to hold tens of thousands of animals each day. Father yelled to the stock yards attendants, "These will be sold by Pracht and Company," the agent who handled our cattle sales to the colossal meat packing plants on the far end of the yards. Father and I followed our cattle to their pen, carefully avoiding the piles of steaming hot manure in our way. We checked to make sure the cattle had fresh hay and water to regain the pounds they'd lost on the trip, and to settle down their panicked spirits. Truck travel is stressful for cattle who often come down with shipping fever the next day. But for these cattle there would be no "next day." Just to settle our own spirits and reconnect with the cattle one last time, we sat on top of the wooden fence and surveyed the scene. Then other stockmen would recognize Father and fall into long conversations about their farms and herds. I was impressed that Father had a reputation as a stockman with good judgment about the selection and care of animals that other farmers wanted to learn from.

Soon a stocky Jewish peddler came down the alley with an insulated box slung from his shoulder. He was crying in a sing-songy voice and a Yiddish accent and his own brand of humor: "Ice cream. Ice cream. I'ff got vite ice cream und chokolat ice cream. I'm out of chokolat. Vat you vant?" I waved him down while father dug into his pocket for some change. We each got an ice cream bar and returned to our perches high up on the plank-topped fence to survey our animals one last time.

This truck load of cattle represented the labor of boys, hired men, father and his brother's crews; growing feed, tending animals through every kind of weather, concentrating the energy of the whole farm into this form of four-legged wealth. We surveyed our pen-full of animals eagerly eating hay and sating their thirst in this small corner of a vast cattle city. There we ate our "vite ice cream" with the satisfaction of a perilous journey fulfilled.

Soon the stock yards attendants opened the gate and moved our herd down another alley and up a wide chute to the scales where they were all weighed in. Then they moved on and out of our sight, on to the slaughterhouses where they would soon be turned into hamburger, steaks, and roasts. In exchange, we took the weight receipt to a six-story office building next to the truck parking lot where Pracht and Company had their headquarters. Before long we exited with a check. Our cattle were deemed top grade, weighing in at 1,300 pounds per head, fetching a better-than-average price of 37 cents a pound. I carefully did the math in my head. We were going home with a little over $8,000. Back in our pens on the farm there were four other truckloads of cattle waiting their turn. All told, that seemed like an immense sum of money to me in comparison to my weekly allowance of twenty-five cents, "If you've been a good boy." Of course, I did not need to pay for hired men, cattle feed, vet bills, machinery, and everything else that a family of six might consume. So, after a little more reflection, I was glad to let father take home the check and keep his responsibilities.

On the way back to "Heck of a Ranch" we stopped at another restaurant where the waitress also knew father by name and asked, "What kind of pie will you have today, Mr. Janzen." Mother did not make pies, so this was our chance to catch up on an accumulated deficiency, with ice cream on top.

The road home was more boring, perhaps because we were tired and the drama of delivering cattle was behind us. By the time I was fourteen years old father was likely to say, "I'm tired and need a nap. Are you ready to drive?" Of course, I was ready. It was my turn to double clutch on uphill shifts and mesh the gears with just the right pump on the throttle. It was my turn to blink the headlights to let a passing trucker pull back into the right lane. I realized with great satisfaction that my headlight signals were respected just as if I were an adult. I tracked the trucks behind me in the mirror and looked far ahead to gauge just when I would need to shift gears on the next hill. As my father slept to my right, I was mastering the skills he had demonstrated for me over the years. I realized that a bond had grown up between us of which we never needed to speak. He trusted me and I wanted to make him proud. On these trips to Kansas City, I learned that he was an important and respected man to many people beyond our little world around the farm. Somehow, without knowing just how, I gained a lot of confidence to face the world because I was a son of the stockman farmer, Louis Janzen.

* * * * *

That, however, wasn't the conclusion of my trips to the Kansas City Stockyards. By the time I was college age I was driving the truck to Kansas City on my own. The trip that I remember best was also my last. In late May 1964, I invited my sweetheart, Joanne Zerger, to accompany me and a load of cattle to the Kansas City stock yards because I wanted to share with her the memories of all these epic childhood trips with my father. Without incident we made it to the stockyards, unloaded the cattle, and let William Pracht's men negotiate their sale.

Then Joanne and I had a day before us in Kansas City, touring the city in a cattle truck. Our best idea was to visit the Nelson Art Gallery, which we did only to discover that it was closed because of an extended Memorial Day weekend. So, with our smelly truck parked in the Art Gallery lot, we lounged around on the grand sweeping lawns overlooking the city beyond. And as we talked, we came to the conclusion that now was the right time for us to get married. I officially proposed to Joanne, and she accepted my offer. We decided that, on getting back to HeckuvaRanch we'd tell my parents and hers that we were engaged, and that we hoped to get married in September. A few days later we agreed on a diamond ring.

Whether riding to Kansas City with me in a smelly cattle truck impressed Joanne or depressed her, it let her know something real about my character and upbringing. Of course, no young couple knows what troubles and joys they are marrying into, but Joanne knew she was marrying a philosopher with manure on his boots, someone with big dreams but also the skill to double-clutch and downshift as needed on the uphill climb of life. And the rest, as we say, sixty years later, is history.

CHAPTER 25

Marrying a Stranger

As a child, I enjoyed the attention of Grandpa Neufeldt who could be a joker and a tease. Once he beckoned me close and confided, "You know, Grandma married Grandpa, and your mama married your papa," then he lowered his voice and added, "But did you know that when you grow up, you'll have to marry a stranger?" What a shocker! That idea took me a while to swallow. The thought of living alone, like some bachelors we knew, did not appeal to me. And I realized I could not forever live with my mama. I'd have to make a family of my own someday, so I looked around to see how this might happen.

In high school I dated a few girls I found attractive, but my social life was cramped because the family car was usually not available, and driving the farm pickup on dates was very "not cool." In college I had more options, but even then, I was usually short on cash and could not impress girls with my lifestyle since, in those days, Brother John and I shared the use of a modest VW "Bug." Still, I did have fun getting to know girls, but none of the relationships became serious, perhaps because I was not serious enough myself.

Then in my senior year at Bethel College, on a trip to Washington, D. C., I had a spiritual awakening as part of a delegation of students who fasted and picketed for three days in front of the White House. We were protesting atmospheric testing of nuclear bombs. I felt God breaking through to this alienated agnostic with a strong sense of calling, which, if translated into audible words might have said, "David, this is the kind of prophetic work I'm calling you to." I had my reservations because I saw many other peace activists righteously motivated by anger at injustice, but their alienated stance seemed to me like a lonely path to burnout. God spoke to my objection by adding, "I will be with you and will give you a soulmate and a community who can share life and uphold you in following a radical peace-making Jesus."

While we were in Washington, I phoned back each evening to the Bethel campus connecting to the peace-movement group who had stayed behind to carry on the witness against nuclear testing locally. The voice on the other end of the line was Joanne Zerger. We'd known and dated each other a few times before then, but this marked a turning point for us both in our friendship; curiosity became serious interest. We could imagine a similar life vocation as peacemakers in Christian community.

During the following two years, while I was at Harvard Divinity School, and Joanne finished her Bethel college degree, we wrote letters daily. Our letter writing was a lot like journaling, a way to pour our thoughts and experiences into someone else's "listening ear." By the end of those two years, we thought we knew each other well.

Elsewhere (chapter 24) I've written about proposing marriage to Joanne on a memorable cattle-delivery trip to Kansas City, getting married three months later on September 4, 1964, and the next day, beginning life together as graduate students at the University of Kansas.

We were married in the Eden Mennonite Church, September 4, 1964.

From the beginning of our marriage, Joanne was often overwhelmed by the feeling that life had too many fragments that "didn't fit together." Was the problem our life together? Was it graduate school? Was it feeling lost as a new homemaker, since she'd never lived alone, apart from her family home or college dorm?

It turned out that I knew a little more about cooking than Joanne did, so I didn't mind taking the lead in the kitchen. My mother had taught us boys how to cook, "So that you won't get married to avoid starvation." Over the years of our marriage, I've made our breakfasts, and usually helped in the kitchen when we had guests.

Gradually, Joanne learned to cope with her times of panic and feelings of fragmentation by two strategies: One was for me to listen till she got to the bottom of her fears, thereby breaking their power. Then she could trust me to help make a plan going forward. For this support, she was invariably grateful and loving. Her second way of coping was to meticulously chronicle the events of each day, and journal her reflections, making a discipline of giving thanks for each gift to counter the downward pull of discouragement. Over the years, these ways of coping have taken her a couple of hours most days but have proven indispensable for her mental and emotional health.

However, I should not give the impression that all our life adjustments were grim struggles. We still loved being with each other and embarked on many adventures to keep life interesting. Despite the undertow, our youthful vitality powered us through many trips, camping adventures and cross-cultural encounters. Our life with a growing circle of friends was rich and satisfying. We continued our peace movement involvement, protesting war taxes, the nuclear arms race, and racial segregation.

In graduate school, Joanne soon realized that excelling in school thus far, while somewhat gratifying, had also been a dutiful way of pleasing her dad and her teachers. Despite a full scholarship for Ph.D. study in English Literature, Joanne never actually read literature for its own sake or for personal enjoyment. Her heart was drawn more to marriage and a life shared with friends in our immediate community of peers, the Lawrence Mennonite Fellowship. Joanne usually had only one way of doing a task—careful attention to detail, no matter how long this took. I was better at time estimates and concise summaries, helping Joanne adjust plans to meet deadlines. Together we finished her papers even as she lent her skills as a careful proof-reader for my writing. After two years of grad school, three years with Mennonite Central Committee, and a year back at the University of Kansas finishing up her program, Joanne, greatly pregnant with our first-born, passed her oral exams and gained a master's degree in English Literature. It felt more like a deliverance than an achievement.

The time with the Mennonite Central Committee began in 1966 with a year of language study in Belgium and France, and then two years of teaching at the secondary level in a village Christian school in the newly independent Democratic Republic of Congo. These were rich and rewarding years of significant learning and service. Joanne taught English as a second language, and I taught whatever gaps needed to be filled—mostly math, and history. Our marriage worked well; we were set free by a cook-housekeeper to focus on our teaching endeavors, and we received much practical help and appreciation from those around us.

Alongside her teaching, Joanne volunteered to serve protein supplements to malnourished children at our Bibanga hospital.

From the beginning, we were determined to have a marriage of equality, different from some of the patriarchal assumptions of our home communities. Mutual submission and consensus-building conversations seemed to work well in our relationship through the time of our return to Newton, Kansas, from Congo and while Natasha (born 1970) was our only child. But once we adopted James (at 15 months) and Natasha was a two-year-old, Joanne quickly felt overwhelmed. At the time we were living in a larger communal household, part of New Creation Fellowship. Our children loved the extra attention and additional playmates of our community. I was glad for the closer companions, but this was a time of intense and complex relationships and growing stress for Joanne, who is more of an introvert. The feedback from people who shared life with us helped untangle our marriage issues to see what agenda each of us had to work on.

Our intentional community, New Creation Fellowship, assessed our growing crisis and stepped in with help. We returned to a less complex single-family life at 418 W. 10th and focused on our immediate family. I was encouraged to quit my work as community organizer on prison issues, which took me away from home more of the time. Instead, I got a job as a local carpenter. The community invited a younger member, Bernard Regier, to move in with us and help us with the need for more childcare. Bernard became a life-long "family member" and "uncle" to our children.

Bernard Regier joins our family from 1980 to 83, as support and instant "uncle" for our children. Mac enjoys lapdog status for the photo moment.

In addition, Joanne and I met every Thursday evening with Jake and Irene Pauls for marriage counseling, encouragement, and prayer. And the community provided a Friday night babysitter so we could have an evening out. This strategic community focus literally saved our sanity, marriage, and family, for which we give thanks to this day.

In 1984, when our children were in middle school, we took a leave from New Creation Fellowship for a "sabbatical" year at Reba Place Fellowship. This turned out to be a permanent move. Joanne, with the help of a Reba community friend, landed an ideal job at Northwestern University as a Library Assistant. There she could work in a quiet, well-ordered environment where her gifts for detailed attention flourished. Our family befriended many of the foreign students whose work Joanne supervised. And with the move to Reba Place, Joanne began meeting with John Lehman, who gave generously of his time and attention as a wise and experienced counselor, often on short notice in times of stress. John also helped identify the "primal wound" which, we came to see, was a likely source of Joanne's recurrent emotional distress.

As a newborn, Joanne was raised according to a (short-lived) theory from child development experts. They convinced pediatricians and new parents that infants who got fed and held only on a strict four-hour schedule would "tough it" out to become more resilient, individuated, and creative adults. After a few months of Joanne crying in one room and her mother crying in another from heartbreak and, counter to all her maternal instincts, Joanne's mom broke down and began to feed and cuddle her baby whenever needed. But severe damage had been done. It turned out that most of the infants who were strictly raised on this theory (many of them in orphanages) ended up institutionalized for life. They never learned to attach to their care givers, nor could they feel secure, trusting that their needs would be met. We thank God, Joanne's mother was inconsistent in her application of this highly-touted but ghastly child-rearing regime and gave it up completely after six months. More than once, with a heavy heart, she confessed to Joanne, "I wish I could have done you over."

In her times of panic, many times Joanne has suggested that I should "find a better wife." But that idea never made sense to me. God had called us together in the first place, and I never heard God change the plan. There is a proverb that says "If you want to go fast go alone. If you want to go far, go together." My personality was geared to go fast. I was good at fast estimates (like most carpenters) and quick judgments (which is about the same as being judgmental). In our times of crisis, I sensed that staying close to Joanne, loving her faithfully, and listening to her whenever she needed me, might change my character for the good, even though it painfully stretched my soul. Slowing down and listening to Joanne taught me to listen to others, too, which has allowed me to befriend and pastor many other people as well. Staying with Joanne, I discovered, could make me wise—not because Joanne would say wise things, but because this path promised to infuse us with the wisdom of Jesus who gave his life for us.

When people are haunted by suicidal thoughts, therapists will ask, "Do you have a plan?" If they say, "Yes," then it is time to take them to the emergency room and commit them to psychiatric care. Similarly, hopeless as Joanne might get about her ability to hang onto life and marriage, she never had a plan to actually "check out." When she said, "You'd be better off without me." I'd reply, "If you ever leave me, I'm going with you." Somehow, that comment broke the spell and allowed us to laugh and make a U-turn before the abyss of hopelessness.

For thirteen years (1984 to 1997) when Joanne was a library assistant at Northwestern University and then Skokie Library, I was the house husband, doing the shopping and cooking, and meeting our children when they came home from school. That worked out because my job with the Overground Railroad was at a Reba office only two blocks away, and as the director, I could arrange my hours as needed. Usually, when we hosted guests, Joanne and I would share the kitchen work until the guests arrived. Then I'd entertain them until she had the food on the table.

By 1997, Joanne laid down her library work because of health challenges and the call to care for others. Joanne went back to Kansas to be with her mother over the final month of her life. Though deeply exhausting,

Joanne found this opportunity, to give and receive love to the very end, as a mysterious balm to her "primal wound."

Our marriage has had key support from quarterly retreats when we get away together from interruptions, review our journals, take long walks in nature, and listen to the Spirit. Our relationship has not been symmetrical—day to day I've done more listening than has Joanne, but these times of retreat allow both of us to report what is going on in our souls and to make plans for the coming season. Joanne's attention to details is a gift to us both, as is my ability to listen to Joanne's many lists and discern an overall direction that seems Spirit-led. Usually, around New Year's Eve we take a retreat where I might assemble 200 cards with high-quality photos cut from National Geographics and Sierra Club calendars. Over the course of the next year Joanne sees that we send off about that many birthday greetings and messages of encouragement to a long list of friends.

Joanne's empathy for others who suffer is a gift that stems from her own life struggles. She has had a hard time completing larger projects because the distractions of basic life maintenance always seem to intrude. Nevertheless, a dozen times a week, this introvert with a strong drive to get life under control, will take initiatives of generosity, delivering gifts of food, cards for special occasions, messages of encouragement, or spontaneous bouquets of flowers from our yard. She is acutely aware of both relational and systemic injustices in this broken world, and constantly looks for ways to bless her less privileged neighbors and friends. She often feels like a failure compared to her professional prospects coming out of college. But that was when she was still a stranger to herself. Her mission as a wounded healer has no status in the world's eyes, but it gives meaning to the days and softens the hurts that come to us all. It's what can be done when not much else is possible—except to make friends and show them love however and whenever the inspiration strikes.

* * * * *

Journal, 8 June '07: One of the ironies of Joanne's character is that she works so hard with lists and schedules and detailed journal entries to plan an orderly and self-protected life. But then things blow up, people in need bring their problems her way, and she succumbs to compassion. Despite her best efforts at getting life under control, she is becoming a "saint."

Yesterday, without advance notice, a distressed friend dumped a seven-year-old child into our hands. This has happened before. But God gave Joanne grace right there in the middle of Seward Street to receive the child and then call on me to make a plan for the rest of our day. That involved us taking turns. I got the child for three hours to prepare supper and do other chores—exactly what the child enjoyed—being in the middle of adult action. More grace given. By the time we returned the child back to the caregiver, we still had the long list for Friday afternoon shopping to do that evening, when we had planned a date. Joanne confessed, "I'm going crazy with fatigue," and began to slump into a puddle of helpless confusion. I assured her of my love and promised that God will see us through. Joanne chose to believe me rather than her own crazy-making feelings. And so it was that we got home late with all our groceries and collapsed into each other's arms. What a crazy, wonderful, affectionate, broken, holy woman!

* * * * *

Since our arrival in Evanston in 1984, Joanne has been legendary in our neighborhood for a couple of reasons that deserve elaboration. Some people refer to her as "The Bicycle Lady."

Joanne, the "bicycle lady" on her way to work at the Northwestern University Library, ca. 1990.

Her old Schwinn three-speed, with coaster-break and wide seat, is Joanne's "pick-up truck." Her ever-present bulging red backpack can haul up to thirty pounds when the bike's side pockets are full. To stay physically fit, Joanne bikes anywhere within the city of Evanston to run errands, redeem coupons, meet doctor appointments, deliver food to friends, or shop for what we need.

Joanne is also famous for her "More with Less" frugality and generosity with food. During Covid we didn't serve a lot of guest meals. Joanne, however, is the local queen of free food distributions. Here is how it works. Our community mate, Nina, likes to dumpster dive and visit the back doors of local produce markets where she hauls away loads of free food to what we call "The Manna Garage." There the goods are stored in a refrigerator or in big animal-proof plastic cannisters. A baker friend and neighbor, Kris, also blesses our Manna Garage with day-old deliveries of otherwise pricey, award-winning bread from Hewn Bakery. Both the rich and the poor of the neighborhood can come by and load up.

Joanne knows a lot about who needs this food and will make deliveries to her friends who are too busy or too disabled to get out and harvest "manna" for themselves. And, of course, Joanne brings home exotic treasures for our table that we could never afford in the store. The food we get isn't perfect; it is more like the produce that came out of our garden when I was a child, when we used to cut the good stuff away from the bad stuff and process it in bulk. In solidarity with the poor, our Reba common treasury gives each member household a food allowance based on what used to be called "Food Stamps," but now is a "Link Card." However, Joanne's food ethic saves us an amazing amount of money each year, which we are happy to donate to needy neighbors and good causes around the world.

* * * * *

How can I sum up this relationship of over sixty years between Joanne and me? So many times, we've almost not made it—but just as often we have been transformed by the gift of love that outlasts all the forces of fragmentation, despair, and sin. We see that other marriages around us have ended in bitter divorce, the death of a spouse, or cold-hearted resignation. Why have we been spared? This has nothing to do with any virtues we might possess. It's true that we have been loved from all sides by a faithful community of family and friends. Apparently, our job is to humbly give thanks for those gifts, enjoy something together each day, and return home from the latest retreat willing to try again, trusting that God's grace will be sufficient for every need.

David and Joanne together in all weather.

Now that we're grey-haired and still together, people ask us, what is the secret to a long and, ultimately, satisfying marriage? We might say you need to recognize that your spouse is not like you. Therefore, try to listen in terms of the other person's experiences rather than projecting your own. Restate often what you hear until you get assent that "Yes, that is what I meant."

We've heard the advice "Don't go to bed angry; Talk it out." That didn't always work for us because the more tired we become, the more likely we are to blow up or melt down. Instead, we take some quiet time apart to figure out what we each can apologize for. And then, usually after a night's sleep, we return to the conversation when we are rested and more centered, to apologize and forgive.

One marriage custom that's worked well for us is called "couch time." We take half an hour each morning to share our feelings, make a few plans, and cuddle as we offer a prayer for one another and those on our minds. Unity of heart often leads to unity of bodies and spirits, something God, apparently, delights in. Joanne calls this "fore-prayer." We've noted how our sexual relationship closely mirrors the quality of our communication.

Our friend, Eric Colbert, used to take us up on our standing invitation to drop by for breakfast and Bible study at our kitchen table. However, ever since the beginning of the Covid epidemic, we've connected at 8:15 AM by speakerphone to read through some book of the Bible, a few verses a day, and then tell each other stories from our lives that reflect on the same themes. Invariably, we see that God has been with us both in the study time and through the day, showing us how Jesus is with us as he promised, to grow in our lives what we have studied together.

We could go on with more lessons we're learning, but lessons don't get to the heart of the matter. Life wisdom cannot be reduced to a few principles that we can grasp once and then routinely follow. Life has contradictions where intellect fails, exposing painful tensions that can only be bridged by love beyond understanding. Mysteriously, Joanne and I are still strangers, and we are still in love. Faithful suffering through the hurts of life has not killed us. Rather, it has widened our hearts more than we thought we could bear, and that's where we've found the truth confirmed: "The light shines in the darkness, and the darkness did not overcome it." (John 1:5)

CHAPTER 26

Natasha in War and Peace

Intuiting the Condition of Souls

IN 1960, AT THE restless age of nineteen, I was stuck on my parents' farm to earn my next year's college tuition by plowing several hundred acres of stubble following the wheat harvest. It was July; every day the sun burned away the clouds and the temperature soared above 100 degrees. Rather than fry my brain, I chose to plow at night and sleep the day shift in the cool basement shade, and plow through a few more chapters in Tolstoy's *War and Peace*.

Like an invisible camp follower, I witnessed and survived the War of 1812, Napoleon's epic invasion of Russia. But as a budding philosopher and historian, I was also enthralled by the various theories of history that Tolstoy marshaled like toy soldiers, battling with arguments to see if he could make sense of all that humans suffer in the throes of so-called history. In Tolstoy's telling, world-stage actors like Napoleon (ever the brilliant tactician), and the Russian generals (stubborn and proudly inept) were entangled, with their swarming millions of troops, in immense and tragic consequences—but never the consequences that anyone intended. In the end, Napoleon was defeated by Moscow set on fire, by the Russian winter, and the immense capacity of the Russian people to suffer. However, within the details of this vast tapestry, in the stories of a few families and their wartime travails, we meet an array of lovingly portrayed characters who, despite their many sins, eventually discover a peace that outlasts war.

So, all night long, as the tractor rumbled across the fields turning over infinite rows of clods and dust, I turned over Tolstoy's ideas, raising dust-clouds in my mind as I pondered the epic past and my imminent future: "Would I throw myself into historic world-changing events, or would I take the humble path of small-scale and unseen service where peace is built from the ground up?" Isolated for a summer from any real social life, I was also captivated by one of Tolstoy's characters, Natasha, who, from a great distance in space and time, somehow won my lonely heart.

As is typical of thick Russian novels, our hopes for Natasha rise and fall with every twist of the convoluted plot. As a thirteen-year-old girl she goes to an opera and, instead of getting caught up in the music and drama, she only sees the painted cardboard stage props, the fantastic costumes of the actors—and finds the whole spectacle false and pretentious. Natasha has a crush on a dashing prince, an army officer whom everyone agrees is destined for greatness, but the war takes him far away and her heart is broken. Meanwhile, Natasha's family arranges an engagement with another officer who goes to battle, disappears, and then is discovered in a wagonload of mortally wounded soldiers returning to Moscow. Natasha and her fiancé's sister nurse him through his final days. Natasha's vitality and infatuations lead to heartbreak, to suffering, and to an early wisdom about life and people.

Meanwhile an older friend of Natasha's family, the widower, Pierre, is captured by French soldiers who proceeded to execute the five men in line ahead of him. Then, without apparent reason, they postpone his death and thus forget about him because soon the French army is fleeing a burning Moscow that could not sustain them through the Russian winter. Later, when the liberated but deeply shaken Pierre told Natasha about his French captivity, she "understood precisely what he meant to convey . . . but also what he could not express in words."

In the epilogue of *War and Peace,* seven years after the horrendous dislocations of the War, Natasha and Pierre are married and at home with little children playing underfoot, talking "as only a wife and husband can talk, that is, grasping thoughts and conveying them to each other with extraordinary clarity and quickness, in a way contrary to all logic."

So, you see why this lonely farm boy fell in love with Natasha that summer. And to remember the love that blessed my solitary days, I resolved that if ever I should marry, and should we have a daughter, we (whoever that "we" might include) would name her "Natasha."

Indeed, two years later I was in a serious relationship with Joanne who was "Okay" with the name "Natasha." But starting a family would have to wait until after a few more years of graduate study and voluntary service in Africa.

Ten years after I conceived the name, on the 9th of October, 1970, Joanne was eight months pregnant (or so the doctor thought), but Natasha was full-sized and ready to join our family and take on the world. That night, as we sat through the wedding ceremony of two friends, Joanne secretly squeezed my hand every few minutes while I timed her contractions. Later, all that good-looking food in the reception hall triggered a sudden urge for Joanne to eat in case she needed the strength for a long labor, and so we downed our share before we hit the road. Then hard and frequent contractions made us wonder if there were more miles between Hillsboro and the hospital at Moundridge, Kansas, than there was time. Doctor Loganbill was most casual, meeting us at the emergency room door with his jogging-suit on, and after glancing at Joanne on the examining table, decided he could finish his run and change before the baby came. Twenty minutes later he returned just in time to catch Natasha. I was at Joanne's side the whole while, something the doctor permitted for the first time in his career because, in those days, no husband ever asked him for the favor.

When I called Joanne's parents that evening to announce the birth of their first grandchild, Grandma Zerger responded to Natasha's name with an incredulous "Na-what?" But they came to love her as soon as they saw her, as did my family too. The name soon lost its foreign accent and exotic connotations, and our Natasha just became who she was.

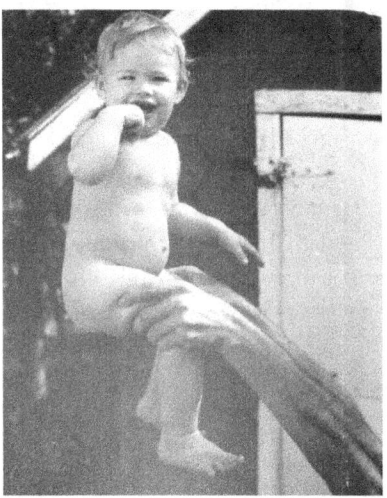

Baby Natasha, ready to take on the world.

When Natasha was a sophomore in high school she spent a pivotal year living back in Newton, Kansas, with our friends, Gordon and Jeanne Houser, at New Creation Fellowship. Natasha missed her Newton friends and the Housers welcomed her as a live-in babysitter and teenage helper. During that year of relative autonomy Natasha made some adult life decisions, choosing her own church youth group at Faith Mennonite, and then deciding to be baptized. Natasha never needed to experience the prolonged phase of rebellion and foolish choices that some of her Evanston peers pursued. Upon her return to live with us in the last two years of high school, Natasha felt the freedom to talk with us as an adult, giving and receiving counsel in ways that sometimes instructed us, her parents.

Natasha graduating from her parents' alma mater, Bethel College, in 1991.

Natasha spent her junior year of college in Germany where she met Ingo Ulbricht in a Baptist Church youth group, which led to marriage a couple of years later. For most of their family life they have lived in Berlin, except for a couple of years serving with the Mennonite Central Committee in Akron, PA, and fifteen months serving in Zambia as educators.

Now that Natasha is in her fifties, I'm wondering what ontological connections might link the character of Tolstoy's Natasha with the one God gave us. Actually, there are more resemblances than we have a right to expect. Our Natasha has an exceptionally buoyant spirit and a level head—in both war and peace. She is attracted to what is authentic, however humble, and ignores what is false, however mighty. Natasha has the gift of intuiting what others are feeling and speaks to their souls as well as their ideas. Faith has transformed life's hurts into early wisdom. She is a thoughtful listener who, without any titles, pastors those around her and, on occasions, her parents as well.

A memorable example of Natasha's ability to discern the condition of souls around her came to us in this story. Her oldest son Tobin was, at the time, grounded for some misdeed. Tobin and his deviously inclined friend schemed how they might snag a couple of cans of soda from the pop machine across the street.

Tobin's friend urged him, "Let's go do it. No one will ever know."

Tobin responded, "No, my mom will find out."

The friend countered, "How will she find out?"

Tobin answered, "I don't know how she knows these things, but she always does."

Meanwhile, on the other side of the wall, over-hearing the proof of what Tobin was saying with her own ears, Natasha danced and pumped her fists in silent exclamation, "Yes! Yes! Yes!" Our daughter could hardly wait to share this minor triumph of parenthood with us on her next call.

When I shared an earlier draft of this essay with Natasha, who at the time was living with husband and two boys in Zambia, she responded with a new factoid about her name and a speculation about how the Russians might have acquired it. "I have learned that here, in the Bemba language, my name means 'thank you.' People are often surprised that I have a Zambian name. I ask if they know that it is a Russian name. I wonder, maybe the Russians came to Zambia and took the best names back with them."

Someday, when Tobin is ready to fully appreciate his mom, I'll tell him the story of her name and how her gift of intuiting souls came along with it. Then he can complete the circle and say, "Thank you," or "Natasha," back to Tolstoy.

Natasha's family in 2019 includes husband Ingo Ulbricht, sons Noah and Tobin, plus Asim Hasani, an Afghan refugee who joined the family as a foster son in his late teens.

As of 2023, Natasha and her husband, Ingo Ulbricht, live in Berlin, Germany, with three grown sons, Tobin, Asim, and Noah. Tobin and Noah are home-made and currently enrolled in local universities. Asim, a refugee from Afghanistan, joined the family at the age of seventeen as a foster child. Following the death and disappearance of his parents he arrived in Berlin at the age of sixteen after a harrowing trek with a few friends across eight national boundaries on foot, hidden in trucks, and by boat on the Mediterranean Sea. He is employed in retail sales. Ingo teaches high school Math and Computer Science. Natasha supervises practice teachers at the Free University of Berlin where she is completing a Ph.D. program in linguistic pedagogy.

Chapter 27

James

A Calling to Rescue the Underdog

"Leo was scared of everyone and everything when he came home with us from the animal shelter." Leo lies with his head on our son, James's, shoe, looking up at his face from time to time to assure himself that his rescuer is still there.

Leo is an eight-week-old Bernese pup with electric grey hair that stands out like an Afro all over his body. His paws are already huge "fists," letting us know he'll become a massive adult, able someday to carry that iconic cask of whisky on high Alpine trails to rescue and revive snowed-in travelers, as his did his legendary ancestors.

James continues with Leo's story. "He's still easily scared because he did not get much love before he was separated from his mother. The animal shelter is not like a quality dog breeder's kennel, where they hope to sell well-trained, pure-bred dogs for a thousand dollars and more. Leo is a big project in building trust."

"By now Leo is eager to communicate with me," James continues, "I just have to 'get' what he's saying. When he lies down by the door, I know he wants to go outside to pee. I clip on his leash, and we tumble down the stairs to go for a walk. He eagerly pulls me wherever we've been before, but not beyond that. If I try to take him into new territory, he'll whimper and balk. Coming over here to your house, where he's never been before, I had to carry him in my jacket. If I do that he settles down and licks my face, letting me know that he's grateful and submissive. But he doesn't always obey—he already knows he'll be a big dog one day and put other dogs in their place. Given all that he eats, I'm going to make sure he's a working dog who earns his keep. I can look forward to the day when he's going to pull my supplies wagon with all my fishing gear plus a tent, table, and chairs. The works!"

"So, why did you pick Leo?" we asked.

"He was the runt of the litter; a little smaller, and he had one ear that flopped the wrong way. He doesn't have exactly the pure-bred Bernese Mountain Dog coloring either. I knew the others in the litter would be chosen, but probably not Leo, so I wanted to give him a home.Joanne and I reflected on the tender heart James has always had for strays, perhaps because he remembers the story of his own adoption, son of an African American father and white mother, coming to our house at the age of 15 months after many moves from one foster home to another.

James continued, "Leo is happy in our home, but insecure. I still sleep with him on a blanket on the floor. Jaden (James and Emily's daughter) thought he looked like a little lion with a ruff of fur standing out around his collar; so she named him Leo."

Joanne and I could not help but marvel at the symmetries between James and Leo's stories, and how James is now passing on this amplified tenderness to a dog who is learning the kind of courage it will take to one day, like his ancestors, rescue lost travelers in the worst of conditions. I can see how James and Leo will love working together, mucking through mud, rainstorms and sleet—whatever it takes to rescue stranded hikers, picnickers and fishermen from a bad-story ending.

There's a son and a granddog we're already proud of.

* * * * *

Years ago, when folks asked about our family, Joanne would explain, "We've got two children—one home-made and one ready-made." Natasha was our first-born. Then, because of our concern about the global population explosion, we considered enlarging our family by adoption rather than another birth. Our friends in New Creation Fellowship, Steve and Wanda Schmidt, had seen interracial children advertised for adoption on TV, and had adopted their daughter, Jalane. They encouraged us to consider doing the same. At that time social workers were eager to find African American families for children like James, but at fifteen months, no such match had been found. Since Joanne and I had lived in Africa, we promised to introduce James to his African heritage and to orient him to the racism he was likely to face growing up in America. An African American social worker approved our visit with James in his foster home in Junction City, Kansas. She warned us to think soberly about our commitment in advance, because she predicted once we saw James, we would fall in love with him and not be able to give him back.

And that is what happened. We bonded instantly, both ways. Not long after, I remember picking up a crying James, holding him against my shoulder and patting his strong, heaving little back. Before long he settled down, stopped crying, and began to pat my back, too. At fifteen months, James was only half Natasha's age, but he was already her equal in speed and physical strength.

James smother-loved by his big sister, Natasha.

As James grew up, he was eager to try on different roles. Give him a carpenter's apron and he wanted to follow me around on the work site. Give him a toy fireman's hat and he recruited his buddy to run with garden hoses and heroically put out imaginary fires all over our yard. With a superman cape he flew to the rescue of everyone in distress. James was, and still is, a kinetic learner who acquires hands-on skills, learning by doing more quickly than by sitting in a classroom or reading a book.

* * * * *

Often at bedtime, especially when we were on vacations, I would tell James and Natasha "Once-upon-a-time" stories about the adventures of their day.

They always settled down to listen intently because these stories lifted their everyday experience into the realm of heroic myth and legend.

"Once upon a time there was a boy and a girl who were taking a vacation with their family in the Rocky Mountains of Colorado. On this day they set out with their father to climb Mount Baldy. But as they got higher and higher, approaching the peak, a violent storm arose with lightning and thunder, and as they ran for shelter, it began to rain chipmunks on their heads."

"No, no, Dad," they'd interrupt with bright-eyed giggles. "There were no chipmunks falling from the sky, it was hail. And it didn't hit our heads, 'cause we ducked into a cave."

I'd protest, "But this is my story. Can't I tell it however I want?"

"No Dad, it didn't really happen that way. You've got to tell the truth."

"Why do I have to tell the truth?" I'd ask.

"Because if we have to tell the truth, you do too."

I always loved these bedtime-delaying theological digressions that followed our stories because the underlying values of how the world is supposed to work would emerge from "the mouths of babes and sucklings" (Psalm 8:2 KJV). I was fascinated to witness a primal wisdom show up in these conversations with our children (and later, with grandchildren), a wisdom far beyond anything we had ever actually taught them. Their minds had been constructing a world view, a moral order, an aesthetic sense of beauty, somehow grasping the basic laws of nature. I imagine that Jesus experienced conversations like this growing up, perhaps with teachers in the temple, leading him to one day say, "It were better for a man that a millstone were hanged about his neck, and be cast into the sea, than that he should offend one of these little ones." (Luke 17:2 KJV) I was awed by moments like this and sobered to realize that how we lived before our children's eyes had transcendent consequences.

* * * * *

As already mentioned, James was physically strong and precocious. He won all the physical fitness blue ribbons in his cub scout den. Everyone wanted James on their team, whatever the sport. At the same time, school was a struggle. He ended up getting a GED rather than finishing high school.

James bearing down on the ball in Evanston High School soccer.

In 1992, at the age of twenty, when James was temporarily unemployed, he agreed to serve our Janzen family by moving to Kansas and helping my mother care for my father as he fought a losing battle with cancer. As difficult as this assignment was, a deep bond grew up between Grandma Hilda and grandson James. They both got a kick out of venturing into public spaces—a silver-haired 84-year-old grannie and a dark-skinned, handsome, muscular 20-year-old with obvious affection for each other. James got to drive grandma wherever she needed to go and then had the car for his own use, to go fishing or for other outings as he wished. James was at hand when my father passed away, and then lived on with his grandma for some more weeks till her life became more stable. Our family is forever indebted to him for this incredible service.

James as his grandpa Janzen's pallbearer in April 18, 1992.

But that was only one of the many worlds that James had to navigate. I went to Chicago's Union Station to pick him up as he returned from Kansas, and while I waited a couple of policemen rushed past me to detain a young man in the distance. I followed them and soon recognized that it was James whom they had seized, frisked, and were aggressively questioning. I approached and asked, "What's going on here?" The police were startled to see me, a tallish middle-aged white man who carried himself with some confidence and sense of entitlement.

"Who are you?" they asked.

"I'm this young man's dad," I said. "I came to meet him at the station and take him home." I asked again, "What's going on here?"

They said, "We're detaining him because he fits the description of someone we were looking for."

I responded, "He's returning from Kansas where he was taking care of my parents until my father died."

"Oh," they said. "We're sorry to hear that." They took their hands off of James and let him stand free.

"Are you done with him?" I asked. "Can he come home with me now?"

They looked at me, then at each other, and replied, "Yeah, he can go." The difference in their attitude and stance toward me and toward James was painfully blatant and spoke volumes about the persistent nature of racism in our society.

In the car ride home I asked James, "How you feeling?"

With his eyes downcast he said, "Rotten, angry, and humiliated," plus a few other hard-edged "#!%h@" words that you can imagine. This was not the first such incident for James, nor was it the last. Some life-threatening encounters have come from police, others from gang members who have their own version of "You fit the description of the one we are looking for." The Black Lives Matters movement painfully fits James's repeated experience of humiliation, danger, and need for respect. At home and at work, James feels mostly safe and respected, where he has an important role that people generally honor and appreciate. But in public he lives in a dangerous war zone that he believes could take him down at any moment as it has for several of his peers. This experience has led him to retreat into a more secluded life, making a priority of protection for himself and his nuclear family. He seldom wants to venture outside that safe circle of mutual respect.

James lets us know that he appreciates our love and the home we gave him. And when we part, he usually says, "Love ya." But he also asserts, "You will never understand my experience, and what it has been like to be me. We are different in so many ways I cannot explain." And there we have to leave it.

* * * * *

Soon after James' stint of service to the Janzen family around my father's death, he disappeared for a few months, only to reappear with Tonya Lewis, with whom he had been living. They asked our approval of their relationship and presence at their wedding in Rensselaer, NY, where Tonya's family was centered. James and Tonya lived for a few years in Aurora, a western suburb of Chicago, where we could visit and grow close to their family—Jahmel who was born to Tonya before she met James, and then Damien and Derrick whose births soon followed. This marriage did not last, and Tonya returned with her boys to live in New York state. We arranged for Damien and Derreck to live with us for a portion of each summer, including memorable family times at Menno-haven, the Mennonite Church camp two hours west of Chicago.

* * * * *

James and Emily Andersen, who had grown up together in the Reba youth group, married in 1999. They have one daughter, Jaden, who (now in 2024) has completed a master's degree in early child development with the University of Illinois in Chicago and is also coaching women's high school softball at Loyola Academy. Emily is an early childhood development specialist who has just completed an M.A. in social work. James has been a highly appreciated long-time employee of Reba Apartments in the Rogers Park neighborhood of north Chicago.

* * * * *

Backing up a few years to tell another story of our relationship with James, we land in July of 2014, when James's post-high-school sons, Damien and Derrick, along with a couple of their friends from Albany, NY, decided to try living in Evanston to be closer to their father and to us. They camped in our house, until they could land jobs and rent an apartment. It was for us both a challenging and a blessed time as we could make some memories together, spending a few intense weeks with them close-in. To provide a little earning, we had this four-some scrape and paint the garage and the fences around our back yard.

On one fateful day, Joanne was out on her bicycle bringing home a load of groceries for the crowd at our table. A van sideswiped her, toppling her bike, and sprawled her knee-first onto the pavement. The couple in the van kindly stopped, picked up Joanne and her bike, and brought her home as Joanne requested. We needed help and called James, who left work immediately and came to our rescue. James, who is always the most calm and resourceful person in times of crisis, assessed the banged-up knee, and based on his history of sports injuries, said, "Mom, you need to go to the emergency room right away." It turned out that she needed immediate knee repair surgery. Joanne spent the next days in the hospital while James supported us and the crowd in our house. Before long, our visitors decided that a move to Evanston was not working out, and they returned to live in Albany, NY.

James and Natasha's families at a BBQ in our back yard. Back row: James Janzen, Kevin Canetta (Emily's son), Natasha and Ingo Ulbricht. Middle row: Damien and Jaden Janzen, Emily Anderson (Jame's wife), Derrek Janzen, Noah and Tobin Ulbricht. Front row: David and Joanne, both recovering from knee surgeries.

One lesson we learned from this intense season of our life is that James is the most compassionate and resourceful person to call on in time of need. In our old age, I've been advised to designate a "circle of care," people who can be called on when I need help, and James has agreed to be on that short list. Ordinarily, James is busy and in demand at work with Reba Apartments in Chicago. There he responds to maintenance and repair calamities in old buildings, and with people often in crisis. Our times with James are fewer than we would wish, but we know that in any moment of crisis or need, he will show up to rescue us no matter what.

* * * * *

In 2022, James and Emily purchased a two-flat bungalow in North Evanston with the down-payment help of an inheritance from the Janzen Family Farm Corporation in Kansas. Soon after, while Natasha, Ingo and Noah were visiting from Germany, James grilled a flock of chickens to feed guests at their house-warming party.

James barbecueing a flock of chickens for his open house guests.

At present our grand-daughter, Jaden, shares the house with James, Emily, and two big dogs. After a career of repairing other people's homes, James is thrilled to fix up his own abode to "Janzen standards." James and Emily are making plans to host a reunion in 2024 for his sons and their families in the basement guest space he is fixing up.

Chapter 28

A Family without Borders
Eric Revises Our Family Tree

In my childhood home, Mother and Father informally adopted other young adults into the family zone—sometimes just for a meal, sometimes for years. But we kids understood our job was to ask curious questions, play with, and integrate life with this new member of the family. Usually, this integration went well but it had its rude surprises too.

In the summer months, when children were home from school and mother had extra work with childcare, gardening, and feeding farm workers, she would hire young women to be "Kindermadchen" (nannies with farm chores and kitchen duty added). Elda Hiebert was a favorite of ours—like an older sibling who blended seamlessly with our family. As a beloved member we kept in touch with Elda over the years. She later became a Mennonite missionary nurse with whom we crossed paths again in the Congo.

Another summer, when I must have been three or four, mother hired a young woman, E. D., to nanny us kids. Of course, we were curious to see her arrive with a couple of suitcases and move into our guest space upstairs. Having no sense of personal boundaries, I followed her up to her bedroom where she began to unpack her clothes. I spied a pair of pink, lacy underwear, grabbed it and held it high asking "What is this?" Never before had I seen such a piece of clothing on our back-yard wash-line, so I thought my question deserved a forthright answer. Instead, I was whisked out of the guestroom by a yank from behind, and the door closed with a slam. It all happened so quickly that, to this day, I don't know who did it to me. It dawned on me that I must have broken some taboo about unmentionables. Apparently, I had missed the orientation lesson on how to be a properly house-broken brat. I don't know if I was the cause of it, but E. D. did not last long in her assignment at our place. Years later I crossed her path again at Bethel College where she served in the cafeteria kitchen. I never introduced myself and hoped she didn't recognize me either from that cringeworthy first encounter.

Usually, however, long-term guests got along swimmingly with us children. There were German prisoners of war (described in another chapter), foreign college students who joined us for holidays, a German exchange trainee after World War II named Wolfgang Fieguth who lived with us for half a year and learned to drive our vehicles. Our family "adopted" Elda Hiebert's younger brother, Leroy, who became a faithful hired man at HeckuvaRanch from his teenage years until retirement in his seventies. Leroy was a basketball star and a strong-man superhero in our cast of imaginary playmates on the farm.

But the fellow who actually lived with us the longest was an older gentleman whom we called "Oom Schmadt," Low-German for "Uncle Schmidt." He was a live-in hired hand on the farm who joined us for meals and slept in the basement. Oom Schmadt spoke slowly, moved slowly, drove his car slowly, and thus was paid a modest $3.00 a day for his work. He would tolerate our questions for a while, and then went off by himself to sit in his car, to slowly shell and eat peanuts, hoping we would leave him alone. One time brother John and I dared him to run a 100-yard dash that we'd marked off on the county road, and he accepted. To our amazement, he beat us handily and then never said a word about it as he returned to shell more peanuts in his auto hide-out. John and I never told anyone either because we were so humiliated. Eventually, Oom Schmadt was let go as our parents deemed it was time for him to retire to an "old folks' home," as they were called in those days. His basement bedroom became the site of our model railroad layout.

In hosting all these guests and keeping up friendships, our parents gave us the idea that family boundaries are flexible, and that adoption happens in many ways to expand our understanding of shared life in community. Joanne and I could name a few dozen companions we have shared our home with besides Natasha and James.

* * * * *

Our extended family is wide-ranging, but one fellow deserves special attention. About ten years ago Joanne met Eric Colbert as he was selling *Streetwise* at our local Jewel-Osco supermarket. Eric, always careful to dress well, did not look like he was homeless. He greeted everyone passing by with a cheerful "You'all have a good day." *Streetwise* was a newspaper telling the stories of homeless people and advocating for their cause. Selling the paper was a creative way for homeless people to earn a meager living while providing a valuable community service. Over time we got to know Eric, and invited him to join us for community workdays, occasional Sunday breakfasts and worship at Reba Place Church. There he discovered that many of the people who had befriended him at his *Streetwise* post were from the same Reba church community. Soon Eric's picture appeared with us in the *Streetwise* magazine, alongside an interview telling the story of our relationship.

As trust grew Eric told us about an early childhood mystical experiences when he felt the overwhelming presence of God in the form of an enfolding light flooding through the apartment window while his teenage mom was away at work leaving four-year-old Eric to care for his two-year-old sister. Ever since then, Eric had an ongoing conversation with a loving God who cares for him, forgives him, and guides him through the hardships of life. It was not, however, until adulthood in prison that Eric began to read the Bible and discover that Jesus was the Son of this God who had befriended him, and that the Holy Spirit was the name of the presence he had known for years. He became an avid student of the Bible, memorizing large passages for his own edification. It was natural for us to talk about what God has been showing us and to pray together on many occasions.

At one point Eric confided to Joanne that he was losing his subsidized apartment on the South-side of Chicago and would once again be homeless. So, we invited him to stay a few nights in our guest room. We weathered the culture shocks and the discoveries of the differences between privileged white Kansas-bred Mennonites and a refugee from the south-side Chicago African American ghetto. We had advanced degrees while Eric only earned his GED in prison and never knew much stability of life circumstances. All this strained our relationship to the point of desperate prayer and tears, but Eric was a storyteller, and telling the stories of our life experiences helped us get through. A few nights of hospitality turned into eleven months of becoming family.

We came to know Eric as utterly respectful, trustworthy, and meticulously clean—but more importantly, a brother in the faith. The high point of our day was Bible study at the breakfast table where we slowly read through the Gospels, told stories from our day, and prayed for one another. Joanne said there was probably only one homeless person in a thousand she could live with, but Eric was that one. He washed our dishes, mowed the lawn, raked our leaves, and cleaned the car. While with us he paid off his debts and soon, with the help of a pro-bono attorney, got his record cleared.

Then when we needed our guestroom for our daughter, Natasha, and her family visiting from Germany, Eric took up lodging with a couple of elderly Reba neighbors, one after the other, who needed support in their declining years. Though Eric has lived in various places, often reduced to sleeping in his car, he counts our home as his address and picks up his mail along with snacks Joanne leaves at the top of our stairs. Like a son, he checks in often to see how we are doing, especially when I am away on trips.

Our relationship took a deeper turn when the Covid-19 Pandemic hit, because we could no longer share our occasional breakfasts together. Instead, we instituted a daily speaker-phone conference call at 8:15 when we could read the Bible, tell stories, and pray for one another. On occasions, our conference call includes Christine, Eric's wife of a few years.

Eric and Christine Colbert making a Joanne sandwich.

To conclude this memoir chapter on "Family without Borders," we want to include a couple of Eric stories as transcribed by Joanne, our local scribe and wordsmith.

* * * * *

> Eric:... Though I did not commit the crime I was charged with, I was rounded up with a group of friends who had broken the law and was taken to the Cook County jail. The police put me in this holding place. When the day came for the sentencing, I got so scared. I knew the sentence for what they accused me of was like forty-five years. I was only about thirty-one at the time. The only private place there was the bathroom, and I was in there cryin' by myself and said, "Lord, I can't do it. Lord, I can't do it, I can't. I don't see no way out. I don't want to do suicide. I'm finding no escape."

> But God talk to me sayin', "I will hold your hand. I will be with you. I will be with you." Soon that got through to my heart and I could believe it. My tears stopped comin' and I could say, "O.K. Lord, let's do this. Man-up. Got to stand and bear the cross. We get through this."
>
> When they put me in the jail, they put me in Division One, maximum security. That was somethin, . . . in with the murderers and the rapists. It was so dark in there, only little square windows at the top of the walls, mices running along the deck walks. But God was with me. I had a Christian cellie (cell mate); he was not a gang guy. We did some Bible studies together. We'd sing Christian songs, and some other guys would join in from their cells. Soon the whole place was rockin'. We saw God turn that whole deck around. God was working with the inmates, and the officers, too. One of the officers got saved. It was amazin', and I just sittin' back and seein' it happen. Wow! And then they redid the Division and get better lights, and put in new windows, and painted the walls.
>
> Later they called me in and said, "We made a big mistake. You were not supposed to be sent to Division One, but to Division Eight. We can move you there. You want to go?" (In Division Eight things were much cleaner, no mouses, even A.C.) But that not what God wanted. God said, "These guys need you." So, I told the officers, "No, God want me in Division One."
>
> I seen a lot of bad stuff happen around me there too, but it didn't touch me. One guy especially, he had fire in his eyes when he look at me cause he seen me getting favor from the officers. I made friends with all the pastors who come in. Once, one of them gave me a bag of candies. So, I was sharing those with the other guys. I passed the guy who did not like me. But then God tell me to go back to him and say, "You want a candy?" He say, "Huh?" But then he took it, and he became a friend. That guy who used to not like me started comin' to Bible study. He was so hungry for the Word.

Eric hoped his move from Chicago's South Side ghetto to north-shore Evanston would be a step up in safety and opportunity. Here's a story from Eric about his "welcome" in the Reba neighborhood.

> I remember the time I was sittin' in my car on Sherman, reading devotions there, next to Tom Roddy's place. This guy, who live on third floor, called the Evanston police on me. Maybe even told them I had a gun. So, all these cop cars came out with five policemen. They had me get out and put my hands in the air

while they searched my pockets. I talked relaxed and friendly with them, and soon they begin to josh back with me, except for one agitated guy who went to look through my car, lookin' and lookin' for some kind of trouble. I wonder if he gonna plant something illegal there. I was thinkin, "Please, somebody give him a hug to calm him down. He so unpeaceful, he about to lose it."

And then Stephen Wilke, comin' home from work, rolled up on his bike. He came and greeted me friendly-like and said, "Hey Eric, how you doin.' What's up?" When the troubled policeman saw this white guy with a smile, he asked, "Do you know him?" Stephen said, "Sure, he's my friend. Lives right here." The agitated policeman was taken aback. Seein' I was Stephen's friend, that just blew his wig, his idea that I was a dangerous bad guy. Everyone wished me well and went on their way. What race people look like, that affect a lot.

* * * * *

In 2019, while our daughter, Natasha, visited us from Germany along with husband Ingo and sons Tobin and Noah, we often ran as a pack including our tall African-American son, Eric Colbert. One day Eric came home excited because he had shagged a promotional coupon from the "LA Fitness" gym for "Member and family." So, we all became Eric's family. Tobin and Noah, papa Ingo, and Grandpa David drove off to work out at Eric's gym. The guy at the desk recognized Eric and checked the coupon, but to his eyes, all us blue-eyed white guys did not look like family with this tall dark-skinned African American. "Let me explain how it is," Eric offered. "My mama's first husband was a cousin to this woman's daughter, and while she lived in Germany they had a passel of kids including this guy's father. So, you see," he added brightly, "We all family!" The "LA Fitness" guy asked Ingo, "Now where are you from?" Ingo laughed and said, "Germany," rolling the "r" for special effects.

By this time the "Fitness guy" was holding his head in pained confusion. "Wait," he replied. "Let me go talk to the manager." A minute later the manager arrives, listens again to Eric's family tree spiel, which is even longer and more entangled than the first time around. The manager then looks at this motley family without borders, throws up his hands and concedes to his assistant, "Aw, what the hell! Let 'em in!"

CHAPTER 29

From Farm Boy to Communal Life

ELSEWHERE IN THIS MEMOIR I have related the boredom I experienced as a teenager doing solitary farm fieldwork. The Thesaurus does not have enough options to describe this melodramatic scene and my lonely feelings about it.

This mind-numbing story, however, was interrupted one day when the farmers of our church banded together to plow the fields of a Mr. Harms who was in the hospital recovering from an emergency appendectomy. So about ten of us neighbors converged on his fields with tractors and plows, making terrific progress. In a couple of days, we finished the job. Mrs. Harms expressed her gratitude by feeding us sandwiches and snacks. It felt great working together, seeing such dramatic results, and all for a good cause. Why, I wondered aloud, didn't we all farm communally? Well, the answer came back that it was inefficient—we all had to drive a few extra miles to make it work, something to only do in an emergency. But I had to wonder why we didn't more often organize our lives and our resources to harvest the joy of common work for a good cause like Amish barn-raisings, or the Hutterites' communal farms?

On June 10, 1958, a major tornado ripped through Eldorado, Kansas, killing thirteen people. A couple of days later, the fledgling organization, Mennonite Disaster Service (MDS born in 1954) was in place to organize Mennonite volunteers (mostly farmers) to help clean up. I was seventeen years old at the time, and went with my brother John, hired-man Leroy Hiebert, our truck, and a box full of tools. As we approached the city, we saw that the police had blocked off sections of town to guard against looters where a path of destruction a quarter mile wide had plowed through the city. We found the MDS bus, got our instructions and approval to pass through the police lines to begin work. I claimed the chainsaw as my tool for the day, cutting up toppled and mangled trees so they could be stacked on the truck and hauled away to a growing mountain of debris in the countryside, awaiting an eventual gigantic bonfire.

What a mighty storm! On the edges of the tornado's path roofs were torn off and trash was scattered about, but in the middle of the destruction, houses were swept away completely, leaving only the floorboards and basements in place. I recall seeing a school flagpole bent horizontal four feet above the ground, a windowless car drifted full of roof shingles, a pickup truck wrapped around a tree, and sorrowful homeowners sifting through the debris to salvage a few mementos.

I remember feeling energized by the significance of our work, clearing the way for folks to rebuild their devastated lives. We made the sawdust fly, but we also took time to talk with the refugees of the storm who thanked us for our help, and praised God for their survival. We understood that our job was not just demolition work, but social work and pastoral care. We were there to listen as long as folks wanted to talk. We shared a common purpose across the generations and classes, erasing social barriers in an intimacy of grief and support that otherwise would have left us strangers to one another.

Common work, I came to see in those years, has the power to redeem our daily struggle for existence, meaningfully connect us with others, infusing our toil with transcendent meaning. It is no wonder that Mennonite Disaster Service has flourished and grown into a far-flung network of solidarity whenever storms and floods have disrupted life, often sticking around for months in relays of volunteers to rebuild what was lost.

Growing up on "HeckuvaRanch" gave me a few indelible experiences of communal life, especially in my early years when small farmers still shared much of the work. But with tractors and mechanization, farms grew larger and fewer, and fewer farm kids chose to stick around. Community was not absent from my childhood, but it was growing increasingly thin. In retrospect, I can see how my experiences of loneliness on the farm transformed into a calling, an impulse to build community wherever I went.

The structure of farm life increasingly pointed us toward individualism while the structure of a liberal arts education and dormitory life in college favored community. I appreciated the history of philosophy courses I took under Dr. Harold Gross which exposed us to the greatest thinkers of Western Civilization whose philosophies I "tried on for size." One week I was a meddlesome Socratic question-asker. The next week I was a Platonist exploring ideal forms. Then I became an Aristotelian systems builder. I was not content to just learn about philosophers for the test. I tried on their philosophical outlooks and methods, looking at the world through their minds to see what answers they might give for current questions. Imitation is, I still believe, one of the fastest ways to learn, because playing with a philosophy soon makes it intuitive and second nature.

In some ways, a circle of intellectually curious friends in college was my first intentional community. This is where we could be "brutally honest" in conversations without boundaries, examining the inadequate answers to life that we'd been spoon-fed as children. However, this vibrant intellectual community naturally dissolved upon graduation. Nostalgically revisiting the campus years later reveals that the place thereof remembers it no more. Thank God, I've enjoyed similar intellectually honest and curious friendships in community to this day.

However, a more lasting impact on our life came from Joanne's firsthand experience of an intentional community led by the Academic Dean. Albert Meyer. His circle of proteges gathered for a "Recovery of the Anabaptist Vision" seminar that tried out in daily life the practices of the Early Church as described in Acts 2 and 4. As my relationship with Joanne grew, I was drawn to that same vision of community life.

* * * * *

The early church in Jerusalem was famous for its thick community life. What, exactly do *The Acts of the Apostles* say they shared? Possessions, the Apostles' teaching, food, fellowship, times of regular prayer. But beyond the outward marks there was a spirit of implicit sharing—*koinonia* was the Greek word for it. "They were of one heart and mind. And no one said that anything they had was their own." As Joanne and I pursued this way of life with others in later years we heard critics minimize these New Testament texts saying they are idealized and that the communal life in Jerusalem did not work out, citing the need for Paul, two decades later, to raise funds for the persecuted mother church in Jerusalem. that thesis with historical examples of the perennial nature of renewal communities. However, when New Testament commentators declare that communal life does not work, this suggests to me that they have never lived it. So, what has been Joanne's and my experience after sixty years of swimming in that pond?

Intentional Christian community, as Jesus and his twelve disciples experienced it,I could refute should not be judged by its institutional longevity, but by its power to transform lives. Blending intense love and high challenges, it is the necessary setting for discipleship formation. Like marriage and family life, thick community reveals quickly what we are made of and how far we are willing to empty ourselves and let in the self-sacrificing love of Jesus for which we were created.

As we see in the Gospel stories, it takes a thick common life of messy interactions, plus patient conversations about those breakdowns, to make disciples of Jesus. Repentance moves us from the world's conventional wisdom of 'Lording it over others' to the Suffering Servant wisdom of the One who died for us and was vindicated by God in the Resurrection.

The Kingdom of God might be an ideal when viewed from a distance. But in community it is a present reality that we respond to imperfectly. We build our house on the rock by practicing the things Jesus taught, and practice produces habits, skills, and eventually, character. We come to community with easily triggered wounds, with blind spots others put up with more or less graciously, with immaturities we are still working on. Our community is always in need of renewal. There are times of refreshing (Acts. 3:20) and times when we long for it. But to dismiss it as idealized is to suggest that we've never experienced love and times of renewal like that. It's like asking, after fifty-plus years of marriage, are we still in love? Well, it's not like one's first romance where Oxytocin levels are booming. But with time a deeper, more tested and ultimately satisfying love makes her home among us.

* * * * *

What did we share in at New Creation Fellowship from 1973 to 1984? Around the 400 block of West 10th and 11th streets in Newton, Kansas, we intentionally lived within walking distance of each other. Many of us had common work on a construction crew and in informally organized childcare. Others worked in their professions, pooling income. We had many community workdays upgrading our homes, gardens, and yards involving children and sometimes neighbors. We had more picnics, potlucks, campouts and parties than any other time in our life. Our children had many young adults intimately involved in their lives. We had exuberant, spirit-filled times of worship that drew others from far and near who wanted to join in open-mic times of intimate sharing, confession, and prayer.

We wore each other out trying to make too many decisions by consensus and then, in our weariness, learned to entrust responsibilities to individuals according to their gifts and maturity. We also ran into the limits of our wisdom as inexperienced leaders who often called on other more mature elders at Reba Place Fellowship who were already in their 40's! We knew from our own experiences the reality of the life described in Acts 2 and 4.

The common purse at New Creation Fellowship came to an end in 1984 because of Regan-era persecution—i.e. the refusal of IRS to grant the community "Apostolic Order" status—resulting in double taxation on what had been donated to the common purse. By that time our family had moved our membership to a sister community, Reba Place Fellowship in Evanston, IL. But our friendships still go deep with those early New Creation members who invited us to return and share memories at NCF's 50th anniversary celebration in October 2023.

* * * * *

David Brooks (*The Second Mountain: The Quest for a Moral Life*) discusses the "two mountains" we face on the path of maturity. The first half of life, he observes, is typically about "resume virtues," making a living, buying a house, accumulating professional honors, accomplishments that the world might value and respect. But those who keep growing in maturity discover that impressing others with our accomplishments is ultimately empty, while growing in what he calls "eulogy virtues" like love, integrity, capacity for service, and sacrifice are what really make life worthwhile.

So, for persons called to community building, our goal is not to stay on a high plateau about community accomplishments, but to see how Jesus uses community to grow us up in love according to the divine image within. That is why we are often surprised by the presence of love in the worst of times as well as the best. The crucifixions and the resurrections, work together for good to those who love God.

* * * * *

Our move to Reba Place Fellowship in 1984 placed us in a larger, more established community than New Creation, with more emphasis on common ministry. There Joanne and I found mentors who could help us grow in wisdom and servanthood. Like at New Creation Fellowship, the dimensions of *koinonia* included living in close proximity; shared possessions like income, houses, cars . . . where "no one said that anything they had was their own." Shared finances encouraged us to seek God's will in major decisions with small groups members where our lives were generally open and known to one another. Reba's main form of common work was managing apartment buildings as low-income housing. But Reba also began various ministries and businesses to meet local needs—a food coop, Reba Early Learning Center, a Ten Thousand Villages fair trade store, Reba Place Development Corp, and Reba Place Church—which all grew from communal seed to flourish beyond their original boundaries, eventually standing on their own feet.

Those outward "resume" marks of Reba might hide the inner life of care for one another and for our neighbors, which flourishes and wanes according to how deeply we have been transformed by the love of Jesus and grown in the wisdom of our accumulated experience. It turns out that our motivations for staying in the communal life move beyond the reasons that brought us in the first place.

Jesus's disciples also tell us how their reasons for following The Master changed over time. At first, they jockeyed with each other to be "the greatest." They joined Jesus in the hope of sitting at the right hand of the One who would kick out the Romans and restore Israel to Davidic greatness among the nations of the world. That ambitious dream was brutally crucified. And yet, the resurrected Jesus returned to ask Peter, "Do you love me?" Do you love me enough to accept my forgiveness for your betrayal? Do you love me enough to feed my sheep?" Do you love me enough to lay down your life for others in the hope of resurrection?

How have my reasons to stick with Jesus and with community changed? Writing this memoir has helped me see more clearly how God uses our shabby motives in order to move us along to deeper levels of commitment, love, and sacrifice. As this chapter illustrates, there was a discernable movement from loneliness to common work, from alienation to joy in intellectual companionship, from trying to impress others to learning how to love in real relationships, from me to we in marriage and community, from public recognition to service of obscure others. And in old age comes relinquishment of all that which we cannot hold onto anyway.

* * * * *

Long-term friendships of virtue, to borrow a phrase from Aristotle, are one of the best gifts of community. I've been intrigued by Jesus's reference to friends in his last discourse (John 15:12 ff.). "This is my commandment: love one another as I have loved you. No one has greater love than this, to lay down one's life for one's friends. You are my friends if you do what I command you. I no longer call you slaves, because a slave does not know what his master is doing." It is in a community of character like this that we find the best friends.

However, in the course of a few months (2019—2020) death claimed my best friend (Allan Howe), my mentor (Julius Belser), and my affordable housing protégé (Adrian Willoughby). For the first time in sixty years, I was lonely. Not profoundly lonely, I still had Jesus and my journal, a community and Joanne. Still, I looked around for new friendships of virtue. Robert (Mike) Buren, who had recently lost his wife, agreed to meet with me. Soon others asked to join, and we became a book study circle slowly reading and telling our stories in dialogue with Charles Moore's collection *Living the*

Sermon on the Mount Together. Recently I wrote in my journal, "Hey, I'm not lonely anymore." We have become "The 6:30 Geezers" (which is when we meet on Thursday mornings.) We haven't talked about everything yet, but I feel like I can ask them anything and get a caring response. The gift of intellectually honest friendship has been renewed.

* * * * *

In 1973, in the era of the Vietnam War, we banded together in New Creation Fellowship, to sustain a witness for justice and peace. Since then, our experience of community and our understanding of justice has grown. Many conservatives understand justice as retribution—something that governments are supposed to do, deal out punishments where laws have been broken. There is a left-wing vision of justice understood as liberation—a vision with prophetic Biblical roots. Jesus also denounced oppression and lifted up its victims. But Jesus's vision of justice was more communal than either of those options. The justice of restoration, reconciliation and redistribution happen best in face-to-face communities. In covenant community we can know intimately what people need in order to find healing for past wounds, reconciliation of broken relationships, and restoration to a thriving shalom way of life. This will look a lot like the Early Church—freely giving and receiving according to gifts and needs. Justice wants to be embodied rather than imposed. This is the work of community at its best.

* * * * *

After an evening of listening to a brother vent his "unholy anger" about mistreatment, a moment comes where the spirit in the room turns. Our brother realizes that his rage has been listened to and is carried, not just by the others in the small group, but by our crucified Lord. He asks, "What do you think I should do?" Together we explore the path of healing, direct conversation, and reconciliation as outlined in Matthew 18:15–20.

After experiencing the worst that the world can do to us, we discover we still are loved and a desire for healing and right relationships is born again. That is proof of the resurrection still active among us. Those are the turning points in a community's life when our sins are brought to the light, lovingly confronted and redeemed, whereupon they lose their power to separate us from God and from each other.

I'm sorry for people who have not known this communal dynamic from their own experience. I'd love to tell more personal stories that illustrate these points of turning, but those stories are too tender and private for this kind of space, and furthermore, they do not prove anything. Finally, our deepest choices are not rationally arrived at. They are shaped and moved by how we are loved and by what we love. As Pascal said, "The heart has its reasons that reason does not know." Such love is not an infatuation, it is not an ideal. It is a painful reality tested by grief shared and love renewed from the One who will not leave us, ever.

Reba members and friends circle up for announcements, prayer, and a potluck at Emmanuel Lodge in Wisconsin.

Mirror # 5

Bearing Fruit in Old Age

Chapter 30

I Remember Beans

From Peasant Village to Urban Soil

JOURNAL: 12-28-08

    Last evening, I sat at the kitchen table shelling our last beans of the season, picked from twenty-five vertical feet of strings that climb the west side of the back porch of our Evanston two-flat. In the cramped quarters of an urban lot, garden space competes with lawn and flowers, so we grab a little extra sunlight with a vertical exposure. During summer and early fall we pluck the green beans from the vine at ground level, from the first floor and the second-floor porch. Joanne or I will wash them, snap their stems, and plunk them into our pressure cooker for three minutes, and they are ready for dinner. In an age when produce typically has traveled about 1,300 miles from migrant field laborers to supermarket shelves, our five steps from the back porch to the kitchen sink helps bring down the average.

    However, there are plenty of beans on our vine that grow beyond our reach, or that grow to maturity when we are gone on vacation. Those we let hang and pick them in December, when the leaves have fallen and the pods have dried to a crisp. Each year I buy a new packet of climbing beans and add them to the seed mix. What comes up, whether planted or volunteer, usually has some surprises. Now, in the pan before me I see at least six varieties—black, red, shades of tan and marble—a pleasure to the hand and eye. The rhythmic work of splitting a pod and rubbing out the beans with my thumbs is surprisingly satisfying to the body and soul. My mind goes still in contemplation, recalling other bean harvests from the past. It is always appropriate, as the years go by, to take time to deepen memories, ponder meanings, and savor the gifts that God has given.

David playing the giant atop our two-storey beanstalk.

I remember a generation ago when our children were in grade school, living at 418 West 10th Street in Newton, Kansas, we had a garden as large as our energy would enable us to tend. That usually included 10–15 rows of green beans about 60 feet long. When harvest time came around, we had to get fully organized as a family. Our children, James and Natasha, of course, would not help for nothing. The argument that they should work if they wanted to eat, did not impress them. They negotiated hard and finally settled on a plan whereby every quart of beans we picked and processed together would yield ten cents in a jar, and from that fund we could go to the Dairy Queen and enjoy some treats.

More than once, as we were all working in the back yard and bragging about how many quarts of beans we had picked, a couple of neighbor kids came by and looked on wistfully at our significant labors. They asked timidly, "Can we help?" "Sure! Grab a bucket." Soon they were each moving down a row and pulling pods off the bushes too. Our kids, who believed their labors were somewhere between child slavery and cruel and unusual punishment, were surprised that other kids felt deprived by not having the opportunity to labor alongside adults who had time for them and their questions. Of course, the neighbor kids would be included in the snack, and our celebration was doubly sweet.

Then from the back yard we moved into the kitchen where an assembly line worked smoothly and persistently toward the last beans in the bucket. A quart every seven minutes moved down the line. I snapped stems, James dunked them into a boiling water bath, Natasha put them into ice-cooled water and laid them out to dry. Joanne filled the freezer bags with blanched and quick-frozen beans. Half-cooked, they could be pulled out of the freezer any time in the following year and, with a quick boil, were ready for the table.

Where did this yen to grow beans come from? I thought I was a normal kid who liked normal things until I wrote a scandalous sentence in our grade school paper. We all welcomed the last day of school, I wrote, so that we could play as much as possible through the summer and work in the garden. My peers jumped on me and wondered what strange demon had gotten into my head to lift up the joys of gardening—something they all hated and of which they did only as little as they had to, or less.

For myself, I recalled working in the garden with my mother, witnessing the wonder of seeds sprouting in the sun and rain, and in a few weeks, feeding our family and feeding my soul with wonder in the process. I remember early one spring, while snow was still in the garden, making a deal with my mother that I would grow as many beans for her as I could and she would pay me seven cents a quart. I don't know why I chose seven cents. Perhaps that was the price in the grocery store for a can of green beans. In any case, my mother must have wanted to encourage my farmer initiative.

So, I planted a big plot of beans and faithfully weeded and watered them till the harvest came on. I learned that beans are best irrigated by dragging a hoe between two rows of plants and setting the water hose to flow down the furrow. By contrast, irrigating from the air with a sprinkler, especially when the sun was shining, would scorch the leaves. The plants should be picked every three days for as long as they bear new pods, until the plants were exhausted. When harvest time came, I learned how to feel the undersides of the plants and pull off handfuls of pods at the right time when they were just full grown but had not yet turned coarse and stringy.

With some pride I hauled one milking pail of green beans after another into the kitchen where Mother worked in a cloud of steam, putting the bean pods into canning jars and dunking them into big vats of boiling water. At the end of the day, I carried the sealed jars down to the basement shelves and Mother settled accounts with me. "Let's see, thirty-six quarts times seven cents is. . ." All afternoon I'd been estimating, then counting the jars and repeating the math in my head. "It's two dollars and fifty-two cents," I announced with assurance.

I looked forward to Mother's canned savory green bean and potato soups that would sustain us through the winter. But more immediately, with the money in hand, my brother John and I would go to our model railroading catalogue and consider which piece of rolling stock we could buy with my hot cash. Maybe a box car or a gondola would be added to our HO gauge layout that sprawled through the basement. Or even better, we'd buy several sheets of balsa wood, 1/32nd of an inch thick, just right for building houses, stockyards and factories along the tracks of our growing empire of mountains, tunnels, planes, lakes and thriving industry. The Santa Fe Railroad and the Union Pacific were built with loans from British Lords and land-grants from Congress, but our basement railroad was financed by beans.

Shelling beans in our kitchen took my mind back to earlier years in the Congo and many weeks in El Salvador, to moments of incredibly gracious welcome and shared food with folks in peasant villages not much different from the life of Bible times and countless other rural villages around the world.

Beans, goatmeat, rice and bidia at a Congolese feast.

In our sister community, Valle Nuevo, in El Salvador, the whole family will sit together under their veranda or a yard-shading mango tree to shell beans for a week or two until the whole crop is stored away in sheet-metal silos under a thatched roof, safe from weather, rats, and mice. Though each peasant family has its own plot and tin silo, the bonds of shared village life and common work mean that the village will starve or thrive together rather than alone. Beans represent social solidarity and gratitude for God's provision.

Bean-filled pupusas on a hot Valle Nuevo griddle.

Beans and corn are planted together. The corn grows fast and tall, giving the beans a temporary trellis to climb on and eventually dry out in the sun. Salvadoran beans turn out ruby red and make excellent filling for corn tortillas, their favorite treat called *pupusas*. So, corn and beans that grow together are eaten together in an ancient, pre-Colombian pattern, producing a balanced vegetarian protein that has meant survival for generations since the dawn of agriculture. I've been privileged to share beans and tortillas with peasant friends in Central America, beans and *bidia* in the Congo, beans and rice in India. Shelling beans, I remembered not just my own childhood, but the childhood of the human race and our solidarity across the continents and generations.

Henry David Thoreau writes about the season of his life when he determined to "simplify, simplify, simplify." Beside his cabin near Walden Pond he tilled a patch of beans. With meticulous accounting, Thoreau determined how much he spent on seed and how many pounds of dried beans he harvested and how much he ate on the way to simplicity.

The beans I shelled last night will only make a few pots of soup, show hospitality to a few guests, and then be gone. Still, they point toward simplicity of spirit, solidarity with the poor, and hope for the earth that is reverenced with food grown a few steps from the table, a way of life that God has given us for peace.

CHAPTER 31

Sorghum Day

How Refugees Remember and Give Back

As a child, I lived a lot in the future, looking forward to the next big event, for which Sorghum Day certainly qualified. It fell on a Saturday in the late 1940's when Grandpa and Grandma Neufeldt drove onto our Janzen family farmyard, their car loaded with great pots, wooden paddles, and other more mysterious contraptions. They led a caravan of elderly friends who had gotten up early to drive an hour from the Hebron Mennonite Church near Buhler KS to HeckuvaRanch for a day of sorghum cooking. But first a little background.

Our grandpa, Dietrich B. Neufeldt, was famous in those circles because he was born in 1878 on a steam ship in the middle of the Atlantic Ocean, adding one more name to the list of several thousand Russian Mennonites immigrants. These emigres brought along their prized Turkey Red Wheat seed and countless other crafts and traditions that transplanted well from the Steppes of Russia to the Plain States of the U.S. Every time the Russian Mennonites of Central Kansas celebrated their immigration, we were proud to note how D. B. Neufeldt got honorable mention because his age always matched that of the anniversary.

So, why did these old folks who should have been in their rocking chairs drive an hour to our farmyard for a communal work day? We had several highly fertile cattle feed lots that stood empty during the summer while the yearlings were grazing in the Flint Hills pastures. This particular year, part of our stock yards had been sown into sorghum which grew fast and tall in the richly manured soil. In a few days the cattle-drive of horseback farmers and their boys would bring several hundred cattle back to their winter feed lots. So, the sorghum had to be harvested now.

Sorghum, which originally came from Africa, has spread around the world in its many varieties (grain sorghum, sweet sorghum, sudan grass, broom corn, and others). Its tall green stalks and leaves resemble corn, but instead of a tassel on top and ears of golden kernels, sorghum raises a thick head of BB-shot-sized grains that cows and chickens love to eat. This sorghum harvest, however, was not about grain but the sweet golden sap. Like sugar cane, sweet sorghum is harvested for its sap, but sorghum has no bitter-tasting edge like molasses.

The sweet sorghum stalks must be cut and crushed to press out the sap, and running a sorghum press takes lots of power. In earlier years this energy was supplied by a team of hitched horses walking in a circle, turning a capstan to drive the sorghum crusher. But Grandpa Neufeldt, who had already retired from the farm to small town living, outfitted a workshop in his horse barn to invent gadgets for every need.

Grandpa came totally prepared. He jacked up the back right end of his Dodge sedan, put a block under the right-rear axle, set the hand brake tight, and proceeded to take off the right rear wheel. In its place he bolted a power hub which was connected to a drive shaft with flexible U-joints permitting the old car to power a sorghum press a dozen feet away. So, with the engine running and the transmission in first gear, grandpa let out the clutch, and, to our amazement, the car went nowhere. Instead, the rear differential gears put all the torque into the loose axel up in the air, which turned the drive shaft and powered the clattering sorghum press all day long on one tank of gas.

At this point the old folks organized themselves into an efficient assembly line of common work—habits that Mennonites had passed on from generation to generation. Seeking religious freedom and better opportunities, they migrated from the Netherlands to Prussia, from Prussia to Russia, and from Russia to the Plane States in America. Persecution forged community. Whether it was threshing wheat, butchering hogs, baking for a wedding or raising a barn, these folks knew about working together with purpose, joy, and efficiency.

One man with a machete cut down the sorghum stalks while a line of bonneted women and straw-hatted men drug the stalks to the press. Plant after plant was pushed between the rollers that squirted, sprayed and squeezed all the sweet juice out of the stalks. Beneath the rollers of the press was a catchment bowl with a faucet, where the sorghum sap ran into buckets relayed hand over hand to big black cast-iron pots and sheet-metal troughs with wood fires going beneath them. The boiling sap had to be faithfully stirred with large wooden paddles and tested with a wooden spoon blown on till it was cool enough to taste with the tongue. When the sugar was concentrated and caramelized just right, the sorghum syrup was ladled into hot and heavy gallon jars to be sealed and cooled in our kitchen. By the end of the day our kitchen was lined all around with rows of gallon jars gleaming as if the sun were still in them, a tawny gold to joy the eye, nose and tongue. Who knew that Kansas prairies had their equivalent to the New England maple syrup season?

This is the way these old folks had sweated together for years and, if they were not dead, they did not want to miss out on the pleasure of community-building common work. Despite the hard labor, they knew how to have fun: practical jokes—hiding someone's glasses, an accidental swat across the rear with a stalk of sorghum, belly laughs at old jokes, and sometimes tears shared remembering those missing from the circle. Fresh-baked coffee cake renewed energy and talk at *vaspa* time. Grandchildren (like me) were honored with jobs that matched their eagerness to learn and belong. Like the sweet stickiness of kitchen floors and doorknobs at the end of sorghum day, we all bonded in the common effort.

When I was eight years old, the unique technology, the communal high and the anticipation of sorghum on breakfast pancakes fascinated me most. Now, seven decades later, I ask other questions and see new dimensions of this rich community life.

Why would these old folks with arthritic joints travel 40 miles to sweat and strain like mules for a day, to harvest and preserve perhaps 30 gallons of sorghum syrup, not for any profit, but to donate to their church's Mennonite Central Committee relief sale, to raise money for resettlement of World War II refugees? And then, at the relief sale auction, they would mischievously bid against each other to jack up the price in order to buy back what they had labored for and donated in the first place.

Why? So they could get together once more as families to bake pungent sorghum-sweetened peppernuts by the flower-sack full, so that every Christmas season guest could share in the blessing and the crunchy mouthfuls of delight.

Why? For love, for community, to give expression to a way of life that blesses those close to home and those far away with signs and wonders of the Kingdom of God, a kingdom for which we may suffer like our Master, but we will not kill. A kingdom which creates a circle that will remember us when we die and welcome us on the other side.

Sorghum Day is a bit of heaven on earth, embodied theology, a foretaste of what is to come, a little comfort in life's sorrows, shared memories of lands where we used to live before we were driven out as refugees, sojourners, pilgrims seeking a better home with God.

Is that all nostalgia for a disappearing way of life? I don't think so. Our relatives in Kansas continue to put in communal workdays preparing quilts, peppernuts, vareneki, and hosting huge auctions for Mennonite Central Committee relief and development work here and overseas. In this way the poor and dispossessed of the world—whom we once were and might again become—also get to sit at the global potluck and feast in the kingdom of God.

And in the city, we, the descendants of D. B. and Anne Neufeldt are called to pioneer new communities with the privileged and the poor. Like ancient prophets and eccentric monks, we're learning by common work and shared mistakes how to grow and spread around tastes of heaven here on earth.

Alas, these days we buy our sorghum at $8.99 a pound from Whole Foods, but we still bake, eat and share oodles of peppernuts among God's friends at Christmas time. Some days I forget that sorghum and peppernuts are not holy—but they do remind us of what is. In community we get to share with all the saints who have put their lives, work and treasure together so the world can know for real the persistence of God's justice and God's peace.

Is it off topic to leap from Sorghum Day to our sister community, Valle Nuevo, in El Salvador? I think not. I hope you will see the connections with me before we are through here.

* * * * *

AN ALIEN IN OUR MIDST:

Revolutionary Reflections from Doña Chunga's Front Porch

> Last night as I visited the outhouse in Chunga's front yard
> > I could tell chickens were roosting in the trees above, cause they'd startle, flap their wings, and water droplets from last evening's rain
> > would fall on my head,
> > > at least that's what I hope it was.
>
> Suddenly, up there, a rooster thumped his wings and crowed,
> > up and down the neighborhood
> > the midnight roosters passed on the code,
> > > "an alien in our midst."
>
> This morning that same *gallo*
> > proudly strutting his iridescent colors, makes the rounds

harassing all the hens in turn,
And each hen, in her turn moves away, scratching
    with studied indifference,
    body language saying, "Bug off.
        When I need your services, I'll let you know."
Chunga's yard is junky
    by suburban North American standards
    but everything belongs in a shaded
Salvadoran village kind of way:
Chipped, used roof tiles stacked in a corner
    patiently await a more useful day;
A solid rectangle of chopped firewood stands straight and proud
    under two sheets of corrugated tin;
Stones laid in tidy rows,
    borders for a few struggling flowers
    rained on daily by dishwater,
        encouragement to not give up.

Eager Valle Nuevo children volunteer to wash our underwear.

Each morning, Patricia, Chunga's daughter, sweeps the sidewalks,
    that make a "Y" between two porch openings
and the street-side gate,
chasing away the leaves that have fallen overnight
    till her broom gently touches guard dog, Turko,
who stands up and slowly stretches,
    first front legs,
    then back,
    and elegantly steps aside
        as the street-sweeper moves through.

Turko bites his rump three times,
expertly scratches his eye with a hind leg,
returns to his outpost with an eye on the house and the road,
then descends with a sigh,
into his guard-dog nap.
Chunga, our host, slaps her mountain-grown corn masa into
    shape,
        laying disks of dough on the out-door wood-fired stove,
        deftly flipping them with bare fingers,
        growing a perfectly cylindrical stack of toasted tortillas
        wrapped in a towel,
        with fried beans and plantains
            for our steaming breakfast.
Jim and I eat with relish and thanks to Chunga
    who does not sit with us,
    but who lingers, knowing what it's like
to be an alien.
We recall our first meeting twenty-four years ago,
    when a hundred guerilla soldiers came down out of the
    mountains
    to lay their guns at the UN Peace-keeper's feet,
    trusting their revolutionary ambitions could be worked out
as a new political party,
trading guns for machetes.
    in civilian life.
I show Chunga a photo of that day
holding her six-month-old twins,
        fragile signs of hope for a life of peace,
For a people reeling from a decade of nightmares,
    a desperate flight of thousands under helicopter fire into
    exile,
    a hot spot in a Cold War that the world soon forgot,
    and then a dangerous return from Honduran refugee camps
    before the war was over,
        "Please do not forget us," they pled.
So, each year we have returned,
    sister communities south and north,
        "God's doing," we agree.

Everywhere we see evidence of Valle Nuevo's gift at community
    organizing,
    learned in the refugee camp,
    and smuggled back past military check-points
    under truckloads of old boards and rusty tin,

from dismantled refugee barracks,
To build their first homes
    where we were welcomed to dirt floors,
    their best home-made beds,
    hot tortillas and beans
    seasoned with bitter tears of each life story,
Treated by landlords as animals and dirt,
    labeled "communists" for wanting schools and fair wages,
    scorched earth and military sweeps drove them
        into exile.
We came hoping to help them rebuild,
    Instead, they wanted to tell their stories.
        late into the night.
    Thank you," they cried, "for listening
        and letting us heal."
    "Where was God?" we wondered.
        As disciples of Romero they had no doubt,
            "He was crucified with us.
            And with him we will rise."

Now Chunga wet mops the gleaming floor
    of her proud Habitat house,
    like dozens of others in Valle Nuevo.
No dust dare come between
    the cool tiles and her bare feet
    where Chunga sits all day at her treadle sewing machine,
    paying off her modest no-interest mortgage
        by turning out smart school uniforms.
Chunga visits with whoever stops by,
    laughing freely at her own jokes and those of her guests,
    changing bobbins, zipping hems, and snipping threads
        without a break in conversation.
Students stride by with their homework,
    wearing Chunga's handiwork,
    proud of the village
    that built its own primary and secondary school,
        a grade at a time,
    pioneering popular education of indigenous values,
    led by their own university graduates,
    raising a generation eager to share their love of learning
        to other still-impoverished villages.
Their university student children return on weekends
    to lead community health workshops.

Everywhere the enlightened practical wisdom of campesino
life
    shows up.
Chickens wander round the yard, scratching at every leaf,
    pecking at whatever moves,
    which keeps us all happily
        bug-free.
In Chunga's *pila*
    the open water tanks for washing dishes, clothes, and bodies
    swim minnows from the creek
    like every pila of the village,
    where the minnows eat mosquito larvae,
    the same mosquitoes that bother
        no one at night.
Black plastic barrels and tanks catch rain water
    under the corner of a roof gutter,
    Chunga thinking ahead
    to the dry season when the village water supply
    trickles into the pila one day a week,
        sometimes.
On a flat rock Patricia beats the sudsy water through her clothes
    then hangs them up to dry in a tree and
    on a kinky wire
        from the roof corner to the border fence.
The *campesino* life is ordered by natural contours
    this Gringo cannot see
    until he slows down and finds a few friends
    who answer his questions,
and kindly do not laugh
    at his kinky Spanish.
No morning hurry here to
    catch a coffee and a commuter train
    for another high-rise
        high-tension day downtown.
Life flows together at a gentler pace,
    forgiving many failings with a laugh,
    that does not rile up at all the stuff that might happen,
    nor the stuff that is bound to happen
        anyway.
But Chunga and her neighbors have time
    and attention for each one passing along this rocky path of
    life
    with a hearty
        "*Buenas dias.*"
Between the two branches of the sidewalk "Y"

Leans a home-made cross of two bound sticks
draped with a lacy chain of scissors-shaped prayers for peace,
preserving the intentions of a holy day
that Chunga, the seamstress, treasures,
and that I hope to remember
    with this poem.

CHAPTER 32

Our Half-mile Cottonwood Tree

Bearing Fruit in Old Age

WE HAVE COME TO the last chapter of this meandering tale of memories and confessions, a story without an end because, thank God, I'm still alive and pondering how to faithfully bear fruit in old age. However, to help wrap up this story for now, allow me to introduce and enlist the aid of my favorite childhood tree.

Once upon a time there was a grandpa who, with his brothers and sister, walked a mile and a half to a one-room country grade school, and every day on the way he passed by his favorite tree. Unlike all the trees in the farmyard that we climbed and built tree houses in, no one ever climbed this tree. Its lowest branches were higher than our house. In art class we carefully drew and water-colored respectful pictures of the tree, and everyone understood why we held it in awe. Most cottonwood trees grow fast, reaching sixty feet in height, live half a century, and then break up in a storm. But this tree was colossal by comparison with everything around it, boasting a circumference of more than twenty feet and easily a hundred feet tall, higher than any of us could throw a rock.

The older a cottonwood tree gets, the thicker is its bark and the deeper are the cracks that form within it. This thick, craggy bark protects the tree from periodic prairie fires that burn off the little trees but renew the grass land's fertility. Our favorite tree was the oldest living thing for miles around with crevices in its bark as deep as my hand. The tree didn't have a name although if we talked about "the half-mile cottonwood tree in the middle of the road," everyone in our part of Kansas knew which one we meant.

Our colossal half-mile cottonwood tree in the middle of the road.

This tree had an aura about it, perhaps because it stood across the road just north of the Zion church cemetery. It would have been ancient already when the first graves were dug by Mennonite settlers in the 1870's. It reminded us of Psalm 1 which compares the righteous person to a tree planted by streams of living water that faithfully bears its fruit in due season.

The fruit of a cottonwood tree is not something you can eat. Instead, its seeds are carried away on fluffy parachutes of cotton from which the tree takes its name. In springtime the Kansas breezes blow these cotton tufts in the billions, like a warm blizzard for miles down-wind until a seed sticks somewhere along a muddy stream, takes root and there begins to reach for the sky.

Pioneers crossing the Great Plains with muel-drawn wagons traversed many dreary miles without seeing a single tree. Before the inventor John Deere figured out how to forge a steel plow that could bust the prairie sod, many travelers, on their way to California or Oregon, called this the Great American Desert. But a line of cottonwood trees in the distance signaled welcome shade, firewood, and a stream of running water since this is a tree that likes to keep its feet wet.

Our favorite cottonwood tree was old enough to remember generations of wolves, deer, antelope and bison, and the nomadic tribes that followed them with horses and teepees. These native-Americans understood that all of nature exists in living mutual relationship so that this tree which they revered, would have known and revered them in return. Thus, as we walked to school, this tree imparted to our imaginations a connection of knowing and being known from an age before roads, plows and white-man sod busters. We looked at our famous local legend and understood why the Cottonwood (*populous deltoids*) was named the Kansas state tree.

A tree in the middle of the road looked weird and out of place. If you drove half a mile south from our farm it seemed like you would run straight into a big tree smack on the mile-line road. Only when you came closer did you notice that the road dipped down into the Henry Creek valley, looped west around the massive trunk, and then turned back to rise out of the valley once again on the mile line. And if you looked back, there stood the tree once more in the middle of the road.

How did this happen? Already in the 1860's when the first surveyors laid out a square mile grid for roads to eventually follow, that tree was so formidable the respectful road builders decided to leave it stand as a landmark right where the survey said a road should have gone. The tree stood next to the Henry Creek which meandered so many ways that the first road had two crooked wooden bridges across it, bridges that proved inadequate in every flood when they washed away and had to be retrieved from our neighbor's pasture.

By the time I came along the tree was approaching two centuries in age and was still majestic, though obviously in decline. I remember one day we walked to school and discovered it had been struck by lightning and lost a major branch so that it looked lopsided now, taller on one side than the other. Eventually the center of the trunk rotted out, making a hollow room large enough for a few children to hide in, but it was damp and smelled like the other critters who had been there first. With every major storm the tree lost limbs that sometimes fell on the road and had to be pulled away by our farm tractor so cars could pass through.

Then in the mid 1960's, when I was away in graduate school, I read the sad news in a letter from home that the half-mile tree with the rotting heart had finally split and crashed to the ground. Bulldozers were hired to shove its tangled branches off the road into the adjacent pasture where the rot and fungi were free to do their composting work.

Mother and Father conspire to take a photo of the new bridge where the half-mile cottonwood tree used to reign.

Soon earth-moving equipment straightened out the creek and the road, and two rotting wooden bridges were replaced by a single span of steel and concrete raised high enough to stand above the floods. Mother and Father Janzen must have conspired to take this photo of the new bridge and send it to me. The cemetery, which once was guarded by this towering sentinel, now looked bleak and unprotected.

In 1992, when my father died at the ripe age of eighty-four—he would have turned eighty-five on the day of his funeral—the family asked me to write his obituary. Like the half-mile cotton-wood tree, I wrote, Louis Janzen was a man of the land who stood straight and tall above the crowd, remarkable in both stature and character, silhouetted year after year against the prairie sky. But now when we looked at the horizon, it pained us to see that our landmark was gone, leaving us bereft, disoriented, somehow undefended. Suddenly my siblings and I had to reckon with the reality that a guardian role had been passed on to us whether we were ready or not. It was our turn to grow into the full stature and character that God intended for us, taking our place on the horizon for our descendants, nourished by streams of living water, bearing fruits of faithfulness and wisdom in this season of life remaining to us.

And now, thirty years later, without our knowing how, we too have become landmarks, rough barked and lightning scared, for another generation that might one day tell stories like this to remember us.

* * * * *

I don't remember if this Half-Mile Cottonwood tree was male or female. The male trees grow catkins in the spring that release pollen into the air in thick enough clouds that some allergic folks have a two-week-long bout of sneezing. A million pollen spores miss their mark for every one that sticks to a tiny red flower on a female tree downwind. Amazingly, each spore carries the entire DNA chain of a billion bytes of information, half the blueprint for another absolutely unique tree. The female trees soon produce billions of little cottony seed parachutes that ride on the breeze like a slow snowstorm. Some homeowners hate the voluminous cotton tufts because they clog window screens, fill gutters, catch in air-conditioner vents, and drift like snow into fence corners. Cottonwood seeds are among the lightest of all seeds—it takes a million to make a pound. In its lifetime each mature cottonwood tree, on average, seeds one mature cottonwood offspring. So, to do the math, that means it takes about a quadrillion of pollen spores to make a billion seeds, to plant and grow one mature cottonwood tree. Is that fruitful, or what?

How else might cottonwood trees be fruitful? Some of the trees end up in the sawmill, but their wood is not used for furniture or house framing because it is too rough and fuzzy. It is good for making the most study and light-weight reusable pallets.

One other use I discovered when a few houses were donated to our Newton, Kansas, construction crew on condition that we move them off-site so a clinic could be built there. We hired professional house-movers who proceeded to jack up the houses and insert cribbing under them to bear their resting weight. This cribbing was made of cottonwood beams about the size of railroad ties built up in crisscross stacks. Because they were light and strong, one laborer could easily toss these cottonwood beams in place by hand. Eventually the house stood high enough on the cribs that a truck could back under it and haul it down Main Street with Yours Truly, riding on top, helping telephone wires pass over without hooking on. Then at the destination lot, the house was lowered, one layer of cottonwood cribbing at time, till it rested on the newly poured foundation. Cottonwood will not build a house, but it will easily hold it up.

But the ultimate fruitfulness of our old half-mile cottonwood tree opposite from the Zion Church Cemetery, came after it had crashed to the ground and begun to rot. On the west side of the road at each funeral, preachers intoned the mournful liturgy, "Ashes to ashes and dust to dust," for each loved one laid to rest in hope of the resurrection. Meanwhile, on the east side of the road, the Creator was orchestrating a different kind of death and resurrection project of insects, worms, fungi, and bacteria, creating the softest, lightest, and richest humus on the prairie. There lies the Half-Mile Cottonwood tree, generously giving away its substance to energize another generation, the resurrection of plant and animal life in ceaseless cycles of carbon and DNA, powered by the sun.

In this living parable of death and resurrection, I find a parallel to the karma of love which has nourished each of us in a genealogy of grace—mentors, mothers, fathers, lovers, forgiven sinners and reluctant saints—who constitute the spiritual earth from which we have grown. And likewise, whatever we have given in love is preserved and passed on to sustain life because, as the Apostle Paul writes, "love never fails." (1 Corinthians. 13:8)

* * * * *

> The righteous flourish like the palm tree,
>   and grow like a cedar in Lebanon,
> They are planted in the house of the Lord;
>   they flourish in the courts of our God.
> In old age they still produce fruit,
>   they are always green and full of sap,
> Showing that the Lord is upright;
>   he is my rock, and there is no unrighteousness in him.
> (Psalm 92:12–15)

* * * * *

How do I understand my calling now at the age of eighty-three to be fruitful in old age? I'm inspired by Psalm 92, which compares the righteous elder to a palm tree or a Cedar of Lebanon, samples of long-lived, upright, and fruitful trees. The palm yields its oil-rich seeds year after year. The cedar was famous in Israel because Solomon made a deal with Hiram, King of Tyre, who sold a forest of famed Cedars of Lebanon, to outfit the Temple in Jerusalem with beams, paneling, doors, and furnishings. The psalmist then transplants the righteous man into the courtyard of God's House where his greatest joy is to worship the Creator and Deliverer of Israel. Such a person will be fruitful in old age, green and full of sap, which suggests to me a bright-eyed grandpa joking with children; a peaceful presence fully attentive in the midst of conflict; someone able to reflect and speak a word of wisdom that fits the moment; a spirit alive in the morning with the good news of what God has been teaching in the night.

The developmental social psychologist and biographer, Erik Erikson (1902–1994), devised a widely used and sometimes contested developmental scheme naming eight life stages. "Generativity versus stagnation" marks the primary challenge of the seventh stage usually reached in late adulthood, which if met successfully, describes the fruitfulness of someone at the height of his or her powers who ably serves family, community, and society as an elder with good judgment that others have come to trust. Such a person does not need to be in charge but leads by sharing a vision of a better future, and invites others to find their place of fitting service within it. Such a generative person finds his or her joy in seeing others grow into leadership and fruitful service, pouring the substance of character into those they mentor.

I became aware of Erik Erikson's landmark book, *Gandhi's Truth* (1969), just in time to use it as a text in a class I taught in "Biography" at Bethel College in 1971. Erikson finds in Gandhi an exemplary leader who experimented with and developed an array of non-violent direct-action techniques to guide his people in the way of justice and independence from the British Empire. For Gandhi, the last brief stage of life, following Independence for India, was that of a sage—a wise man who could reflect on experience, to share wisdom and to inspire with a self-less model of sacrifice for the common good.

* * * * *

In recent years Joanne and I have been awakened by Sarah Augustine's regular column in *The Anabaptist World* and her book aptly titled *This Land Is Not Empty: Following Jesus in Dismantling the Doctrine of Discovery*. This prophetic testimony by an indigenous-American Mennonite activist, traces the devastation brought by the White European's doctrine encoded in law, that whatever belonged to non-white "pagan" peoples could be "discovered" and stolen under a divine mandate.

Now that it is our turn to be old, Joanne and I see opening before us a small role in undoing a portion of this genocidal history by which our ancestors bought or inherited land in Kansas; a history embodied and symbolized for us in this Half-mile Cottonwood Tree. The next step we see in that dismantling process involves discovering the details of who occupied or used this land before the arrival of the Europeans.

In the case of "HeckuvaRanch" that path is not immediately clear. According to the Kansas State Historical Society's web site, before the disruptive arrival of White folk, this region around our farm was occupied by four tribes—the Kansa (north-east), the Osage (south-east), the Pawnee (north-west), and the Comanche (south-west). The earliest historical records show that the typical occupation pattern before the white man was that indigenous tribes had permanent village settlements along major water ways such as the Kaw and the Arkansas rivers. But the upland prairie surrounding the landmark "Half-Mile Cottonwood Tree" was likely visited from time to time by nomadic hunting parties from these Kansa and Osage villages, according to the seasonal migrations of bison and other game. Later, other indigenous people groups who were displaced by fighting and colonial settlements to the east also ended up on reservations in Kansas. But plagues of small-pox, the Indian-Removal Act of 1854, military incursions, Congressional land grants to railroads, and other forms of racist imperialism cleared the way for European settlers in the Midwest where our ancestors found favor.

It seems right to Joanne and me that a portion of our inheritance should be invested into some repentance and restoration project yet to be explored with the descendants of those peoples who were displaced, acknowledging our undeserved security, wealth, and privilege. Three generations downstream from our settler great-grand-father, Johan Janzen, we feel called to return a portion of what did not belong to us—unfinished business that remains after this memoir is written. I have signed up to walk a few segments of the "Potawatomi Trail of Death" from Indiana to Oklahoma, with fourteen others in June of 2024. God willing, this might launch another late-life chapter similar in theme to our earlier Jubilee calling to partner with dispossessed Central American refugees and folks closer to home in need of affordable housing.

* * * * *

How shall we conclude this rambling and eccentric series of farmer-boy stories and their trajectories into older age, these seeds that God planted and a community of friends have tended from fragile wind-blown cottonwood tufts to full-grown tree. The hard work of character development and the pursuit of justice is never done so long as we have breath. In December 2023, my achy body could still show up on a cold winter day with fifty others in Mennonite Action, calling for a permanent ceasefire in Gaza. Now it's time for others to organize, but I'm still glad to lend my body in public witness. I still have energy to listen to the dreams of a few young leaders and encourage them to faithful witness.

We follow in faith the One whose life ended on the cross and who trusted God for the resurrection. We are the seeds of that hopeful planting. Likewise, we trust God for the resurrection of whatever we have given in love for the blessing of further generations.

So, for now this over-grown children's story must end with a hands-on bedtime benediction: "The Lord bless you and keep you. The Lord make his face to shine upon you and be gracious to you. The Lord lift up his countenance upon you and give you peace this night and always."

Meanwhile, the larger story remains, the final stage of character development and relinquishment is still unfolding. Someone else will make the ultimate judgment about our lives. Fortunately, our experience in following Jesus this far sustains the hope that our final editor is honest, forgiving, and wants to be with us forever.

Appendix

A Chronology of Selected Writing Projects

WRITING HAS NEVER BEEN my primary role, but alongside my main job, I have always had some writing projects in the works. Here are a few samples from the decades of my life:

1969: While teaching in the Democratic Republic of the Congo, a few years after Independence, when most text books still came from the former colonial overlord, Belgium, I managed to compile a collection of primary sources for teaching African and Congolese history (in French). For a few years, this amateur collection was used as a history sourcebook by other teachers until something better came along. This gave me the idea that I should get a graduate degree and return to Africa as an historian. That dream did not go further than a Master's Degree at the University of Kansas, because, before long, I felt a stronger call to major in Christian intentional community and peacemaking.

1972 to 1974: *Liberty to the Captives Newsletter* was a "spasmodical" compiled and edited for the Mennonite Central Committee on the emerging theme of prisoner rights and alternatives to incarceration.

1984 to 1992: *The Overground Railroad Newsletter* was a quarterly of news and articles from and for the network of communities that assisted refugees fleeing Central American to find asylum in Canada and the United States.

1991 to 1997: *On the Way* was a monthly devotional co-edited with Susanne Coalson, that gathered contributions from Shalom Mission Communities and friends as a common prayer and reflection guide for each day of the month.

1996: *Fire Salt and Peace: Intentional Christian Communities Alive in North America*, published by Shalom Mission Communities, was the fruit of a year-long series of visits to thirty communities, profiling their character and charisms in a time when most people believed the community movement was dead.

1996 to 2010: *Shalom Mission Communities Newsletter* shared news, photos, and essays from the Shalom association of communities, and included articles that spoke for the wider Christian community movement. The newsletter goes on, but a decade ago, I passed the torch on to a younger generation.

2012: *I Remember: Bonded Labor, Quicksand, and Good News for Thousands*, an imprint of Wipf and Stock publishers, is the story of our dear family friend, Das Maddimadugu who with his wife, Doris, was an innovative Indian pastor, educator and peacemaker among the outcasts and tribal people of Andra Pradesh in India. This memoir also includes tales and reflections from a dozen of Das and Doris Maddimdugu's international co-workers.

2013: *The Intentional Christian Community Handbook: For Idealists, Hypocrites, and Wannabe Disciples of Jesus*, was published by Paraclete Press. It gathers up testimonies and reflections on the stages of seeking for community, founding communities, their healthy growth, and times of renewal. It has become a standard reference book of the movement.

2020: *Seven Radical Elders: How a Failed Civil-Rights-Era Storefront Church Launched Seven Lifetimes of Faithful Communal Witness*, by Wipf and Stock Publishers, contains the memoirs of an amazing group of folks who bonded in an interracial community in the 60's and 70's, and stuck together to become an exceptionally wise and durable group of community leaders. These seven memoirs are wrapped in a series of essays by persons these elders mentored and who carry on their radical legacy. It seeks to answer the question of how do saints like this happen?

2024: *Once Upon a Time There Was a Three-Year-old Grandpa*, is the book you hold in your hands and needs no further introduction.

www.ingramcontent.com/pod-product-compliance
Lightning Source LLC
Chambersburg PA
CBHW060556230426
43670CB00011B/1842